7.αν

THE SKEPTIC'S DICTIONARY VOLUME TWO

Robert Simmons

THE SKEPTIC'S DICTIONARY VOLUME TWO

Copyright 2004 Robert Simmons   ISBN 0-9666039-1-5

Library of Congress Cataloging-in-Publication Data 2004093457

Printed in the United States of America

AUTHOR'S PREFACE

I was encouraged to write VOLUME TWO of THE SKEPTIC'S
DICTIONARY by the warm reception given the original. This new work,
as does the other, contains original and classic definitions and verse. It
is guaranteed to lift the spirits of all but the most
pathologically-depressed reader. But, even those sad wretches
should find enjoyment, here, when taken with their medication.

The Skeptic's Dictionaries were written for the millions of
educated readers who enjoy literate laughs, caustic comedy, and
sharp satire. They are also intended as resources for
toastmasters, speakers, authors, and conversationalists everywhere.
All those who wish to enliven their communications with pungent
metaphors, rollicking puns, and memorable verse, will find rich
pickings in these pages.

It has never been my aim to displace standard dictionaries on
library shelves. They are important works and should be there.
But, each suffers from a common failing--there is not one laugh in
a thousand pages! By contrast, this new edition of THE SKEPTIC'S
DICTIONARY holds at least one laugh on every page.

For readers who know that humor is as much a tonic as sex
(without the health risk); who enjoy twisting the tails of sacred
cows and poking fun at stuffed shirts; who prefer irreverence to
servility--to you, this work is dedicated. Finally, to those who
may need another reason to part with the purchase price, modern
medical science tells us that good humor promotes good health.
This being so, readers will find strong therapy in these pages,
with the only possible side effect--sore ribs.

Acknowledgement must be made of the invaluable help and
unerring judgment of my close friend, the late Jack Winer, on whom
many entries were tested. If he mustered just a smile, I threw
them out. Only when he laughed did I know they were finally right.

Robert Simmons
San Diego, California

A

ABASEMENT (v) Showing a proper reverence for power, celebrity, or
money. Nineteenth Century sociologists wrote that this trait was
most pronounced among children, toward their parents; college
students, toward their professors; Republicans, toward labor
leaders; Democrats, toward captains of industry; pickpockets,
towards the police, and everybody toward lawyers. It seems that
sociologists lied then, too.
>A reverent fellow in Fife
>Banished all greed from his life.
>He turned in his Mum
>As a tax-cheating bum,
>And gave the reward to his wife.

ABDOMINAL FLU (n) A microscopic protein that causes the brawniest
man to head for the head and the loveliest woman to shun her
toilette for the toilet.
>A feverish fellow, named Lou,
>Was stroked by his saucy spouse, Sue.
>When she saw, with dejection,
>No sign of erection,
>He explained, "all my heat is from flu."

ABORIGINES (n) Persons of little worth to explorers, who find
them cumbering the soil of newly-discovered countries. They soon
cease to cumber. They fertilize!

ABORTION   (n) The yeast in America's political bread,
producing so much fermented gas that it often explodes. The
sourdough variety is much admired by partisans on both sides of the
issue. Combining caustic soda, toxic sweeteners, vitriolic
binders, copious salt, and large bundles of green dough, it is
especially good for making baloney sandwiches.

ABRIDGER (n) One who separates fat from meat and uses the fat.
>Said an editor, Imogene Guest,
>Who abridges for Writers Digest,
>"Of the feats which I'm liable,

4

"Condensing the Bible
"To twenty-one pages was best."

ABSCOND (v) To disappear mysteriously, usually with the property of another.
"Spring beckons; all things to the call respond.
"Trees are leaving and cashiers abscond."
Ambrose Bierce

ABSENTEE (n) Someone who has exposed himself to slander.

ABSENTMINDED (adj.) A mental condition distinguishable from senility by such examples as these:
--A man is absentminded if he forgets to zip up his trousers, afterward, while he is senile if he forgets to zip them down, beforehand.
--A woman if absentminded if she forgets to use her credit card to pay for a purchase, while she is senile if she forgets that she has a credit card.

ACCIDENT (n) An intentional act of Satan designed to force survivors to blaspheme, sell overpriced insurance, produce plaintiff lawyers, and motivate perjurers. Following are common applications of the term:
1. A wife's explanation to a jury of how a shotgun she held discharged to kill her adulterous husband.
2. A young man's explanation to his date of a fondle.
3. A young woman's explanation to her mother for making-out the latter's credit card.
"An attractive young woman is an accident of nature, but an attractive old woman is a work of art."
George Kaufman

ACCORDION (n) An instrument that, when squeezed, produces sounds that are sometimes musical. It is shaped like a bellows, operated like an exerciser, and often employed as an instrument of torture. Literally translated, the name means
"maker of harmony," thus belying claims that our language is humorless.
A Navy accordionist, Mort,
Grew so fat that his arms were too short.
Since his paunch was the trouble,

5

He folded it double
And stapled it starboard and port.

ACCOUNTANT (n) Someone whose calculations of clients' tax
liabilities disprove the adage: "figures do not lie."
   An accountant, in Hell, says that Satan is swell;
   "I've never been over-heated.
   "It seems to me true that His favor is due
   "To the masterful way that I've cheated."

ACHIEVEMENT (n) An event that follows ambition and precedes

disappointment.
   "My uncle invented a new soft drink which he called, 'Five-
Up.' Soon after, he improved the drink's formula and re-named
it, 'Six-Up.' Then he died, never knowing how close he came to
achieving success."
                                        Victor Borge

ACRIMONY (n) The second of three related stages in a typical
American marriage. The first stage is called "matrimony", while
the third is called "alimony".

ACTIVIST (n) One who, engaged in a tug of war, pulls for the good
of a snoring public against one who pulls for his own profit.
   "Everyone is just one tragedy away from being an activist."
                                        Donna Frye

ACUPUNCTURIST (n) A person who gets paid for needling people.
      An acupuncturist, Chu,
      Stuck Lola to cure her of flu.
      But, quite unexpected,
      Himself got infected.
      Now, he's sneezing his name 'til he's blue.

ADAGE (n) A moral truth that is accepted by all and obeyed by
none. Following are superior examples, by the practice of which
all readers of this lexicon will profit:
      1. Only brush the teeth you want to keep.
      2. Essential to wisdom is knowing the faults you share
that must be overlooked.
      3. A temper is too valuable a possession to lose or waste

6

on others.

4. We wouldn't worry so much about what other people think of us if we knew how seldom they think of us at all.

5. People should not marry for money. They can borrow it cheaper.

6. It is better to remain silent and appear stupid than to open your mouth and remove all doubt.

7. If people take an instant dislike to you, it may be their way of saving time.

8. If you have trouble making up your mind, it may be because you are in unfamiliar territory.

ADDER (n) 1. An IRS employee whose function it is to calculate tax deficiency bills. Added items include principal, penalty, interest on the principal, interest on the penalty, and interest on the interest.

2. An especially venomous snake.

These two definitions prove how closely language mirrors life.

A taxpayer, Will, found his IRS bill
Excessive by more than a tad.
Said the agent, McFinn, with an insolent grin,
"I can multiply better than add."

ADDICT (n) Someone with an unpopular habit.

Said a corporate CEO, Moffitt,
"I'm compulsive and can't seem to stop it.
"Though my habit is real,
"To lie, cheat, and steal,
"I'm no addict. I just like the profit."

ADDRESS (n) A location where things of value may be found and stolen.

ADOLESCENCE (n) A stage of child development characterized by its own language, pimples, hostility toward parents, blindness to litter, addiction to fast food, magnetic attachment to the telephone, amnesiac responses to parental requests, and knowledge of everything.

Said a stern adolescent, named Bloom,
Filling his mother with gloom,
"Strike me if it's just!
"Kiss me if you must!
"But, don't make me cleanup my room."

ADULT (n) Someone old enough to know better.
Two adults, from the Bronx, being Artic Club wonks,
Went swimming despite freezing rain.
Said a child, at the sight, "growing old is not right.
"It will certainly scramble my brain."

ADULTERATE (v) To commit adultery.

ADULTERY (n) The only sin that cannot be committed by an unmarried person.

ADVERTISING (n) A branch of marketing whose goal is to irritate prospective purchasers so much that they remember the product name long after the reason why they remember it has been forgotten. The tactic has been especially effective in overseas markets, as exemplified by the following true stories:
1. Advertisers for the dairy industry launched their popular slogan, "Got Milk?", throughout Latin America, where, in Spanish, it was understood as "Are You Lactating?".
2. A Coors Beer slogan, "Turn It Loose!", in Spanish, was understood as, "Suffer From Diarrhea".
3. Advertisers for the Scandinavian manufacturer of Electrolux vacuum sweepers disseminated the slogan "Nothing Sucks Like Electrolux" throughout the U.S.
4. Clairol advertised its "Mist Stick" product in Europe only to learn that in German, "mist" means manure.
5. Colgate introduced a new toothpaste in France and called it "Cue". Later, the company was shocked to learn that it is the name of the most notorious porno magazine in France.
6. When Pepsi's "Come Alive With The Pepsi Generation" slogan was introduced in China, its Chinese language translation was, "Pepsi Brings Your Ancestors Back From The Grave."
7. Pepsi's rival, Coca Cola, made a sensational entrance into China. When it was first widely marketed on the mainland, its name appeared as "Kekou Kela", which translates into Chinese as "Bite The Wax Tadpole."

ADVICE (n) A recommendation, made to another person, that requires action too inconvenient to be followed by yourself.
"The only thing to do with good advice is to pass it on."
Oscar Wilde

AEROBICS (n) A type of exercise during which there is movement in all parts of the body except the bowels.

Big Mary is fat; there's no doubt of that.
But aerobics, she manages fine.
She jumps, skips, and hops, then at eight o'clock, stops,
While her thighs stop at quarter to nine.

AFFLUENCE (n) "An attribute that signals the death of diligence and the birth of boredom."
Ambrose Bierce
"One church congregation I visited in California was so affluent that when the wine was passed around, it was sent back for a better year."
Clark Anthony
She: "Before we got married, you said you were well off."
He: "I was, only I didn't realize it."

AGE (n) The duration of an object's life, measured in years for all but women over forty. According to insurance actuaries, women live longer than men. From this fact we may conclude that while, as the Bible says, "Man will inherit the Earth," a woman will inherit it from him.

AGED (n) Persons so seasoned by the years as to be distasteful to the young.
A French woman in Paris lived to be 114. When interviewed on her birthday, she attributed her long life to caring for her skin. She said she had only one wrinkle and that was the one she sat on.
Despite his age, the Reverend Jerry Folwell cannot remember a time when he did not deserve a whipping, while former President Clinton is old enough to have known better.

"When just a girl," said actress Pearl,
"Sex made me quite afraid.
"So old I've got, I'd give a lot
"Just once more, to be laid."

AGEING (adj.) A natural process by which humans slowly rot. Gerontologists have identified the following infallible signs that tell us when the process is well advanced:
--You get winded playing chess.
--A dripping faucet causes an uncontrollable bladder problem.
--You look forward to a dull evening.
--You sit in a rocking chair and can't make it go.
--Your knees buckle and your belt won't.
--The best part of your day is over when the alarm clock goes off.

--Your back goes out more than you do.
--Your memory is the second thing to go.

AGNOSTIC (n) Someone who doubts the existence of God because
She cannot be seen nor heard. Archbishop Oley Saw, of the Holy
See, scoffs at these unbelievers. He points out that by the same
test, we should doubt the existence of electricity. The doughty
cleric is no doubter. He once made a short circuit of
Switzerland and was electrified by what he saw.
   Said an agnostic from Deal,
   "Although I'm not sure God is real.
   "Whenever there's strife
   "Or a threat in my life,
   "I admit that I pray a good deal."

AIRLINE (n) A business that is up in the air most of the time,
loses its cool on descents, has to combat fluctuating pressures,
and services its customers in the following peculiar ways:
   1. It flies them from Point A to Point C, where they are
rushed to a gate at the opposite end of the terminal for a flight
to Point B--the destination they had passed on the way to C.
   2. It makes them breathe air that everyone else has just
exhaled.
   3. It feeds them the cheapest food that complies with the
American Heart Association standards of good health and bad taste.
   4. It Seats them in spaces designed for anorexics.
   5. It scares them witless with security precautions, then
proclaims the skies to be "friendly."
   Due in large measure to stresses induced by the foregoing,
flight crews are not noted for their sense of humor. Fortunately,
there are welcome exceptions, among which are the following true
accounts:
   1. Upon arriving at Kennedy Airport, a flight attendant
announced: "Thank you for flying Delta. I hope you've enjoyed
giving us the business as much as we've enjoyed taking you for a
ride."
   2. Welcoming passengers on a flight to Chicago, the pilot
said: "We're proud to be able to say that American Airlines has the
best flight attendants in the industry. Unfortunately, none of
them are on this flight."
   3. After a bumpy landing, a Southwest Airlines flight
attendant announced: "Please remain seated with your seat belts
latched until Captain Kangaroo bounces us to the terminal."

4. After an extremely rough landing at Amarillo, Texas, a little old lady passenger, walking with a cane, asked the pilot: "Did we land or were we shot down?"

ALIEN (n) 1. A human from another part of the world who is not a citizen of America. Our federal government spends billions trying to identify and expel them.

2. A non-human from another world. Our federal government spends billions trying to identify and welcome them.

When an alien, Jose, from old Monterrey,

Was about to be caught in a raid,

He painted on stars, said he landed from Mars,

And was given a ticker parade.

ALLERGIC (adj.) Prone to react badly in the presence of an irritant, e.g., an oil company executive confronting an environmentalist.

Said a wife to her husband, named Lou,

"My allergy doctor came through.

"The cause is not weeds;

"Neither dogs, dust, nor seeds.

"He says I'm allergic to you."

ALLERGY (n) The cause of an injurious reaction to a natural condition, as, for example, a strange perfume on a husband's undershorts.

It's Spring! A time when tiny spores

Emerge from trees in myriad scores.

When allergies in any number

Awaken from their Winter slumber.

When perfume from blooming roses

Open valves in reddened noses.

"Oh, would to God that I just might

"Sleep without a sneeze, tonight."

ALLIGATOR (n) Teeth encased in shoe leather.

A fat gator hunter, named Blade,

Capsized in the South Everglade.

When he finally emerged,

After being submerged,

He was found to be gator foliated.

ALLY (n) Someone who will stab you in the back only if he needs your blood. This compares with a stranger, who will do it only if he can sell the blood, and with an enemy, who will do it because of the blood.

ALTRUIST (n) Someone who believes in giving something for nothing. This differs from a Republican, who believes in giving something only to himself, from a Democrat, who believes in getting something for nothing, and from a Libertarian, who believes that all those who are getting something should give it back.

ALZHEIMER'S (n) A progressive brain disease that causes a loss of neurons and memory. Perhaps the simplest diagnostic test is the one currently used at the famous Mayonnaise Clinic based on car keys. If a patient can't remember where his keys are, he is considered merely forgetful. But, if he has his keys and doesn't know what they're for, he has Alzheimer's.

AMATEUR (n) An athlete who is paid less than a professional.
    Said a graduate track star at Rice,
    Providing young athletes advice,
    "Whenever you run,
    "Do it only for fun,
    "Though your shoe sponsor's money is nice."

AMBITION (n) What many men mistake for ability and some women choose above honor.
    "Women who seek equality with men lack ambition."
    Betty Fridan

AMNESIA (n) A mental condition that explains why a woman has sex after childbirth and a man remarries.
    An amnesiac Mayor, a Texan,
    Seduced women to win an election.
    When charged with exposure,
    He said, with composure,
    "I forgot that I had an erection."

ANCIENT (adj.) Anyone more than twenty years older than you. The condition is imminent in yourself when any one of the following occurs:
    1. You wink at a pretty girl and she laughs at you.
    2. You think that pinching your wife's bottom is stupid.
    3. The sight of your double chin in the bathroom mirror is not caused by your double vision.
    4. Your husband tells you to stop wrinkling your forehead and you weren't.
    5. Whenever you have to bend over to tie your shoes, you

always look around for something else to do.

6. Whenever you need an x-ray, your doctor just positions you with your back to a bright light.

7. You get compliments for your alligator shoes when you are walking barefoot.

8. The face in the mirror looks like the face in your passport photograph.

ANCIENT HISTORY (n) A time in the past when the following were accepted truths:

1. A "web" was a place where a spider hung out.

2. A "keyboard" was part of a musical instrument.

3. An "application" was a request for employment.

4. "Memory" was what you lost with age.

5. A "log on" was a piece of wood added to the fireplace.

6. A "hard drive" was a tiring auto trip.

7. "Backing up" was what a motorist did to get out of the driveway.

8. "Cut and paste" were what people did when making a scrapbook.

9. A "virus" was what caused diseases and a "fix" was a personal problem.

ANONYMOUS (adj.) The most prolific author who ever lived. Many of his humorous or wise utterances are credited to writers who lack the wit or time to have conceived them. If all the aphorisms attributed to Ben Franklin, for example, were actually coined by him, he would have had no time to invent electricity.

An ubiquitous fellow, Anonymous,
Has a name that is clearly synonymous
With concealing who said it,
Whom to praise or discredit,
And the meaning for history is ominous.

ANNULMENT (n) A miracle performed by the Catholic church, by which a marriage is caused to disappear. This blessing enables one of the spouses to renounce the Biblical injunction: What God has joined together, let no man put asunder." As the Holy See sees it, God made a mistake in joining the two and is properly rebuked by the Pope's sundering.

Parents' marriage annulled, John Simpson felt gulled,
By suddenly being a bastard.
"My life's now a sin," he said with chagrin,
And went to his pub to get plastered.

ANTICIPATION (n) The first of three successive emotions. The other two are "realization" and "disappointment".

ANTIPATHY (n) An emotion that commonly follows any close association with a politician.

> Said a prudent young mistress from Dove,
> When asked why she married her guv:
> "My antipathy's great,
> "Cause his habits, I hate!
> "But, his bank balance merits my love."

APHORISM (n) Regurgitated wisdom for people unwilling or unable to think for themselves. It is a medium favored by those who cannot swallow sermons, whole, only read abridgements, and find reality television more real than their own lives. Here are several examples that Ben Franklin missed:

1. It is better to have loved and lost--much better.

2. "When I entered a room, I used to be behind, before, but now I Am first, at last."
Bess Truman (describing life after leaving the White House)

3. Where there's a will, there's a way, and where there isn't, there's an excuse.

4. "You should believe that God will answer your prayers only if you also believe that the answer will be 'No!'".
University of Michigan Professor Charles Stevenson

5. All stings come to those who wait.

6. Learn from the mistakes of others. You won't live long enough to make them all yourself.

7. No good deed ever goes unpunished.

APOTHEGM (n) (SEE APHORISM) Dehydrated good sense repackaged for people with poor memories, as in these examples:

1. The majority of us start out with nothing and still have most of it left.

2. As we age, our wild oats turn into oatmeal.

3. By the time you finally get your head together, your body is starting to fall apart.

4. I don't remember ever being absentminded.

5. I wish the buck stopped here. I sure could use a few.

ARGUMENT (n) A dispute warmer than a dialogue and cooler than fighting words. If it is between husband and wife, she must always have the last word. If he says anything relevant afterward, it is the beginning of a new argument.

"My wife and I have never exchanged cross words. The flow has always been in one direction."

Richard Mansfield

ARSON (n) A self-help remedy that enables property owners to cure their insolvency.

Said a broke building owner named Hatch,
Who was saved by the flame of a match:
"When the fire took hold
"It could not be controlled,
"Though it took thirty minutes to catch."

ARTIST (n) An aesthetic person with an anesthetic effect on others. This explains why so many people sleep at operas and grow numb in the presence of modern art.

Modern artists engage in a scam
When they take money from Uncle Sam.
Their sculptures are junk,
Their poetry's bunk,
And they can't draw a shape worth a damn.

A wealthy and disdainful woman was being guided through a modern art exhibit by one of the curators. At every painting, she expressed harsh criticism. Near the end of the display, she stopped and, pointing to a frame in front of them, said: "That's the ugliest and most grotesque portrait I have ever seen. Is that a new acquisition?" "No, madam," her guide replied. "That's a mirror."

ASS (n) 1. The South end of a person facing North.
2. A four-legged animal named "Jack".
There's a beautiful girl in Madras
With a perfectly wonderful ass.
It's not rounded and pink,
As you, perhaps, think,
But gray, with long ears and eats grass.

ASSEMBLY (n) A gathering of diverse elements in one place for the purpose of achieving a goal with the greatest possible difficulty and delay, e.g., a State legislative assembly.

"When I look for a toy to buy for my boy,
"There are some that I pass by, unheeded.
"It isn't the price, but this printed advice:
"'Some simple assembly needed.'"

ASSERTIVE (adj.) To be mistaken at the top of your voice.

asteroid (n) The only type of steroid the International Olympic Committee has not yet banned.
>Said the IOC's Rand, "asteroids must be banned
>"And athletes with contacts, disgraced.
>"You can depend upon it, all those who are on it
>"Will be, most assuredly, spaced."

ASTROLOGER (n) 1. A believer in the power of heavenly bodies to influence our lives. "A ridiculous theory!" scoffs Sir Archibald Phipps, biographer of Helen of Troy, Cleopatra, and Marilyn Monroe.
2. One who, in the course of finding fortunate astrologic signs for her clients, finds her own fortune in the illogic of asses.

ATHEISM (n) A doctrine that denies the existence of God on the assumption that the trillions of star and planetary systems in the Universe were all created when a kernel of matter popped with a Big Bang. The doctrine does not explain who created the kernel.
>Said an atheist teacher in Kiel,
>"Although I know God isn't real,
>"When you're over the brink
>"And starting to sink,
>"I suggest that you pray a good deal."

ATHEIST (n) One who believes, without knowledge, in the denials of those who speak, without proof, about things they cannot comprehend.
>Said a wealthy old atheist, Long,
>"My scorn of religion is strong."
>But to churches, while dyeing,
>He gave his wealth, sighing,
>"Just in case my opinions are wrong!"

"An atheist is someone who watches Notre Dame play Southern Methodist without caring who wins."
>Johnny Carson

ATHLETE (n) Someone who has developed his muscles at the expense of his brain. The impact is exemplified by the following true stories:
1. A Florida State University coach offered this advice to one of his star athletes (who had just received four F's and one

D on his report card): "Son, I think you're spending too much time on one subject."

2. Asked by his football coach at the University of Nebraska why he appeared so nervous during practice, a player gave this explanation: "my sister is going to have a baby, today, and I don't know whether I'm going to be an uncle or an aunt."

3. "I don't know the names of any of the basketball clubs I visited when I was there," said a member of the Los Angeles Lakers professional basketball team, when asked by a reporter if he had visited the Parthenon.

4. "I wasn't graded on English," James Brooks (former star running back for the Cincinnati Bengals professional football team) told a judge, who asked how it was that he was nearly illiterate although he had graduated from a university.

ATONEMENT (n) The price paid for the pleasure of sinning and for the right to repeat it.

"My atonement for sinning just marks the beginning
"Of planning to go and repeat it.
"To make me less liable, don't read from the Bible,
"Just show me a sin that will beat it."

AUCTION (N) A form of selling that relies on a complex pattern of hand signals and gestures. It can result in financial disaster to those who suffer from palsy, spasms, poison ivy, hives, or jock itch.

A corseted woman, named Nash,
Had a terrible itch from a rash.
At an auction, she bought,
Never having the thought,
A toilet for five hundred, cash.

AU GRATIN (adj.) A rich French sauce that is reputed to have killed more of its nation than all wars since Charlemagne.

Potatoes au gratin are quite misbegotten;
They ruin a person's insides.
Salted to please, dripping with cheese,
They're things cardiologists prize.

AUSTRALIA (n) A nation continent whose seasons are weird. It resembles the United States in two respects:

1. Like people in the South, Australians speak a language that is vaguely similar to English.

2. Australia, too, has always treated its aborigines with reservations.

A wonderful country, Australia,
Whose people grow sturdy and tall.
Where the whites are all talked of as "dinkum"
And the blacks are not mentioned at all.

AUTHOR (n) A person who rewrites something he has read and publishes it as his own. The process is called "evolutionism" by authors and their agents, but "plagiarism" by everybody else.

Fyodor Dostoyevsky wrote about a young Russky
Who behaved much like Christ, named Alexei.
As the author, he's liable for this theft from the Bible;
So, to fireproof his soul, let us pray.

AUTOBIOGRAPHY (n) A type of fiction in which the author lies about his subject with no risk of a libel actions.

An elderly actress, named Mavis,
Her autobiography gave us.
While the stories were hot,
The truth, they were not.
They were really about Betty Davis.

AVERAGE (adj.) In the middle of the pack. Free of the stress of leadership, it is a desirable position, except in the case of a dog team, where only the lead dog has a good view.

"The average American thinks there's nothing average about him."
Will Rogers

B

BABY (n) "A creature with a loud noise at one end and no sense of social responsibility at the other."
Reverend William Howland

BACHELOR (n) Someone fortunate enough to have loved and lost.

Says a chauvinist bachelor in Wolde,
"About marriage, I'm really not sold.

18

"My trained female Setter
"Is certainly better.
"She's a bitch who will do what she's told."

BAIL (n) A procedure in our Justice System whereby relatives of
a criminal pay for his release from jail so he can steal enough to
pay his lawyer.

> Said a barrister in old Dundee,
> Of a prostitute client named Bea,
> "I'll arrange for her bail
> "So she gets out of jail.
> "How else can the girl raise my fee?"

BALLET (n) A type of dance designed to keep the performers on
their toes. In a typical composition, male dancers hop about as if
their shoes were on fire and catch the female dancers when the
latter get dizzy from spinning. Many of the males seem not to
enjoy this experience, perhaps because

> their tights have been too tight for too many years.
> A Los Angeles fellow, named Ray,
> Has a passion for dancing ballet.
> Once, leaping with zest,
> His tights stayed at rest;
> Critics called it: "Moon over L. A.".

BALLOT (n) One vowel away from its martial counterpart, it is
more lethal than the other, regularly killing off all but one
candidate for each political office. In its "One Man, One Vote"
decision, the U.S. Supreme court ordered that each ballot cast be
given equal weight. Unfortunately, The decision has been corrupted
in every State by the practice of giving the same weight to a
woman's vote.

> Said a very sick Democrat, Mac Tiff,
> To make thoughts of his death more attractive,
> "Plant my bones in Chicago,
> "Then register me so
> "I stay politically active."

BALONEY (n) The name White House reporters give to Presidential
speeches for their blend of beef, chicken, corn, oil, sugar, salt,
vinegar, guts, gall, and coloring agents--not to mention
additives intended to control bad taste and smell.

> Said a White House reporter, named Tony,

Told the President's speeches seemed phony,
"To all friendly noses,
"They're as fragrant as roses.
"But to me, they are tainted baloney."

BANANA (n) 1. A fruit enjoyed by monkeys and their descendants.
2. An acronym that is the battle cry of today's urban anti-developer activists. Standing for "build almost nothing anywhere near anybody", it is more honest than its deceptive forerunner, "nimby" ("not in my backyard"). Members of the latter groups do not oppose development in your backyard.

BANKRUPTCY (n) A legal process by which an attorney helps a client discharge all his debts--except for attorney fees.
> Dan White never frets about his mounting debts:
> "Frugality never restrains me."
> Each seven year stretch, to court goes the wretch
> And wipes them all out in bankruptcy.

BAPTISM (n) A watery ceremony in Christian churches during which the "original sin" of the person blessed is washed away. The volume of water used varies from a simple touch with wet fingers to the sinner's total immersion. Southern Baptists are especially fond of the latter method, giving God the opportunity to purge His church of unworthy candidates.
> Said Napoleon Street, when asked by Saint Pete,
> What had happened to bring him up there.
> "I was being baptized in a white church I prized
> "When I suddenly ran out of air."

BARBER (n) A hair-razing cutup who works in a clip joint and gets shear pleasure from saying, "hair today, gone tomorrow."
> (1)
> In the town of Jackson Hole,
> There's a barber as tall as a troll.
> "Suplinski" is his name
> And his chief claim to fame
> Is that he's the town's barber Pole.
> (2)
> Said an ex surgeon, Timothy Stack,
> Telling why he's a barbering hack:
> "My incisions, quite often,
> "Led direct to the coffin,

"While my present mistakes grow right back."

BARTENDER (n) A type of pharmacist with an all-liquid stock, whose concoctions affect his customers in the opposite way--consumption is better than the consequence.

BASSET (n) A dog with the heart of a lover, the soul of a poet, the courage of a fighter, and the face of a suicide.
>Bassets are fearfully stressed
>And need to be often caressed.
>With bowlegs, poor dears,
>Fat ass and big ears,
>It's no wonder they look so depressed.

BATHROOM (n) In a modern American residence, a place where there is neither bath nor room.
"The only time the world beats a path to your door is when you're in the bathroom."
>Fred Allen

BEACH (n) A place where young people discard their condoms and old people expose why only the young procreate.
>Said a literate litterbug, Keach,
>When charged with befouling the beach,
>"Like Wonderland's Hatter,
>"My trash doesn't matter.
>"I just push it in somebody's reach."

BEAGLE (n) A small dog with the appetite of a bishop, the instincts of a thief, the tongue of a slut, and the face of a lover. Unfortunately, this last impression is marred by a view from the rear, which suggests that its genitalia is housed in parentheses.
>A beagle, called Irma, I tend
>Has parts at the front that transcend.
>But, her back legs curve so,
>Like the sides of an "O",
>That she pees without having to bend.

BEATNIK (n) The name given young urban adults in the Sixties who took drugs, were promiscuous, littered streets, aggressively panhandled, abandoned their children, and cursed the police--for which they were severely scolded. Many of them also demonstrated

21

against the Viet Nam War, for which they were given jail sentences and criminal records.

> A middle-age beatnik I know
> Sowed some seeds into Beth years ago.
> She gave his surname
> To the harvest that came,
> Adding "Bruce", "Tom", "Jill", "Joseph", and "Flo".

BENCH (n) An elevated wooden structure in a courtroom where all judges sit and many sleep. It is equipped with a wooden mallet, called a "gavel", the purpose of which is to knock good sense into erring lawyers. That this remedy has proved an utter failure is amply shown by the fact that so few lawyers have sense, despite centuries of knocking.

> Judge to Criminal Defendant: "Do you want a jury trial or a judge-only trial?"
> Defendant: "I want a jury trial."
> Judge: "Do you know what the difference is?"
> Defendant: "Yes, sir. The difference is that twelve ignorant people decide my fate instead of one."

BENEFACTOR (n) What the first party in a giving relationship is called. The second party is called "ingrate".

> A Boy Scout at Pershing and Hyde
> Pulled a woman across, as her guide.
> Far from thankful, instead,
> She whacked him and said:
> "I was waiting, you twerp, for my ride."

BETRAY (v) To violate one's duty to show good faith and fair dealing toward another. The duty does not extend to love, war, and the used car business, in that treachery is inherent in all three.

> Judas was paid for the Man he betrayed,
> Thirty pieces of coin, says the story.
> Had he known, you can bet,
> The bad press he would get,
> He'd have given Saint Peter the glory.

BIBLE (n) Fiction or sacred truths, depending on the path your prejudices take. Making sense of it is especially hard for children, as these comments by several Catholic school third-graders attest:

1. "Noah's wife was called 'Joan of Arc'."

2. "Lot's wife was a pillar of salt by day, but a ball of fire by night."

3. "Jews are a proud people and through history, they've had problems with bad genitals."

4. "Jews make unleavened bread, which is bread without any ingredients."

5. "The Egyptians were all drowned in the dessert and afterwards, Moses went to the top of Mount Sinai to get the Ten Amendments."

6. "The Seventh Commandment is 'Thou shalt not admit adultery.'"

7. "The greatest miracle in the Bible is when Joshua told his son to stand still and he obeyed him."

8. "Solomon, one of David's sons, had 300 wives and 800 porcupines."

9. "Jesus was born because his mother, Mary, had a immaculate contraption."

10. "The helpers of Jesus were the 12 decimals and the epistles were the wives of the apostles."

BICEPS (n) Upper arm muscles that women admire in men and deplore in themselves. Men flaunt them to enhance their sex appeal, while women conceal them for the same purpose. Neither strategy is worthwhile, since sex between them involves a lower muscle group in a man's third arm, called his "triceps".

BIFOCALS (n) Eyeglasses with partitioned lenses designed so that the wearer's sight is differently impaired through each section, thus qualifying him for a disability parking placard.

BIGAMIST (n) A glutton for punishment whose "ayes" are bigger than the law can stomach.

BIGOT (n) Someone who is color-blinded.

"I am not a bigot. All I want to know is whether a person is a human being. If so, then he can sink no lower."

> Mark Twain
> When a colorblind fellow, in Bryte,
> Was cured by a doctor one night,
> He saw, with disgust,

That the girl of his lust
Had skin most decidedly white.

BIGOTRY (n) How an Italian tourist describes a California Redwood.

BIOGRAPHY (n) The story of a celebrity's life, edited so as to qualify as fiction. Whenever the scope of the myth-telling is too brazen to be left to another, the work is called and "autobiography."

"You ain't what you ought to be; you ain't what you're goin' to be; but thank God, you ain't what you was."
(old Afro-American homily)

BIRTH (n) The end of a nine month ordeal and the beginning of a lifetime of sacrifice. On balance, it is either a blessing or a curse, depending on which of the following conditions prevailed at the time:

1. (blessing) To a childless couple.
   (curse) The couple already has 10 children.
2. (blessing) To a spinster who poked a hole in the father's condom.
   (curse) To the man who relied on the condom.
3. (blessing) The father was a Pope during the Renaissance.
   (curse) The father is a Catholic priest in Boston.
4. (blessing) The mother is a homely unmarried woman from the hills of West Virginia.
   (curse) The father is her father.

"Girls, birthing is tough while dying is mean.
"So get lots of love spread out in between."
Langston Hughes
"Why is it that we cry at a funeral and rejoice at a birth? Is it because we are not the person involved?"
Mark Twain

BISEXUAL (adj.) Having one's cake and eating it, too.
A fine intellectual, very bisexual,
Has a dilemma I know.
When he's romantic, his problem, semantic,
Is whether to come or to go.

BISHOP (n) "An official of the Christian faith who has attained an eminence higher than Christ ever reached."

H.L. Mencken

An indolent bishop from Bray,
His roses neglected to spray.
His wife, more alert,
Bought a powerful squirt
And said to her spouse, "let us spray."

BITCH (n) The mother of a dog or a woman with an attitude.

When a married man cheated, at Boone,
His pregnant wife, mad as a loon,
Bought a funeral niche
For the son of a bitch
And vowed she would put him there, soon.

BIZARRE (adj.) Behavior so different from what is normal as to defy rational explanation, as in the following examples:

1. A politician who does not lie about his opponent.
2. A pigeon who chooses a dirty car to dump on.
3. A Pit Bull with dry mouth.
4. A cab driver who stops for you during a thunderstorm.
5. A freeway service attendant who does not puncture a tire while checking it.
6. A young man on his first date who does not make a pass at her.
7. A young woman on her first date who does not expect a pass.

BLIND (adj.) Having to substitute foresight, hindsight, and insight, for eyesight.

A seeing-eye dog led a blind lawyer off the curb and into traffic. Hearing his danger, the man hurried back to safety as soon as he could, pulling the dog behind him. Then, he took a snack from his pocket and fed it to the dog.

A pedestrian, who had witnessed the incident, tapped him on the shoulder and said: "Pardon me, but do you know that your dog almost got you killed?"

"Yes, I know," the lawyer replied.

"Then why are you giving him a snack?"

"I have to find out where his mouth is," he said, "so I can kick his ass!"

"Oh, take my arm, my bonnie lass,
"And lead me straight and true.

"When e'er we reach a plot of grass,
"I'll lay you on your bonnie ass
"And then we'll have a screw."
Richard Mansfield (parodying Robert Burns)

BLONDE (n) A woman with hair to dye for.

According to the eminent British neurologist, Ms. Ann Thrope, the yellow dye migrates to the woman's brain, where it clogs neural receptors and impedes her reasoning processes. There is plenty of anecdotal evidence to validate the Thrope Theory, among which are the following examples:

1. An attractive blonde repeatedly looked in her mailbox, then slammed the lid shut and returned to her house in obvious vexation. Seeing this, a neighbor called out, "is anything wrong, Marilyn?" The blonde replied, "you bet there's something wrong; my stupid computer keeps telling me that I've got mail."

2. Man to God: "Why do you make blondes so lovely?"

God: "So you will fall in love with them."

Man: "Then, why do you make them so stupid?"

God: "So they will fall in love with you."

3. Q. What do you call an attractive blonde?

A. "Golden Retriever".

4. Q. What did the blonde say when she was told that she was pregnant?

A. "Are you sure it's mine?"

5. When a young brunette woman complained to her doctor that she hurt all over, the latter asked her to point to the places that hurt the most. She obeyed, using her right forefinger, and cried out each time she poked herself. "You're really a blonde, aren't you?" the doctor asked. "Yes, but how did you know?" she replied. "Because you're finger is broken," he explained.

6. A husband gave his blonde wife a cell phone for her birthday and called her the next day while she was shopping at Sears. "How do you like your phone?" he inquired. "It's wonderful," she enthused, "but how did you know that I'd be in Sears?"

BLUSH (n) A slight reddening of the face once associated with feelings of shame or immodesty. Now that both have become obsolete, the word identifies a white wine with high blood pressure.

"Man is the only species that can blush, or has cause to."
Mark Twain

BODYBUILDER (n) An extroverted narcissist who wears his muscles on the outside and delights in watching them play with each other.
> A famed bodybuilder, named Mize,
> For muscles defined, won first prize.
> His various creases
> Can hold all the greases
> From fifty-eight burgers, with fries.

BOERS (n) A minority ethnic group in South Africa with a one-track mind about the majority Blacks--a sidetrack. Their frequent diatribes on the subject has convinced several expert orthographers that their name is misspelled.
> "South Africa has a serpent, strong,"
> Says a racist white depicter.
> "It's black, about one hundred million feet long,
> "And it's called a 'Boer Constrictor'."

BOMB (n) A device for controlling the world's population.
> Said a Chinese malthusian, Fay Shon,
> After setting-off bombs through the nation:
> "I may be quite mad,
> "but I'm not wholly bad.
> "I'm controlling excess population."

BOOK (n) One of the most effective narcotics ever invented. The time it takes the average reader to fall asleep is inversely related to its size. The Congressional Record, the multi-volume set of President Coolidge's speeches, and the Collected Wit and Wisdom of Adolph Hitler, for example, are guaranteed to overcome the most stubborn case of insomnia.
It does not necessarily follow that small books will always keep readers wide awake. Following are several thin titles that will induce a quick stupor:
1. "A Guide to Arab Democracies"
2. "Journey Into the Mind of George W. Bush"
3. "Career Opportunities for History Majors"
4. "Strategies of Contraception", by Pope John Paul II
5. "A Vacationer's Guide to Detroit"
6. "Tips on World Dominance", by Fidel Castro
7. "Guide to Dining Etiquette", by Mike Tyson
8. "Directory of Mormon Divorce Lawyers"
9. "Tasty Spotted Owl Recipes", by the Pacific Lumber

Company's dietician
> 10. "Staple Your Way to Success"
> 11. "The Amish Phone Book"
> 12. "What Men Know About Women"
> 13. "Twenty Ways To Wok a Dog."
> A book in a library I know
> Tells how to make love on the go.
> Seems a couple can couple,
> If sufficiently supple,
> And their walk is sufficiently slow.

BORDELLO (n) A house with many bedrooms, but no sleepers.
> A weary young fellow in a Vegas bordello
> Was pinched by police, that's a fact.
> When he slept with Miss Keep,
> Seems he really did sleep.
> Now he's charged with an unlicensed act.

BORE (n) Personification of a TV commercial, prescription
for insomnia, enemy to thought, and assassin of solitude, this
parricide can be found among both sexes expressing opinions
contrary to yours. Several classic definitions of the species have
been written by eminent critics (who were themselves the enemy they
decry), among which are these examples:
  1. A bore is..."someone who insists on speaking when you want
him to listen."
> Ambrose Bierce
  2. A bore is..."a fellow who constantly opens his mouth and
puts his feats in it."
> H. L. Mencken
> "Mine eyes have seen the ruin from the coming of the
bores.
> "They are stomping out the vintage from their sour grapes
in store.
> "They have loosed the vapid chatter that all sane men

should ignore.
> "Democrats! Keep whining on."
> (excerpted from the famous patriotic song, "Battle Hymn of
> the Republicans.")

BOWEL (n) The lower intestine of a human, including the colon and
semi-colon. Its movement is one of life's greatest satisfactions
and that it is achieved while sitting on a throne lends it majesty.

BOXING (n) An unsportsmanlike business in which lower-class black men endeavor to pound each other's brains out for audiences of cheering white men completely devoid of class. The frequent success of this endeavor proves that some black men have no brains and some white men are sick.

> A boxer, named Sam, can't fight worth a damn;
> One would think his career would be fleeting.
> But, promoters pursue him and TV shows woo him
> 'Cause he takes such a colorful beating.

BOWLEGGED (adj.) Having legs so concave that the knees are strangers.

> "What ho! What manner of men be these,
> "Who carry their balls in parentheses?"
> (Texas doggerel imitating Shakespeare)

BRIDE (n) A woman who ties the knot in marriage. Nowadays, it is a slipknot she ties, whereas formerly, it was a noose.

A little girl asked her mother, at a wedding reception, "why is the bride dressed all in white?" Wishing to keep it simple, her mother replied, "white is a happy color and this is the happiest day of her life." The daughter thought about that and said, "then, does that explain why the groom is dressed in black?"

BRAGGART (n) Someone who over-gilds her lily. She is distinguishable from an egotist, who believes that her lily cannot be improved by gilding it; from a cynic, who believes that the gilt will not hide the wilt; from the gullible, who thinks that gilding a weed will look the same; from a Republican, who is convinced that he is already solid gold; from a Democrat, who will accept gilding only if a Republican pays for it; and from a wise reader of this work, who knows that to gild a lily is to kill it.

> Said a braggart, named Arthur McGee,
> Whose wife got a water bed, free:
> "When we love, it's so frantic
> "That it's like the Atlantic."
> But, his wife thinks it's like the Dead Sea.

BRAIN DRAIN (n) A natural process by which the neural cells of some people are liquefied and flow out through their brain stems down to their hind quarters, which then becomes the seat of their intelligence. The process is most prevalent among national politicians and explains why there are so many asses in Washington.

Here are several true stories illustrating the effect on a cross-section of the public:

1. A woman in Pensacola took her new motorboat out for a spin and was dissatisfied by its sluggish performance. She brought it back to the dealer, whose mechanic inspected it thoroughly and found everything in good working order. On a hunch, the mechanic dived into the water at the mooring to check the bottom. When he surfaced, he nearly choked with laughter, explaining that the trailer was still clamped to the underside of the boat.

2. In Detroit, a man gave the clerk at a convenience store a $20 bill and asked for change. When the clerk opened the cash drawer, the man pulled a gun and demanded the contents of the drawer. The clerk complied and the robber ran out, leaving his twenty behind. When he was caught running from the store, police discovered that the cash from the drawer totaled $15.60. The police posed this question to the Prosecuting Attorney: "If a robber gives you more money than he has taken, has a crime occurred?"

3. A man in Los Angeles, who later said he was tired of walking, stole a steamroller and drove it through city streets at its top speed of 5 miles per hour. He was finally arrested when a policeman stepped aboard and placed him in handcuffs.

4. A young man in Atlanta was arrested after giving a department store clerk a $15 bill and asking for change.

5. In Phoenix, a man was found violently sick at the rear of a parked mobile home. He admitted to a security officer that he had tried to siphon gasoline from the gas tank and, by mistake, had stuck his hose into the sewage holding tank. The owner of the mobile home declined to prosecute, saying it was the best laugh he'd had in years.

> A prominent judge in Rose Hills
> Was shot by his spouse through the gills.
> 'Cause he paid a tart, Lisa,
> By charging his Visa,
> Forgetting his wife paid the bills.

BRIDLE (n) An apparatus for controlling a horse. A variation of another word, "BRIDAL", it is thought to have been coined by a disgruntled husband in 19th Century England. The relationship illustrates how closely language mirrors life.

BRIEF (n) The droll name given to a written legal argument that commonly runs to thirty pages or more. It refutes the accusation that lawyers are humorless.

But spin, more than humor, is at work here. The word derives from an ancient tradition of the legal profession that bases a lawyer's fee on the number of words in his document, rather than the number of worthwhile ideas in it. If the latter was the standard, lawyer fees would be much lower and the nation would still be covered by vast forests.

"Don't marry that lawyer, daughter. All he cares about is in his briefs."

John Tomlinson, Esq.

BROKER (n) The most candid of all professions, whose very name identifies the consequence clients are sure to suffer.

A commodity trader, named Dowe,
Explained why he's called, 'Broker', now:
"I took my advice
"And invested in rice.
"Now I am broker, and how!"

BROMIDE (n) A thought that soars in a phrase that snores. Following are several classic examples:

"A snitch in crime saves him time."
"Absence makes the heart go yonder."
"A woman's word is never done."
"One who lives in a glass house should never throw nude parties."

BUCOLIC (adj.) The tendency of rural life to prove that City living is not so bad, after all.

Two lovers, Linda and Lance,
Were jarred from their bucolic trance.
In a field where they lay,
He observed, with dismay,
That the passionate bites were from ants.

BUG (n) A class of animals that is inferior to humans in that it lacks a conscience. Because of this, it has no reason to lie, cheat, steal, or blush.

Though bugs are small, they give their all,
From heads down to their butts.
They dive to stop my car and plop;
They sure have lots of guts.

BUMPER STICKER(n) Contemporary wisdom displayed on the rear bumper
of automobiles, the front bumper being reserved for pedestrians.
Following are several noteworthy examples of the genre:

1. "I miss my ex, but my aim is improving."
2. "I'm smiling because I don't know what's going on."
   3. "Honk if you love peace and quiet."
4. "I'm not spoiled, just well cared-for."
5. "I may be fat, but you're ugly and I can lose weight."
6. "I may be drunk, madam, but you're ugly and I'll be sober in the morning."
   (attributed to Winston Churchill)
7. "My husband and I understand each other, which is why we're divorcing."
8. "If moonlight becomes you, utter darkness will do even more."
9. "I'm suffering from mentalpause."
10. "If at first you don't succeed, don't take up sky-diving."

BURNOUT (n) A disabling condition that afflicts many people in stressful occupations. Strangely, those who are threatened with layoffs appear to be immune.

Here are several classic signs to help you diagnose the condition:

1. You tried to enter your password on the microwave.
2. You haven't played solitaire with real cards for years.
3. You have a list of fifteen phone numbers to reach your family of three.
4. You frequently e-mail your buddy, who works at the desk next to you.
5. You speak to a stranger in South Africa several times a month, via the Internet, but you haven't spoken to your next-door neighbor in two years.
6. You've sat at the same desk for four years and worked for three different companies.
7. The nameplate on your office door is attached with velcro.
8. When your system crashed, you felt worse abut losing your jokes than losing your customer information.
9. You know precisely how many days are left before you retire.
10. The only way you can remember how your kids look is by glancing at their pictures taped to your desk top.

BUSINESSMAN (n) Someone active in commerce and dedicated to making
the largest possible profit by selling the cheapest product or
service possible, then rewarding himself with what is due to
others.
      "First, you must learn how to lie with a straight face.
"Next, you must be able to cheat without a guilty conscience.
"Finally, you must learn how to break laws without getting
"caught. Now, you are ready to go into business."
            Mark Twain (advice to a young man thinking about
                  a career in business)

BYSTANDER (n) Someone who takes a bye on taking a stand.
            A bystander, white, disregarded the plight
            Of a homeless young child he could see.
            Said the man, "I'm resolved that I won't get involved
            "Unless the one suffering is me."

                              C

CAD (n) 1. A software product for designers.
      2. A soft-soaping product with designs.
            "Young woman, don't yield to a cad;
            "Avoid him as if he's a curse.
            "To let a fool kiss you is bad.
            "To let a kiss fool you is worse."
                  Alexander Pope

CAESAREAN (adj.) An operation that makes a woman bearable.

CALIFORNIA (n) A State in our Union that is in a state of
disunion due to a state of war within itself. Its Northern half is
Democrat, liberal, loose, and wet (in all its meanings), while the
Southern half is Republican, conservative, uptight, and dry
(weather only). Wrested from the Mexicans by a military invasion,
Southward, during the last Century, it is now in the process of

being returned to them by a civilian invasion going the other way.

"In California, whiskey is for drinking and water is for fighting over."
Mark Twain

CALLING (n) A vocation to which one is summoned by a higher power, as in: "Priests are summoned by their soul to answer the calling of the spirit." Nowadays, an increasing number of priests are being summoned by courts for answering the calling of their flesh.

"Every calling can be great if it is greatly pursued."
Oscar Wilde

CANDY (n) One of God's greatest gifts to womankind, it is the best chronic treatment for chronic depression, the only reward for obesity, and a sure-fire expiation for marital misdemeanors.

"Candy is dandy, but liquor is quicker."
Dorothy Parker

Said a corpulent lady, named Sandy,
"I know that hot sex is just dandy.
"But, because of my tummy,
"No man can get chummy,
"And, in truth, I would rather have candy."

CANNIBAL (n) An aborigine who has learned to stomach missionaries. He carries the symbolic practice of the Catholic Church to "eat the body of Christ" to the next logical stage for true believers. He eats the body of the missionary who ate the body of Christ.

To Heaven go priests and to Hell he who feast
On people he boiled into jelly.
But, what I don't know is where they both go
When the priest's in the other guy's belly?

CANT (n) Piety confined to the tongue. This kind of religious fervor is often displayed by leaders of nations to justify action that is especially vicious. A notable example is the exhortation of Saddam Hussein in Iraq, who assured his soldiers that their invasion of Iran would "bear sacred fruit." He was right, for many thousands of them stayed as fertilizer.

Before Paul was sainted, he saw God and fainted.
Then, his preaching was thought to be cant.
But, he crowed to his critics, "by my gaseous emetics,
"I will rise up to Heaven, but you shan't!"

34

CAPITOL (n) The "seat of government", so-called because there are so many asses there.

CARNIVORE (n) Someone who loves carnival food. This person is distinguishable from an "herbivore" (an eater named "Herbert"), and a "broccolivore" (someone who likes broccoli). The last of these is nearly extinct.

There are other lesser known categories, among which are "mommyvore," who consumes everything near her; "billygrahamivore," who only eats missionary preachers, and "sadistivore", who has an appetite for downtrodden Republicans.

An unsavory family is Vore.
There are Carney, Herbie and more.
Carney's flesh is half rotten.
Herbie, boiled, tastes like cotton,
While the rest are a terrible bore.

CARPEL TUNNEL (n) A painful disorder of the wrists and hands that can ruin a man's sex life.

CAT (n) An incompletely domesticated animal with the morals of an assassin and the affectionate nature of a Lizzie Borden.

"Dogs have owners, while cats have staff."
George Carlin

CATHARTIC (n) An effective method of clearing clogged intestines of waste.

A famous explorer, Sir Fay,
Was clogged from September to May.
While in the Antarctic,
He took a cathartic
And jetted himself to Bombay.

CATHOLIC (n) Someone who believes in the divinity of Christ with all her heart, but not with her mind, and in His precepts with all her mind, but not with her heart.

"I'm a Catholic," said Angela Hutch.
"Attend mass, pray daily, and such.
"But, ask me to mix
"With Afros and Spics--
"Oh, please, you are asking too much."

35

CAVIL (v) Generous with ungenerous criticism.
> "I certainly don't mean to cavil,"
> Said he to the judge one day.
> "But, when you just pounded your gavel,
> "My fingers were in the way."

CELEBRITY (n) Somebody who is a somebody to everybody.
> "I always wanted to be a somebody, but I should have been more specific."
>> John Wilkes Booth

CELIBACY (n) A vow taken by priest and nuns of the Roman Catholic Church to eschew marriage. Pursuant to it, nuns are deemed to marry Christ, who never asserts His conjugal rights, while some priests assert conjugal rights without breaking their vow. The latter believe, with some truth, that this is the only way they will ever know Heaven.
> "I'm not at all surprised to see
> "That some priests spurn celibacy.
> "How can they disdain vile Satan's path,
> "Unless they have seen a woman's wrath."

CENTENARIAN (n) Someone who has lost money on his life insurance policy.
> A pert centenarian, Greer,
> Celebrated her birth with a beer.
> Said she, with a twinkle,
> "I've only one wrinkle
> "And that one I'm sitting on, here."

CENTURY (n) One hundred years, or any one of the following equivalents:
1. One month in Kiev.
2. A two week visit with your spouse's relatives.
3. One week aboard a cruise ship during an Atlantic storm.
4. Two days substitute teaching at a middle school.
5. One night baby-sitting an infant with the flu.

CHAMBERS (n) A judge's private office. It is spacious enough to accommodate the occupant's ego, crown, halo, dunce cap, and privy (where they do their best thinking). The offices are inaccessible to the general public, to avoid their discovering that they rarely work past three in the afternoon.

A Common Pleas judge in Poughkeepsie
Stays in his office a lot.
It's not that he's shy; he's just tipsy
And won't stray from his chamber pot.

CHANGE (n) Something that is inevitable in life, except from a vending machine.

All philosophers tell us, from Plato to Sullus,
That change is a part of our lives.
But, some things never change, though it seems very
strange:
All those PBS fundraising drives.

CHAPERONED (n) An adult supervisor at a social event for minors, whose presence inhibits sex, drinking, drugs, and attendance.

CHARITABLE (adj.) Moved by and altruistic purpose that includes getting a tax deduction.

CHARITABLE ORGANIZATION (n) A philanthropist with the funds of others, less 80% for administrative salaries and bonuses.

CHARITY (n) What conscience supplies when effort and the dole are insufficient.

The law's notion of charity is based on strict clarity
In the status of donor-donee.
What the tax people mind is that often they find
That both donor and donee are me!
"The trouble with beginning charity at home is that, too often, it ends there."
Theodore Roosevelt

CHASTE (adj.) An alternative form of the word, "chased". Once, the terms were synonymous, but in our corrupt age, the meanings has deviated somewhat. Now, a woman may be homely and, therefore chaste, without ever having been chased. Conversely, most attractive young women, who are chaste and chased, seem to hit a speed bump at about age fifteen and are caught.

CHAUVINIST (n) One who believes in the superiority of men. The belief is thought to have originated with God, who made a woman out of a man's minor bone. This is the earliest example of a divine ribbing.

George Bernard Shaw was a renowned and implacable chauvinist. During a dinner party at which he was expounding his conviction, Shaw turned to his wife and asked if she didn't agree that men were smarter than women. "I certainly do," she replied, with conviction. "After all, you married me and I married you, didn't we?"

Q. Is there anything worse than a male chauvinist pig?

A. Yes, a woman who won't do what she's told.

Following are several examples of male comments that entitle men to the chauvinist label:

1. "First, God made the Earth, then rested. Next, God made Man, then rested. Finally, god made Woman and, since then, neither god nor Man has rested."

2. (wife) "What's on the TV?"

(Husband) "Dust".

3. (Son) "I hear that in Africa, a man doesn't know his wife until after they're married."

(Father) "That's true in every country."

4. A man placed a classified ad that said, "Wife Wanted." Over the next few days, he received more than a hundred replies that said the same thing: "You can have mine."

5. "My wife is an angel. She's up in the air most of the time, always harping about something, and never has anything to wear."

CHECK (n) A pay order on a bank. Normally of paper, it is sometimes made of rubber to improve its bounce.

Said Congressman Hughes, in response to the news,
That he paid for sex favors by check:
"Don't raise up a squeal, it's not a big deal;
"I'll simply stop payment, by heck."

CHICKEN (n) The main ingredient in a popular salad, it is also a participant in the classic American breakfast of ham and eggs. In the latter guise, it joins the pig as a metaphor for The extent of immersion in a project. The chicken is said to be "involved", while the pig is said to be "committed".

Over the years, various authorities have commented on one of life's great mysteries, i.e., why did the chicken cross the road? Here are several noteworthy examples:

1. (Reverend Martin Luther King) "I dream of the day when nobody will question the right of a chicken to cross the road."

2. (George W. Bush) "Ask me after I've been briefed on the matter."

3. (Fidel Castro) "It crossed where I told it to cross."

4. (Colonel Sanders) "It got away."

5. (Mexican President Vincente Fox) "It was just trying to find work."

6. (Reverend Jerry Folwell) "It escaped from a yard full of Godless and lesbian chickens, and decided to go straight."

7. (Bill Clinton) "First, you'll have to define 'cross'."

8. (Any Eight-Year old child) "To get to the other side, silly."

CHILD (n) The product of a momentary pleasure resulting in a lifetime of imposition. If all aspiring parents could forecast the misery, grinding deprivation, nervous exhaustion, an premature aging that their procreation would cause, homo sapiens (abbreviated to "home saps") would have become extinct long ago.

CHILDREN (N) (See CHILD, this volume, then multiply) These people are featured in many of literature's wisest
proverbs, among which are:

1. Listen to your children while they still know everything.

2. Live long enough to be a burden to your children.

3. "Children in America always give their elders the benefit of their inexperience."

Oscar Wilde

Children are featured in some of literature's greatest classics. Here are several lesser-known titles that are certain to be future best sellers:

1. "You Are Different and That is Bad"

2. "The Boy Who Died From Eating All His Vegetables"

3. "Dad's New Wife, Robert"

4. "Fun Four-Letter Words To Know And Share"

5. "The Kids' Guide To Cutting Things"

6. "Kathy Was So Bad Her Mother Stopped Loving Her"

7. "Curious George and the High-Voltage Wires"

8. "The Little Sissy Who Snitched"

9. "Some Kittens Can Fly"

10. "That's it! I'm Putting Myself Up For Adoption"

11. "Grandpa Gets a Casket"

12. "The Magic World In The Refrigerator"

13. "Teacher Gets Screwed"

14. "Fun Games With The Microwave"

15. "Tantrums That Really Work"
16. "What Mommy And Daddy Do In Bed"
17. "God Doesn't Like Boys"

CHIROPRACTOR (n) A health professional whose principal treatment consists of emptying the patient's wallet, thus relieving pressure on the latter's lumbar vertebrae and his own cash flow.

Said a chiropractor, named Slack,
To a patient with pain in her back:
"I must straighten your spine
"So all parts are in line,"
Then, he fastened her onto the rack.

CHRISTIAN (n) A straggler after Christ who practices what the latter never preached, whose faith is housed in his tongue, and whose favorite sacrament is called, "sanctimony".

"More people have been slaughtered in the name of Christ than for any other cause."

Mark Twain

Said a Serbian Christian, Mikhail,
Interrupting his killing to pray,
"Thanks, Jesus, for giving
"Me so many living
"Moslem mothers and children to slay."

CHRISTMAS (n) Once a Holy day, now a hollyday, we formerly celebrated spiritual gifts and devoted the next year to discharging debts to God. Now, we celebrate commercial gifts and devote the next year to discharging credit card debts.

According to the Jesuit scholar, Father A. Bartlett Pare, Satan moved the "n" in his name in front of the "t" to deceive us as to the person responsible for the change of purpose.

CHURCHILLISM (n) A timely retort by a master of invective wit, Winston Churchill. Here are several blistering examples:

1. Quarreling with Lady Astor during a cocktail party, Astor angrily erupted: "Sir, If you were my husband, I'd put poison in your coffee." Churchill promptly retorted, "Madam, if I was your husband, I'd drink it!"

2. Churchill received 2 tickets from his political enemy, George Bernard Shaw, to the opening night of the latter's new play, "Major Barbara", together with the note: "One ticket is for you and

the other is for a friend, if you have one." Churchill returned the tickets with this note: "Sorry, but a conflict prevents me from using your tickets. Please replace them with tickets to the following night's performance--if there is one."

3. During a hot argument with a society matron at a cocktail party, She became infuriated and said, "You are drunk, sir!" He replied, "I may be drunk, madam, but you're ugly and I'll be sober in the morning."

4. When a companion asked why he would not rise to join in a standing ovation for an eminent politician, Churchill explained: "The only sound reason for a standing ovation is so the audience can adjust their underwear."

CIGARETTE (n) The most popular instrument of suicide in the United States, it combines the advantages of legality and reliability with the allure of uncertainty (the precise year of death cannot be accurately predicted). The primary ingredient, tobacco, is subsidized by the United States government, which regards it as an effective guardian against overpopulation.

> A famished old fellow in Stoke
> Sought Heaven because he was broke.
> He OD'd on cigarettes
> And left with no regrets;
> You might say he went up in smoke.

CINEMA (n) An industry in which the unprincipled market the unedifying to the uncouth.

> Oh, how sad to our heart is the cinema's art;
> As a cultural tool, it's distressing.
> Where never is heard an enlightening word
> And all that is seen is undressing.

CIVIL ENGINEER (n) An engineer with manners.

CLASS ACTION (n) A type of lawsuit in which a lawyer represents many claimants for money damages. If the suit fails, neither the lawyer nor his clients get anything. If, however, it succeeds, the claimants get chicken feed and the lawyer gets the chicken.

> Oh, give me a home where the sharp lawyers roam
> And assert phony claims of all sorts.
> Where their clients don't hear a discouraging fear
> About losing class actions in court.
> In this home on the range, no one thinks it is strange

41

That only the lawyers grow rich.
'Cause your lawmaker blinks at a practice that stinks
From the smell of those sons of a bitch.

CLASSIC (n) "A book praised by everybody and read by nobody."
    Mark Twain

CLASSIFIED AD (n) Newspaper and magazine advertising in a print
so small that the only people who can read it are too young to
afford to buy. Following are several actual ads demonstrating that
newspaper humor is not confined to the comic strips:
    1. "Almost new snow blower for sale. Only used when it
snows."
    2. "Wire mesh butchering gloves for sale; one with five
fingers and one with three fingers. Discounted for quick sale."
    3. "Ten cows and never-bred calves for sale. Also one
gay bull for sale, cheap."
    4. "Full-size mattress for sale, like new; twenty-one
year warranty. Slight urine smell."
    5. "New parachute for sale; never opened. Only used
once."
    6. "Help wanted at $9.75 per hour. Have Flexible
schedules and good working conditions. Compensation at $7 to $9.25
per hour."
    7. "35 volumes of Encyclopedia Britannica for sale, like
new. Recently married and wife knows everything."

CLAUSTROPHOBIA (n) A fear of being alone with Santa in a confined
space.

CLICHE (n) "An idea that sizzles in words that snore."
    Ambrose Bierce

CLOTHES (n) Body covering that is said to make the man. Lack of
it will often make a woman.

CLUB (n) An association of persons who joined for the sole purpose
of selling something to each other.
    "I would never join a club that would have me as a
member."
    Groucho Marx

42

COINCIDENCE (n) An unexpected coupling of events, as in the following examples:

1. A wife, the housekeeper during her marriage, gets to keep the house in her divorce.

2. A clergyman, after throwing the Sunday collection Heavenward to God, gets to keep it all when god rejects the offering.

3. through 10. Among the oddest coincidences are those linking Presidents Lincoln and Kennedy:

3. Abraham Lincoln was elected to Congress in 1846. John F. Kennedy was elected to Congress in 1946.

4. Lincoln was elected President in 1860. Kennedy was elected President in 1960.

5. Both wives lost a child while living in the White House.

6. Both Presidents were shot in the head and on a Friday.

7. Lincoln's secretary was named Kennedy, while Kennedy's secretary was named Lincoln.

8. Both were assassinated by Southerners and both were succeeded by Southerners named Johnson.

9. Andrew Johnson, who succeeded Lincoln, was born in 1808, while Lyndon Johnson, who succeeded Kennedy, was born in 1908.

10. John Wilkes Booth, who assassinated Lincoln, was born in 1839, while Lee Harvey Oswald, who assassinated Kennedy, was born in 1939.

11. Both assassins were known by their three names, which comprise fifteen letters.

12. Booth ran from the theater and was caught in a warehouse. Oswald ran from a warehouse and was caught in a theater.

13. Booth and Oswald were both assassinated before their trials.

COLLEGE (n) A place where young people, who cannot think well, are taught by older people, who cannot do well, about things that will not help either one to think or do better.

> A young miss from Maine, with quite a good brain,
> Got pregnant in college, at Stowe.
> She studied Descartes, advanced Physics and Art,
> But never learned how to say "no!"

COLON (n) The name given the human large intestine. The small intestine is called the "semi-colon".

COLOR COORDINATE (v) What single men do when they launder their clothes.

COLUMBUS (n) An Italian explorer who did not know where he was going, got lost going there, did not know where he was when he got there, was considered insane by his crew, and never set foot in America--where he is celebrated by a national holiday. This fondness for failure explains America's Presidential choices.

COMEBACK (n) A second chance to fail.
"It's hard to make a comeback if you've never been anywhere."
George Carlin

COMMERCIAL (n) The creative part of a television program.
An Iowa village, named "More,"
Has two doctors that people adore.
Drug ads on TV
Often cite them, e.g.,
"More doctors use X when they're sore."

COMMITTEE (n) A group of people chosen for their ability to confuse the issues, avoid relevant facts, disagree about the solutions, and adopt recommendations that every member dislikes.
"A committee is like an overstuffed chair--easy to get into, but hard to get out of."
Robert Wallace

COMMON SENSE (n) "The kind of sense that is very uncommon, because everybody is convinced that only he possesses it."
Jonathan Swift

COMPLACENCY (n) The state of mind of one who, falling from the top of a ten story building and reaching the fifth floor, says "so far so good."

COMPOST (n) A vegetative banquet for worms and maggots. Excrement from the feast is much prized by farmers, who use it to produce vegetables for our dining room tables.
When all is dead except my smile,
Throw me on a compost pile.

And when on celery stalks you munch,

You may be having me for lunch.

COMMUNITY COLLEGE (n) A place where illiterate young people are trained to become semi-illiterate adults. Proof that the improvement is not achieved by every student is supplied by the following excerpts from actual compositions submitted in an English Literature class:

1. "American Indians passed their traditions down to their ancestors, which caused multiple people to be sleeping in each bed."

2. "Martin Luther King, an aspired(sic) leader of Brown and Black people, started the civil rights movement when he ate at a lynch(sic) counter."

3. "Those that could afford it used wet nurses with foul(sic) breaths(sic).

4. "Her past relationship with her father infects(sic) her present relationships with men of the opposite sex."

5. "To train a dog properly, one must have eatable teats (sic)."

7. "Modern heart sturgeons(sic) are doing wonderful things with the culinary(sic) arthuries(sic)."

COMMUTER (n) One of a class of motorists who monopolize highways, thereby preventing retirees from enjoying a pleasant drive.

A commuter, named Sam, in a huge traffic jam,
Started to boil and get surly.
Then, he ran from the car to his office, not far,
And arrived there a whole hour early.

COMPUTER (n) 1. A machine for processing words and data that enables its operator to greatly increase the number and speed of his mistakes.

Said a talking computer, named Poole,
When asked why he's mum, as a rule:
"A human, Doc Pew,
"   Taught me all that he knew.
"If I speak, folks will know I'm a fool."

2. An electronic device that women identify as belonging to the male gender, for the following reasons:

1. In order to get its attention, you have to turn it on.

2. It has a lot of data, but is still clueless.

3. Although it is supposed to solve your problem, most of the time, it is your problem.

4. As soon as you commit to one, you realize that had you waited a little longer, you could have had a better one.

Men, on the other hand, consider a computer to be female for these reasons:

1. Nobody but its creator knows its internal logic.

2. The language it uses to communicate with other computers is unintelligible to anyone else.

3. Even your slightest mistake is stored in long-term memory for eventual recall.

4. As soon as you make a commitment to one, you find yourself spending half your paycheck buying accessories for it.

CONCEIT (n) The conviction that you are as good as me.
>A scruffy old mongrel, named Pete,
>Was pumped with a sudden conceit.
>Because he was wooed
>And madly pursued
>By an elegant poodle in heat.

CONCEPTION (n) Either a new idea or a new being, depending on whether the cortex or the cervix was involved.
>Christian believers are taught
>That Mary's conception was brought
>By God's holy blessing.
>If that's so, then I'm guessing
>That Joseph's enjoyment was naught.

CONDOM (n) The scabbard of a sword, cap of a propellant, dam of a river, wrap of a pipe bomb, and a cannon's spike. Formerly, if a young woman did not carry one on a date, she remained impregnable. Nowadays, if she does not carry one, she is likely to be impregnated.

CONFUCIUS (n) A celebrated Chinese philosopher who authored famous proverbs, among which are the following notable examples:

1. "Better to remain silent and appear a fool than open your mouth and remove all doubt."

2. "A man who is full of himself needs a good laxative."

3. "A young woman who makes a clean breast of it will get many offers."

4. "Better to have loved and lost--much better!"

5. "Experience is a harsh teacher, but fools will learn from no other."

CONGRESS (n) The Federal legislature, from which laws are passed like gas. They are malodorous; are immediately disowned; lack substance; relieve pressure; are often accompanied by much noise; and come from guts rather than brains.

CONNOISSEUR (n) Someone who knows a lot about one thing and nothing about anything else.
>   An old Milwaukee brewer
>   Is renowned as a connoisseur.
>   After tasting Bud beer,
>   He said, with a sneer,
>   "Its proper repose is the sewer."

CONSCIENCE (n) That part of you that hurts when everything else feels so good.
>   Caligula, sadly, treated both sisters, badly;
>   Of conscience, the man had a dearth.
>   Still, their habits, promiscuous, were very conspicuous
>   And they got what their virtue was worth.
>   "A good conscience is a sure sign of a bad memory."
>   George Carlin

CONSERVATIONIST (n) One who advocates that other people keep their property undeveloped so he can enjoy the scenery.
>   A Sierra Club member, named Mack,
>   Received an award for his knack
>   Of conserving much water
>   By saying folks oughter
>   Use privy pits dug out in back.

CONSERVATIVE (n) A former liberal who now suffers from hardening of the arteries.
>   "Nothing in the world is more ridiculous than a young conservative, unless it is an old liberal."
>   George Bernard Shaw
>   Cried Conservative Gail, when sentenced to jail,
>   For swindling clients with lies.
>   "It's not for my crime, but just because I'm
>   "A believer in free enterprise."

CONSISTENT (adj.) Repeating the same baloney or folly over and over again. A prime example of this behavior is Galileo's repeated insistence that our Sun is the center of the Universe. He was quite rightly excommunicated for this heresy by the infallible Pope, who knew that it is the Earth.

"A foolish consistency is the hobgoblin of little minds;
"beloved by teachers, philosophers, and divines."
Ralph Waldo Emerson

CONSTIPATION (n) An organ composition without a single movement.
"Of all the vile words supremely hated,
"The vilest are these: 'I'm constipated!'"

CONSULTANT (n) Somebody who has failed on his own and now advises
others how to do it right.
"A consultant is like a man who knows 100 ways to make love and doesn't have a girlfriend."
Garrison Keeler
A courtroom consultant, named Pree,
Never states his positions for free.
Says he, "since laws bend,
"My opinions depend
"On which side is paying my fee."

CONTINENTAL DRIFT (n) The slow movement of the Earth's land masses
toward and against each other. The term is sometimes confused with, "incontinent drip", which identifies a malady common to elderly men.

CONTINGENT FEE (n) A type of compensation arrangement favored by plaintiff lawyers. Under its terms, if the case is lost, the lawyer gets nothing, while if it is won, the client gets nothing.

CONVENTION (n) A gathering of out-of-town men for the purpose of drinking, eating, and whoring, excessively. All expenses are tax deductible, leading one critic to comment: "A convention is like a gold mine, with the conventioneers getting the gold and Uncle Sam getting the shaft."

(1)

"I love every kind of convention,
"Though it's hard on my back, I should mention."
So said a cute hooker,
Seeing men queue to book her,
As part of their boredom prevention.

(2)

A political convention, it is my contention,
Has an evangelist's pull.
By promises, puffing, and vanity stuffing,
It markets its own kind of bull.

COOL (adj.) Current slang for "rad", which was slang for "super", which was slang for "hip", which was preceded by "swell". All have substituted for "good", which has a moral flavor that youth has always found repellant.

"If you are keeping your cool while all around you are losing theirs, perhaps you are missing something."
Joey Bishop

COUNTERFEIT (adj.) A false identity fashioned to deceive. Several obvious examples leap out:

1. An impoverished clergyman.
2. A smiling boy going to school.
3. A medical doctor in a TV commercial for a laxative.
4. A first-run movie on videotape with Chinese subtitles.
5. A Politician with a good conscience and a good memory.
   Things are seldom what they seem;
   Skim milk counterfeits as cream.
   Altered facts and clever lies
   Conceal the truth and fool the wise.

COUNTRY-WESTERN (adj.) A style of music created in the South for the express purpose of avenging the Civil War on Northern ears. Following are the Top Ten Country-Western songs of all time, according to Outhouse Magazine:

1. "How Can I Miss You When You Won't Go Away?"
2. "Your Face May Look Like My Butt, But Your Heart Is Made Of Pure Gold."
3. "I Wish I Never Met You Before I Got To Know You So Well."
4. "I'm So Miserable Without You It's Like Having You Here."

5. "If I'd Shot You When I Wanted To, I'd Be Out By Now."

6. "My Wife Ran Off With My Best Friend And I Sure Do Miss Him."

7. "She Got The Ring And I Got The Finger."

8. "You Done Tore Out My Heart And Stomped That Sucker Flat."

9. "You're The Reason Our Kids Are So Ugly."

10. "I Haven't Gone To Bed With Any Ugly Women, But I Shore Woke Up with A Few."

COUNTY SEAT (n) Where county politicians and bureaucrats sleep.

> Chardon's an old county seat
> Where rural politicos meet.
> They drink lots of booze
> And, after a snooze,
> Decide which non-voters to cheat.

COW (n) A domesticated animal that eats constantly and gives off lots of gas. See HUSBAND, infra.

> "A cow is of the bovine ilk,
> "A moo in front and behind it, milk."
> Ogden Nash

COWARD (n) Somebody wise enough to know all the contingencies possible in heroic behavior.

> "A coward dies a thousand times;
> "A hero, once," 'tis said.
> But, heroes die in violent climes,
> While cowards die in bed.

> "A cow is of the bovine ilk,

COWARD (n) Someone who realizes all the contingencies.

> Screamed the Sergeant at young Ben Lafarge,
> When the latter held back from the charge,
> "You're a damnable coward
> "For not running forward!"
> Said Ben, "I stayed next to you, Sarge."

CREATIONIST (n) One who believes that Man's innate viciousness should be blamed on God, rather than on evolution.

CREDIT (n) An intangible asset that is most abundant when it is least needed.

> There's a fun-loving fellow, Tim Rhetts,
> Who, a bank credit card, never gets.
> Though the townspeople sneer
> And say that he's queer,
> Tim's the one man in town with no debts.

CREDIT CARD (n) The means providence has given us to spend money we do not have for things we do not need and pay usurious interest for the privilege.

CRITICISM (n) An opinion expressing how a work strikes a critic when the author cannot strike back.

"Your book is both good and original. Unfortunately, the part that is good is not original and the part that is original is not good."

> George Bernard Shaw (replying to an author who
> had submitted a manuscript for his opinion)

CROSS-EXAMINATION (n) A courtroom procedure in which a lawyer for
one side questions a witness of his opponent in such a way as to strengthen the latter's case. Following is a memorable example of the technique often employed for the purpose, excerpted from the transcript of an actual murder trial in Chicago:

"PUBLIC DEFENDER: (Q) Did you perform an autopsy on the victim, doctor?

PATHOLOGIST: (A) Yes

(Q) Was he alive at the time?

(A) No

(Q) How did you know that? Did you take his pulse?

(A) No

(Q) Did you check his other vital signs?

(A) No

(Q) Well, then, how can you be so sure he was dead?

(A) Because his brain was in a glass jar sitting on my desk.

(Q) Isn't it possible, doctor, that the rest of his body was still alive at that time?

(A) Yes, it's possible that he could have gone somewhere and practiced law."

CUR (n) 1. A dog on the lowest rung of the canine ladder.

2. A man who acts like a dog. Intended as an aspersion,
the latter usage actually is a compliment, Not even the most
debased dog lies, cheats, steals, rapes, and makes war on his kind.

> Two fellows had words in Big Sur.
> Said one, "you're a damnable cur!"
> Said the other, "that's rot! A dog I am not."
> Lifting high his left thigh, he let fly at the guy
> And punished the terrible slur.

CYNIC (n) One whose knowledge of what goes into life's sausage
prevents him from enjoying it. So, whenever he smells a rose, he
looks for a funeral. In this, he differs from an idealist, who
looks for a wedding; a Los Angelino, who looks for a gay; a New
Yorker, who looks for a prostitute; a Londoner, who recognizes his
deodorant; a Parisian, who looks for an Italian; and a Muscovite,
who has
never smelled a rose before.

> When a cynical father in Hilton
> Found his daughter in bed with one Milton,
> She explained, "I was cold
> "And, although it was bold,
> "I laid Milton instead of a quilt on."

D

DAM (n) A structure built by the Federal Government to take
water from fish, who do not vote, and give it to rice farmers,
who do.

> Cried a salmon, whose spawn was cut short,
> "I should bring a class action in court!
> "My eggs, I can't lay
> "'Cause a dam's in the way
> "And my scruples won't let me abort."

DAMN (v) Part of a common prayer in America, usually preceded
by "God" and followed by the name of some person for whom His
rival's special attention is sought.

> An ambitious young priest, Father Ted,

Sought promotion from Rome, people said.
But, his sermons on tithing
Set his audience writhing
And ten percent damned him, instead.

DAMNATION (n) A state of perdition, often found in the State of
Mississippi, that can be alleviated by a liberal deposit of money
into the palm of a preacher. In rural parts of that enlightened
State, Bible-thumpers put souls of the dear departed into holding
patterns around Heaven until relatives pay the landing fee.

DEAFNESS (n) A physical condition that enables its
beneficiaries to ignore rap music, television commercials,
requests for money from relatives, telephone solicitations, cute
stories about friends' children, spousal snores, and political
bullshit.

DEAN (n) Head of a college department, so long as it pleases
the President, Provost, faculty, students, trustees, donors, and
alumni, to keep him. In practice, it does not please them long.
    "A college dean is like a mushroom. You're continually kept
in the dark, periodically covered with manure, treated like a
fungus, then cut off in your prime and sent packing."
    Former University of San Diego Dean, Donald T. Weckstein

DEATH (n) 1. What happens to us after we had planned something
better.
    2. The end to the only life or the beginning of a better
one, depending on whether you believe your bartender or your
bishop. It is incomprehensible to children, impossible to
youth, frightening to the middle-aged, a statistic to the
military, a business to morticians, a half-expected visitor to
the elderly, and a blessing to the terminally ill.
        Since they wed, Anna's spouse was her chief.
        When he died, she bought clothes for relief.
        She wept through her facelift,
        Bought bras with an uplift,
        And dyed her hair gold in her grief.

DEBATE (n) In Congress, a verbal exchange between members that
features the opposing opinions of a staff person. By this means,
the officeholders get on television without paying for the time,
boost their fund-raising, inflate their egos, and fire the

staffer if any opinion proves unpopular with voters.

> In Washington debates, they often say
> This phrase: "when all is said and done."
> What angers me is not the dumb cliché,
> But that so much more's said than done.

DEBAUCHEE (n) An immoral person who enjoys what you miss out on.

> Groaned a young debauchee, Dennis Braining,
> As even fingernails on him were paining,
> "My nights, I confess,
> "Are filled with excess;
> "Except an excess of abstaining."

DEBTOR (n) One who is under a duty to repay his creditor with something more than ingratitude.

> Said a free-spending dude in Orleans,
> Whose property sagged under liens,
> "I think it's much better
> "To be a big debtor
> "Than not to have cash in my jeans."

DECAFFEINATE (v) What happens to a pregnant cow.

DECEIVER (n) A person who can tell you to go to Hell in such a way that you look forward to the trip.

> "Deceive me once, shame on you. Deceive me twice, shame on me. Deceive me three times, shame on my parents."
> George Goebel

DECOMPOSE (v) What Beethoven and Mozart are doing.

DECREASE (v) What a fat girl does to her date's trousers when she sits on his lap.

DECREPIT (adj.) Obviously devastated by age. To a teenage girl, the class includes any woman more than twenty years older than her. To her mother, it includes a middle-aged woman who wears no makeup in public, and an elderly woman who does.

> Said an elderly fellow, Joe Toth,
> To his frisky young wife, "I am loath
> "To admit I'm decrepit.
> "Let's just say, with my pep it

"Must be dancing or sex, but not both."

DEED (n) A legal document that entitles the named party to occupy real property until the mortgagee bank is ready to repossess it.

> An angry young couple, named Brace,
> Was expelled by the mortgagee, Chase.
> "We're deed owners," they screamed,
> But, the banker just beamed,
> Saying: "you only borrowed the place."

DEFAME (v) To lie about another as it strikes you when he cannot strike back. The safest results are achieved if he thinks the tongue belongs to someone else.

Most famous people in history are not celebrated because of their long achievements, but because of their longevity. They outlived their defamers.

DEFICIT 1. (n) Something less than nothing.
2. (adj.) A type of financing much loved by credit card banks and the Federal government.

> Said a doc to a drag-racer, Raines,
> Who was mending from fractures and sprains:
> "First, I thought you lacked fear.
> "But now, it seems clear
> "That your deficit really is brains."

DEFUNCT (adj.) Although it has much more punch, when expressed, than its innocuous synonym, "dead", this word has not caught on with the public. Perhaps it is because so few know its meaning or that of its opposite, "funct".

The word was coined by poets for the sole purpose of rhyming with "debunked", as in this poignant protest:

> Old Molly McBride was fit to be tied
> By reports that her husband was dead.
> "That Tom is defunct is a slur I've debunked,
> "Though it's true he's much slower in bed."

DEGENERATE (n) A person with declining energy.

> A hardworking fellow in Tate
> One night, disappointed his mate
> With a muscle quite limp,
> Sobbed he, "I'm a wimp!"
> She demurred, "just a degenerate."

DELICATESSEN (n) A business establishment that sells and serves meat products. The name combines a contraction of the English words "delicious," and "cat," and the German word "essen," (to eat). Thus explained is the original meaning and bill of fare: "To eat a delicious cat." Still today, wherever one of these establishments is located, the cat population is remarkably thin.

DELINQUENCY (n) That stage of human development when children begin imitating adults.

DELIVER (n) How a New Yorker refers to his organ.
>Said Anthony Monks, from deep in the Bronx,
>"When I thirst, I could drink up deriver.
>"Now my doc says to choose; either give up the booze
>"Or I'll soon have to give up deliver."

DELUGE (n) What often is happening outside a television studio during a Spring day in the Midwest as, inside, the weatherman is predicting "a 20% chance of rain."
>All media weathermen suck;
>Their forecasts, as worthless as muck.
>My mother's arthritis
>And nasal rhinitis
>Are better predictors, with luck.

DELUSION (n) A belief at variance with yours.

DEMOCRAT (n) Someone who believes that government has the duty to provide those persons less fortunate than Republicans with advantages that the latter possess, so long as they are paid for by Republicans.
>The typical male Democrat has a colon full of vegetation, a heart full of envy, a chip on his shoulder, a voice box full of complaints, and a brain full of schemes. The typical female is propelled by three Constitutional ideals: the right to abort her mistakes, the right to tyrannize over her husband, and the right to marry an inferior man or a superior woman.
>>A Democrat governor, Keefe,
>>Is compassionate past all belief.
>>From achievers, he'll take
>>Extra income they make
>>And give it to Dems on relief.
>>"I am not a member of any organized
>>political party. I am a Democrat."

Will Rogers
"If you want to live like Republicans, vote for Democrats."

Harry Truman

DENTIST (n) A professional who empties your wallet while
filling your teeth and sticking his tongue in your ear.
>   A prosperous dentist, named Will,
>   Won't work on his patients until
>   He knows, with precision,
>   Their fiscal condition,
>   Hence, whether to crown or to fill.

DEPRESSION (n) (economic) What results when Congress acts to
end a recession.
(psychological) What occurs after anxiety has been treated
by a psychiatrist and his bill arrived.
>   Said the shrink to a patient named Lese,
>   "I can cure your depression with ease.
>   "By long consultation;
>   "By strong medication,
>   "Or by shock, when I bill you my fees."

DESIRE (n) What women mistake for love in a man and compensate
for with candy when the truth is known. Men mistake calculation
for it in a woman and abate it with liquor when she has scored
him 0.

DETOUR (v) To change the route to a planned destination.
Sometimes it is inadvertent, as when NASA is involved.
>   When a woman named Sarah McClure
>   Found her fiancé a boor,
>   She was asked, "will you alter
>   "Your trip to the halter?"
>   She replied, "I intend to detour."

DEVELOPER (n) "Someone who cuts down trees then names streets
after them."
>   Richard Armor
>   "I think that trees, in any number,
>   "Are most appealing when they're lumber."
>   (Rebuttal to Joyce Kilmer's poem)

57

DIAGNOSIS (n) First in a sequence of two medical opinions about a patient's illness; the second is called "prognosis". If the patient is uninsured or in a nursing home, there is a third opinion, called "post-mortem."

"My diagnosis is right," said young Doctor Brite,
"The patient is fiscally ill.
"Since none will insure him, his prognosis is sure grim,
"Since all he will get is a pill."

DIAPER (n) The only garment designed to serve both the beginning and ending stages of life.

"Diapers and politicians have one thing in common. Both should be changed, regularly, and for the same reason."
Steve Allen

DIARRHEA (n) An activity that induces both monarchs and commoners to mount the nearest throne.

"Give a cheer for Imodium, pill of the millennium,
"Pharmacology's blessing to Man.
"Without it, I fear, I'd spend much of the year
"Afraid to stray far from the can."

DIET (n) A method by which entrepreneurs add weight to their assets by removing it from client asses. It is said to be a triumph of mind over platter.

DILEMMA (n) Unable to choose between two alternative actions that would inflict equal pain on an enemy.

Said a masochist, Terry, when asked which she'll marry
Of two very odious guys:
"My dilemma," she sighed, "is that I can't decide
"Which one of them I most despise."

DILETTANTE (n) A person who peels the skin off delicious fruit, then eats the skin.

Said Molly McFee to her husband to be,
"You may kiss me as much as you want.
"But, until we are wed, you can't take me to bed;
"Until then, I'm a sex dilettante."

DIMINUTIVE (adj.) Tiny

There was a young lawyer named Rex,
With diminutive organs of sex.
When charged with exposure,
He said with composure,
"De minimus non curat lex."
("The law does not regard trifles", a maxim of Equity)

DISAPPOINTMENT (n) The last of three emotions a woman usually feels after sex. The other two are "anticipation" and "performance".

DISCHARGE (v) To liquidate an accumulation or relationship, as exemplified in the following newspaper headline: "Marine Captain Lewis Burnette got a dishonorable discharge from his act of adultery."

A couple in Reading spent bucks on their wedding.
They spared no expense, it was said.
Now, with savings discharged and billings enlarged,
They're up to their keesters in red.

DISCRIMINATION (n) The practice of denying some people rights intended for all people.

"War is the worst form of age discrimination. Younger
men are sent to fight and die, while older men send them there."
Martin Luther King

DISGUISE (n) The means by which truth is concealed. See COSMETICS

After kissing the nun, Clifford cried,
"When I said I was Catholic, I lied!"
Said the nun, with a grin,
"What you did was no sin.
"I'm an FBI agent, disguised."

DISINTEGRATE　　　　　　(v) To re-segregate.
Said Governor Dobbs, kicking blacks off State jobs,
"Affirmative Action is dated."
Said one of the sacked, understanding the act,
"I've just been disintegrated."

DISORIENTED (adj.) What has happens to a refugee from the Far

East.

DISSEMBLE (v) To conceal an urge to kill when tact is required,
e.g., a new wife toward her critical mother-in-law.
> Cried a man to his mate, who glared down from above:
> "In the past, you forgave my affairs.
> "It may have been to dissemble your love,
> "But, did you have to kick me downstairs?"

DISTRESS (ancient, v)(modern, n) Originally, to cut off a
woman's hair. The meaning changed following the ride of Lady
Godiva to denote misery. Lexicographers of the era attribute the
change to the many men who watched the ride and shouted for her
to be "distressed." At the same time, the more numerous women
and homosexuals in the crowd cried "miserable" so lustily that
contemporary dictionaries adopted the altered meaning.

Less well known is the fact that the word "disfigure" was
coined at the same time to denote the concealment her tresses
provided the lady. On the other hand, a newly-discovered
affidavit from a servant who watched her bathe suggests the word
was intended to describe her actual appearance under the hair.
> In England, a Lady's long tresses,
> Her modesty saved from distresses.
> That's the story we're told,
> But, in truth, she was old
> And she sagged in key places, my guess is.

DIVORCE 1. (n) A legal proceeding that enables a married woman
to try her luck and a married man to risk his.
> Said a lady from Troy, when asked was her joy
> Due to tying the knot as a bride:
> "Oh, no! The delight is from winning my fight
> "To make the damn knot come untied."

> "My divorce gave me the feeling that I had finally done
something good with my life."
> Sza Sza Gabor (commenting on her divorce from
> actor George Sanders)

2. (v) A more humane choice that society affords a
woman to get rid of her spouse.
> Said a much abused wife, Audrey Picker,
> After shooting her spouse, drunk on liquor:
> "While it's true that divorce
> "Was a more humane course,

"My way was both cheaper and quicker."

"Forty three percent of marriages end in divorce, while the other fifty seven percent fight it out to the bitter end."
Steve Allen

DIZZY (adj.) A condition common to young men after a night of heavy drinking and to old men when they suddenly stand. The comparison attests to the fact that some things can be done cheaper and faster by old people.

DOBERMAN (n) A breed of dog renowned for the affinity of its teeth with human flesh.

(Q) What is brown and black and would look good on a well-dressed lawyer?

(A) Two Dobermans.

DOCTOR (n) A marketing agent for pharmaceutical companies trained to diagnose the maximum number of pills a patient can tolerate in a day.

> An HMO doctor, named Stan,
> Is every pharmacy's fan.
> If you have an ill
> He can't cure with a pill,
> He will let it get worse 'til he can.

DOG (n) Called man's "best friend" because, unlike his wife, its bark is always worse than its bite, it never wants to go out to dinner, it already has a fur coat, it never minds being put on a short leash, it prefers a ring made of rubber rather than one made of diamonds, it lies down on command, and it never complains of a migraine when he wants to pet it.

> A divorcing young couple, named Sog,
> Were mired in a custody bog.
> With a dog and son, Mort,
> They appealed to the court,
> Which awarded the winner--the dog!

"The great pleasure from a dog is that you can make a fool of yourself and, not only will he not scold you, he will make a fool of himself, too."
Samuel Butler

DOGGEREL (n) Poetry with neither rhyme nor reason.

DOGMA (n) The entire body of a religious doctrine, so-called because, no matter what the creed, it is always a bitch to comprehend.

> The Catholic dogma is hidden in fog ta
> all of its millions of fans.
> The Pope, in his satin, explains it in Latin,
> Which only the priests understand.

DOGMATIC (adj.) Stubbornly holding onto an opinion that differs from yours, like a pit bull with your leg in his jaw instead of the one you sicced him onto.

> A patient, Ben Green, called his treatment "obscene"
> And was known through the clinic as "moxie Ben."
> But, not being dogmatic, he stopped all his static
> When they started unplugging his oxygen.

DOLE (n) 1. (Republican) Charity wasted on shiftless people who lack the intelligence, ambition, connections, or inheritance, sufficient to live like Republicans.

2. (Democrat) Compensation to the unemployed just sufficient to enable them to remain unemployed and vote Democratic.

> Said Republican Senator, Shirks,
> "I'm against paying dole to poor jerks.
> "Where the money makes sense
> "Is for Missile Defense.
> "We should spend all we've got 'til it works."

DONEE (n) Someone who receives money from another under conditions that create only a debt of ingratitude.

DONOR (n) Creator of two disappointments by one gift. The donor expected gratitude and the donee expected more.

> "Do not be a donor or even a loaner,"
> Polonious said to his son.
> "Both will cost you a friend and, worse in the end,
> "You will windup losing a ton."

DRAMATIC (adj.) Capable of eliciting real emotion, as distinguished from "theatrics", which is the mere pretense of emotion. The difference is illustrated by the following optional lines spoken by a husband to his wife during a play about marital infidelity:

(dramatic) "I have not cheated on you. I am impotent, remember?"

(theatric) "I have not cheated on you and I won't do it again."

> On stage, a young actress, named Radick,
> Played a scene in a manner dramatic.
> She leapt from her chair
> With a scream and a glare.
> It seems she'd been goosed by strong static.

DRIVEL (n) Words without ideas. It is a specialized form of communication common to lawyers, politicians, preachers, psychiatrists, consultants, and publicists. By its rules, they are able to say a lot, in general, without saying anything in particular, and charge by volume rather than weight.

> A verbose young lawyer, Sam Privvel,
> Was so proud that he started to snivel.
> Seems a judge sent this note,
> Re. a brief that Sam wrote,
> Saying, "Sir, you're a master of drivel."

DRUDGE (n) A woman who is worth more than her wages. Her opposite is called a "sludge," because the latter is thick, slow-moving, and entirely a waste.

> A drudge in Fort Dix works from seven 'til six.
> Though she's eighty, she's feeling just fine.
> Her husband, perversely, worked her hours, reversely,
> And died of angina at forty-nine.

DRUNK (n) Someone whose barf is worse than his blight. Although the addled fellow is the curse of the nation and costs more in dollars and sense than any other drugee, jokes about him abound--of which the following are examples:

1. A Cleveland woman told a judge that, although she had been married to her husband for 27 years, she never knew he was a drunk until he came home sober one night.

2. Mike made so much noise climbing the stairs that he woke up his wife. When she complained, he explained that he was having trouble getting a keg of beer up the stairs. "For the love of God," she said, "leave it downstairs until morning." "I can't," Mike replied, "I drunk it."

3. Two drunks in a Dublin pub where arguing whether Irish or Scotch whiskey was the more potent. "Oh, Irish whiskey,

for certain," cried one. "I was drinkin' Irish whiskey all night, last Saturday, and the next morning, I went to mass." "That don't prove anything," the other man said. "Most Catholics go to mass on Sunday morning." "You don't understand," said the first man, "I'm Jewish."

    4. While in his cups, comedian Joe Frisco emerged from a Hollywood liquor store, where he had purchased an expensive bottle of scotch. On his way out the door, he tripped and fell. As two friends helped him up, Frisco felt something running down his leg and staining his trousers. "Oh," he moaned, "I hope to God that's blood."

DUMB (adj.) 1. Unable to speak. 2. Unable to think.

    The second meaning is vividly depicted in the following real-life examples.

    1. A young man in Florida, who was unable to learn how to water ski because he could not find a lake that sloped.

    2. A young blonde woman in Phoenix, who returned a scarf to the local Saks store because it was too loose.

    3. A 63 year old man, in Cleveland, who was trapped for hours on an escalator because of a power failure.

    4. A young man in New York City, who explained to police that he couldn't call "911," because he couldn't find "11" on his telephone.

    5. A young woman, in Little Rock, who lost the breaststroke event at a YWCA meet and complained to the referee that the other swimmers used their arms.

DUMDUM (n) A hollow-core bullet, so-called because of the effect a head wound has on the target's intelligence.

DUNG (n) The name Biblical writers have given to the world's most abundant manufactured product. Other names relate to specific places or professions, to wit., feces (hospitals), "waste" (sanitary engineers), fertilizer (garden shops), "manure" (farmers), and "shit" (inner cities).

        Dung raises no smile; it stinks and is vile.
        Concealment's been history's answer.
        But, if you cancel the smell and package it well,
    You can market it as "soil enhancer."

EASTER (n) Once a holy day celebrating the ascension of Christ over Mankind, it is now a holiday celebrating the ascension of candy over Christ. Religious communities respond in different ways, for example:

1. (Lutherans) On their knees, observing the Ascension depicted in church.

2. (Agnostics) On their backsides, observing the depiction of golf on television.

3. (Catholics) Playing golf on the same courses they played during Lent.

4. (Moslems) Doing the same things that Christians are doing and condemning them for it.

5. (Jews) Do not observe this holy day, but Passover it.

"When I was your age," shouted dad in a rage,
"I prayed on my knees during Easter."
Said his son, airily, turning on the TV,
"I'd much rather watch sports on my keester."

EAVESDROP (v) How to avoid deception.

"To eavesdrop is bad, so avoid it, my lad,
"It is mean and a stain on your high soul."
So said Preacher Dan, a God-fearing man,
As he watched the girl bathe through a spy hole.

ECCENTRIC (adj.) Behaving rationally and, therefore, in a manner different from the rest of society.

An eccentric attorney, named Reed,
Makes his colleagues in town mighty peeved.
To clients, he's just,
Suing just when he must,
Billing only for value received.

ECSTASY (n) Intense pleasure that is felt at least twice during the life of every parent. The first time occurs at the moment a child is conceived during intercourse. The second time is when the child is an adult and leaves home for good.

Ardent Willie McGee was ecstatic to see
Nubile Jennie respond to his glance.
But her mother, no fool, caused his passion to cool
By slipping ice cubes down his pants.

ECSYDIACIST (n) The scientific name for a stripper. Less

scientific were the names adopted by Gertrude Best and Myrtle Davis
to further their careers, to wit., Helen Bedd and Norma Vincent
Peale, respectively.

     Ecsydiacists wear very little;
     No more than two jots and a tittle.
     Their strip teasing acts

     Expose all the facts,
     Except what is under the tittle.

EDUCATION (n) A system of supply, without demand, by which empty
heads are filled with information that is mainly useless or
obsolete. It is accomplished by a process that transforms the
teachers' notes into the notes of the students, without disturbing
the thoughts of either group at any time.

     "George W. Bush is to education what Jack the Ripper was to
surgery."
               David Letterman

EGOTIST (n) A person who is me-deep in conversation. When two of
them converse, it's an I for an I.

     Said a handsome guy, Bruce, trying hard to seduce
     A beautiful girl at the sea.
     "I'm an egotist, yes, but, you'll have to confess,
     "That no man deserves you like me."

EINSTEIN (n) A brilliant physicist whose theory of the relativity
of time, during his life, was understood by only one other man and
he was a Bohr.

     "Time is relative for all people on Earth except women, for
whom it is absolute. They are always late!"
               Will Rogers
     "A wonderful family is "Stein."
     "There's Eck and there's Gert and there's Ein.
     "Eck's sculptures are junk.
     "Gert's poems are bunk.
     "And nobody understands Ein."
               Anon Y. Mous

ELASTIC (adj.) Possessing the ability to conform itself to an odd
size and shape (See GIRDLE).

     A certain young co-ed at Mass Tech
     Is called by the fellows, "fantastic!"

Her mind is first rate,
Her figure is great,
While her morals are somewhat elastic.

ELECTION (n) 1. A contest between political candidates in which
the ability to govern is never an issue.
An election in Boyce provides voters a choice
Between Frederick, Samantha, and Neal.
Neal hasn't a brain, Samantha's a pain,
And Fred can't decide what to steal.
2. A harvesting process in which voters separate the wheat
from the chaff and keep the chaff.
"You helped elect Ladd," said the son to his dad,
"Yet, you always say, 'vote for the best.'"
"I was true to my word," the father assured,
"For there's no better crook in the West."

ELECTRON (n) A sub-atomic particle that physicists deem to be the
wife in the nuclear family--for these reasons:
1. It is always negative.
2. It sometimes spins out of control when excited.
3. Its behavior within the family is unpredictable.
4. When it unites with the center of the family, i.e., the
always positive proton, baby neutrinos are born.

ELOQUENT (adj.) The ability to fill people's ears in
a way that fills their eyes and the speaker's pockets.
Reverend Dent is an eloquent gent
When he speaks about fetal rights.
But, kids in despair, lacking food, homes, and care,
Are not in his charity's sights.

EMETIC (n) A method for ridding oneself of what cannot be
stomached, such as broccoli, a vegetarian meal, a newlywed's
casserole, or a politician's speech.

EMPATHY (n) The ability we have to share another's distress
without having to share anything of our own.
Said a businessman, Beggs, to a man with no legs:
"The sight causes many a sob.
"So, I'll give you good cheer and five bucks for some
beer,
"But, don't ask me to give you a job."

ENCUMBRANCE (n) A home mortgage or a welfare recipient,

67

depending
on whether you are a Democrat or Republican.

> Say affluent troops and conservative groups,
> "The poverty class we should ration.
> "Because of their number, they simply encumber
> "And should be suppressed in the nation."

ENDS (n) The moral imperative of immoral people.

> "Means are always in our power; ends are seldom so."
> > Henry Fielding
> "Ends justify the means,"
> Says Boston Mayor Greene.
> "So flatulence,
> "Although intense,
> "Justifies baked beans."

ENEMA (n) What children sometimes call their mother after a spanking.

A pharmaceutical company researcher, in Africa, was shown a plant with large fronds that his witch doctor guide said was a sure cure for constipation. The researcher was elated at the find and said, "with fronds like these, who needs enemas?"

ENEMY (n) Someone who took the last parking spot you were heading for.

Dramatist, George Kaufman, and a friend were discussing the motion picture producer, Daryl Zanuck. "He's his own worst enemy," said the friend. "Not while I'm alive, he isn't," replied Kaufman.

> "Friends come and go, but enemies accumulate."
> > Franklin P. Adams

ENGLISH (n) A language spoken in parts of the United Kingdom and the United States. It is understood, but not spoken, in Scotland, the hills of West Virginia, the Deep South, the Bronx, and throughout the City of Oakland. Teachers of the traditional language are not now appreciated.

> On hearing a knock at the gate,
> Saint Peter asked, "who's coming late?"
> Came a voice in reply,
> "Let me in. It is I,"
> "English teacher!" Pete groaned, "damn my fate."

ENIGMA (n) An impenetrable mystery to all but children. After seeing a copy of the Mona Lisa painting and being asked by his parent what he thought of the lady's smile, eight year old Billy Martin had a ready answer. "She's getting ready to fart," he said, matter-of-factly.

"My mom is my stigma, a constant enigma,"
Complained Lucy Jean to friend Dot.
"She wants   me to date and find a good mate,
"But, won't let me show what I've got."

ENTREPRENEUR (n) A business person who was able to delay the company's bankruptcy until all his stock options were sold.

An entrepreneur from a town near Big Sur
Is envied for profits that last.
His wages are low, bill payments are slow,
While his products are made to fail fast.

ENTROPY (n) A law of physics holding that change is inherent in nature so that physicists should not be blamed if today's theory is shown to be goofy, tomorrow.

Said a physicist, Sludge, to a feminist judge,
When accused of a bigamous game.
"The entropy law caused my adding Miss Shaw.
Said her Honor, "five years, just the same."

ENVIRONMENTALIST (n) Someone who has a closed mind about open space and conserves everything except her opinions of developers.

An environmentalist, Salk
Is renowned as a militant hawk.
His tree-hugging ways
Bring him national praise
And the splinters cause nary a squawk.

ENVY (n) Pain from not having what another person has, without pleasure.

"I envy your class and your beautiful ass,"
Said Gail to her friend, Susan Plinchitt.
"Don't be silly," said Sue. "It's all black and blue.
"Every guy in the class has to pinch it."

EPIGRAM (n) A serving of concentrated wit, either full or half, depending on how savory it is to the person served. Following is a smorgasbord for every appetite:

1. On the other hand, you have different fingers.

2. Learn from your parents' mistakes, use birth control.

3. Rehab is for quitters.

4. Be nice to your kids, they'll choose your nursing home.

5. Employ teenagers while they still know everything.

6. Those who love themselves will never have a rival.

7. The ocean would be much deeper without sponges.

8. A day without sunshine is--you know--night.

9. 42.5% of all statistics are made up on the spot.

10. You have the right to remain silent. Anything you say will be misquoted, anyway.

11. "Whenever anyone agrees with me I always think I must be wrong."

Oscar Wilde

EPITAPH (n) Posthumous praise that is engraved in granite to prevent those who know the truth from Substituting it.

EQUITY (n) That branch of law that gives a judge discretion to do whatever the hell she wants to do.

"I'm an equitable judge," said her Honor, one Trudge,
"So my sentence is just thirty years.
"Since you're an old man, do the best that you can
"And I'll waive any prison arrears."

EROTIC (adj.) Capable of shifting a sex drive from "neutral" into "fast forward" without the active participation of the driver.

An eighty-year old man asked his doctor to "lower my sex drive." The amused medical man replied, "at your age, don't you think your sex drive is all in your head?" "I know it is," responded the old fellow. "That's why I want you to lower it."

McCloud has a problem, despotic.
Whenever he sees things, erotic,
His form-fitting kilt
Starts to rear up and tilt.
Then, what happens is truly chaotic.

ERROR (n) A mistaken performance, as in this example: "The politician's error was in being caught in bed with a woman who was not his wife and a man who was."

In law, a judge's mistake is called "harmless error" when it hurts your opponent's case and "prejudicial error" when it hurts your case.

ERUPTION (n) A violent outburst, observable in these situations:

1. A wife tells her husband she is pregnant and does not know who the father is.

2. A wife finds a bra two sizes larger than hers in the back seat of her husband's car.

3. A teenage daughter has been denied access to the family telephone and modem.

4. An unmarried female executive who has just been told that the rabbit died.

5. A husband who has just been told that his wife's mother will arrive the next day for a month's visit.

The following variation on a famous nursery rhyme has helped millions of girls accept one problem of puberty:

(Q) "Mary, Mary, quite contrary,
"How do your pimples grow?
(A) "From oily pores and picking sores,
"And eruptions all in a row."

ESTROGEN (n) A powerful hormone which, when given to men, results in a more social creature, makes them more talkative and emotional, enables them to ask for directions when they are lost, and inhibits them from admitting error when they are wrong. When given to women over fifty, it ends their pause with men, but makes them impregnable.

A big, burley, trucker named Jake
Took estrogen pills by mistake.
Before he gave birth,
His friends roared with mirth,
Believing his pot was just Jake.

ETERNITY (n) The interval of time spent waiting for a live person to interrupt the endless repetition of this recorded message: "All our representatives are helping other callers. Your call is very important to us, so please stay on the line."

ETHICS (n) The last resort of a hypocrite.

EUPHEMISM (n) An endearing word or phrase for something gross. Here are several examples of perfumed words for odorous things:

1. "Peacemaker", for the world's most lethal nuclear missile;

2. "Sanitary engineer", for a unionized garbage collector;

3. "military justice," for court martial procedures that deny Constitutional rights like juries, a presumption of innocence, and a civilian court appeal;

4. "Defense Department," for what has historically been called the "War Department" (when America only went to war to defend itself), until its offensive activities made spin necessary;

5. "Honorarium," Payment for a political speech, where the size of the payment and the quality of the speech reflects rare honor on nobody;

6. "Hero" Formerly, a title that was bestowed on one who exhibited outstanding bravery in battle, it now denotes anyone who served in the military, never fought in a battle, was shielded from solicitors, bill collectors, and gouging landlords, was housed, fed, and cared for, at taxpayer expense, and returned home fitter than when he left.

Several years after President Truman retired to Independence, Missouri, his wife hosted her bridge club. At one point, Harry appeared in overalls, greeted the ladies, and told his wife that he was going out to spread manure on the garden.

After he left the room, a friend urged Bess to get him to say "fertilizer", a more respectable term. "Well," replied Bess, dubiously, "I can't tell you how long it's taken me to get him to say "manure.""

EUTHANASIA (n) 1. Homicide with a friendly face.

2. the ultimate analgesic.

3. The name given an HMO's treatment policy toward elderly patients on Medicare. The name is a contraction of an earlier phrase, "youth and ancients," which extended the same policy to cover young patients with no insurance.

With this policy in mind and recalling that "HMO" is an acronym for "Health Maintenance Organization", nobody can accuse these companies of lacking a sense of humor.

EVANGELIST (n) A minister in the Babylonian wing of the Christian Church, who captures souls for God by the expedient of beating them into submission with his tongue.

> A fiery evangelist, Skagg,
> Is known as a windy gas bag.
> One night, while orating,
> He started inflating
> And lifted off down to Fort Bragg.

EVERYBODY (n) Any number of people, varying in size from zero to the world's entire population, depending on the context. For the skeptical reader (in whose honor this work was written) who questions the definition, common examples are provided herewith:

(zero) "Everybody knows that a husband always tell the truth."

(world's population) "Everybody knows that husbands are liars."

"If you think there's good in everybody, you haven't met everybody."

H. L. Mencken

EVICTION (n) Action that leaves its target displaced, disjointed, and arreared.

EXAMINATION (n) (College Academic) A series of questions designed to keep the student in school and the parents paying.

(HMO Physical) A series of probes and prods designed to miss any condition that requires expensive treatment.

(Court Witness) A series of questions that reveal what a simpleton the average lawyer is. Since no lawyer regards himself as "average", proof is herewith supplied in the following actual courtroom examinations:

1. Lawyer: "You have lived in New York your entire life, isn't that true?"

Witness: "No, not yet I haven't."

2. Lawyer: "What is your date of birth?"

Witness: "July 15th."

Lawyer: "What year?"

Witness: "Every year."

3. Lawyer: "You say that the accident affected your memory. Just how has it affected it?"

Witness: "I forget."

Lawyer: "Well, then, tell the jury something that you think you may have forgotten."

4. Lawyer: "Now, doctor, isn't it true that when a person dies in his sleep, he doesn't know about it until the next morning?"

5. Lawyer: "Were you present when your picture was taken?"

6. Lawyer: "Was it you or your younger brother who was killed in the war?"

7. Lawyer: "Now, doctor, when you performed the autopsy on the victim, are you certain that he was dead?"

Pathologist: "Yes, he was dead."

Lawyer: "But, how could you be certain?"

Pathologist: "His brain was sitting on the next table in a jar."

Lawyer: "But, isn't it possible that some part of him was still alive?"

Pathologist: "Yes, I guess it's possible that part of him

73

was alive and practicing law somewhere."

EXERCISE (v) To force a human body into a shape unnatural to it. Advocates should remember that round is a shape, too, and was chosen by God for every body in the universe.

> "Whenever I feel like exercising, I always lay down until the feeling goes away."
>> Jack Benny

> Said a fitness instructor, named Hand,
> To his exercise class in South Grand:
> "As far as I see,
> "You're as fit as can be.
> "Since you are still able to stand."

EXERCISING (v) Punishing the body for the overindulgence of the mind.
Following are several vital rules to keep in mind.
   1. If you take up cross-country skiing, start with a small country.
   2. Exercise daily so that when you die, people will say how good you look.
   3. Don't risk injury by trying to touch your toes. If God had wanted us to do that, he would have put them higher up on our legs.
   4. Taking long walks away from your neighborhood is especially good for neighbors who irritate you.
   5. If you walk with a straight back and your head held high, you are likely to kill yourself by falling down stairs or over something.

EXERCYCLE (n) A bicycle whose rear wheel has been removed and replaced by a nut.

> Fat Dexter Michael Tutt is an exercycle nut;
> He rides in his kitchen each night.
> "Though I travel a mile," he says with a smile,
> "I am never too far from a bite."

EXITCOURSE (n) The type of sex a husband is relegated to once his wife experiences menopause. Highlights are a closer intimacy with her back in bed and the opportunity to massage the temples during her many headaches.

EXPECTATION (n) An emotion that follows hope and precedes

disappointment.

"From those who have much to offer, much is expected."
Adlai Stevenson

"Expectation is fine," said Sylvia Klein,
"But, be certain before you start gloating.
"I expected a baby, then, it dawned on me, maybe
"My swelling is really from bloating."

EXPEDITOR (n) Someone who wants to procrastinate, but has not gotten around to it yet.

A lax expeditor in Brill
Expedites logs to the mill.
To save him some trouble,
He counted them double;
Resulting in less trees to kill.

EXPENSE (n) The sole destination of income.

"It's not hard for me to meet expenses. They're everywhere."
Phyllis Diller

EXPERIENCE (n) "The name we give to our mistakes."
Ambrose Bierce

"Experience is a harsh teacher, but fools learn from no other."
Winthrop Scott Slocum

A NASA nabob has a high-paying job
Getting rid of uranium bars.
Experience prevailing, off Earth it goes sailing
To poison all life forms on Mars.

EXPERT (n) Someone who holds himself out as not knowing less about a subject than anyone else.

It was an expert who discovered that the Earth is flat; that stars are lights hung on a tall ceiling; that Napoleon was a great man; that humans descended from Adam and Eve, who came into the World with belly buttons; that Man is rational, but dogs are not, and that Republicans have a conscience.

"An expert is someone who knows everything about something that has no value."
Mark Twain

A credit card expert, named Ladd,
Wrote a prize-winning book that was rad.

75

His treatise was praised
For the moral it raised;
That being a bankrupt is bad.

EXPURGATE (v) An act of editing by which composition is
seasoned to the taste of a Puritan--i.e., lots of sugar and oil,
but no salt, pepper, or spice.

Said an editor, Susan Hewitt,
"I expurgate curses and rue it.
"For the words that aren't nice
"Give the story some spice
"And I'm damned if I know why I do it."

EXTINCT (adj.) No longer alive, if animate, or no longer active,
if inanimate, as in: "For modern men, gallantry is extinct, but
adultery is instinct."

A volcano is said to be extinct if it is not known to have
blown its top according to recorded history. But, since recorded
history covers only two thousand of Earth's five billion years,
that is as absurd as saying that a politician must be truthful
because he has not yet been caught in a lie.

The eruption of an extinct volcano surprises everyone but
geologists (all of whom later claim to have predicted it) and is
widely thought to be an ecological disaster. This view is
rebutted by the eminent British scientist, I. M. A. Stonehead,
who points out that volcanic soil is invigorated by nutrients
coming from buried bill collectors, tax auditors, lawyers,
preachers, politicians, mothers-in-law, and geologists.

The Arts, too, are stimulated. Vesuvius, alone, accounts
for tens of thousands of air brush paintings on sweatshirt.
As for music, the Mount Saint Helena eruption was inspiration for
several unforgettable songs, such as these hits:
"Lava, come back to me"
"Oh, pumice me that we will never part"

EXTREMISM (n) The belief that too much is better than just
enough.
"Extremism in the fight against extremists is no vice, while
moderation in their defense is no virtue."
Gore Vidal (paraphrase of Vice-President Spiro Agnew)

EXTREMIST (n) Someone who either leads a crowd or is chased by it, depending on the latter's point of view.

> An extremist, named Marx, must have OD'd on narcs,
> Saying all employees should be healthy.
> This Communist view conflicts with what's true,
> That all employers should be wealthy.

Issue advocates shudder when extremist supporters join their ranks, knowing the latter are likely to demand a "perfect" result and oppose a "good" one.

> Extremist supporters are cursed;
> Of all campaign roadblocks, they're first.
> By demanding the "should"
> And opposing the "could",
> They often result in the "worst."

EYEWITNESS (n) Someone who can be counted on to ruin a good story.

> Said a self-proclaimed hero, named Tushed,
> "I jumped in the fight and saved Kushed."
> But, an eyewitness, Sling,
> Said, "I saw the whole thing.
> "The guy didn't jump--he was pushed!"

F

FACELIFT (n) A type of cosmetic surgery that greatly improves the patient's appearance and the surgeon's assets. The result may, however, have unintended consequences, as illustrated by the following account:

A middle-aged woman had a "near-death" experience in which she appeared before God. "Is this it for me?" she asked. "No," God replied, "you still have 44 years to live"--and she awoke.

Several months later, reflecting on God's words, she decided that, since she had so many years left, she ought to make the best of them. So, she went to a cosmetic surgeon and got a facelift, hair dye, tummy tuck, breast augmentation, and liposuction. On her way back to her car after the surgery, she was struck by a car and killed. Again, she found herself before God.

"I thought you told me I had 44 more years to live," she reminded Him, indignantly.

"I know," God replied, defensively, "but I didn't recognize you."

FACULTY (n) A body of teachers whose collective head is in the clouds; whose tongue is wagging; whose hands are outstretched, palms up;
whose legs are moving to avoid student questions, and whose ideas are half-baked and cannot be stomached by persons with discernment.

Said a faculty spokesman, named Pike
(Showing what many teachers are like),
"Teacher rights are the concern
"And this Board had better learn
"To meet our demands or we'll strike!"

FAILURE (n) Not to get what you desire, or to get it.
"If you think that God has failed you, then do it yourself."
George Santayana
"Your failure in math," fumed his mother, with wrath,
"Is pain I should not be allotted."
"But, I didn't fail, mom," said her son, very calm,
"I planned to get 'F' and I got it."

FAIR (n) A fun-filled annual event consisting of farm animals heading for slaughter, prize-winning canned recipes that are inedible, gadget salespersons that are intolerable, kiddy-rides that are unaffordable, and loud speakers that are unendurable. It is so-called because, as entertainment, although it is not as good as a circus, it is better than a hanging.

Beverly Ridds had six noisy kids
Until two disappeared at the fair.
Said she, with a tear, "they're goners, I fear,
"In time, I'll report on the pair."

FAIRIES (n) Magical people once limited in number and seen only by children and Irishmen. In recent times, they have multiplied prodigiously and are seen everywhere, showing a marked preference for the company of men dressed in pastels.

FAITH (n) 1. Beliefs based on hearsay, assumptions, and speculation, that no court would admit as proof, motivated by the expectation of a Heavenly reward that discredits the conclusion.
2. "Belief, without knowledge, in what is said by one who speaks, without evidence, of things without precedence."

Ambrose Bierce
> Said a Catholic wife, Donna Odell,
> Within a confessional well,
> "My faith was quite buried
> "Until I got married;
> "But now, I'm convinced there's a Hell."

FAITHFUL (adj.) Character trait of a man who lacks enterprise and a woman who is homely.
> "Young men want to be faithful and are not, while old men want to be faithless and cannot."
> Oscar Wilde

FALSEHOOD (n) A lie, retouched and shaped for better circulation.
> "Falsehood flies and truth comes limping after it. When you are finally undeceived, the rescue comes too late to repair the damage. It is like thinking of a good retort after the company has parted, or like a physician, who discovers a cure after his patient died."
> Jonathan Swift

FAME (n) Celebrity based on achievement and notoriety, deodorized.
> "Fame is the spur that the noble spirit doth raise
> "To scorn delight and live laborious days."
> William Shakespeare

FAMILY PLANNING (n) The art of spacing children so as to maintain your position on the brink of financial disaster.

FANATIC (n) Someone who, upon seeing that he is heading for a chasm, accelerates.
> A Moslem fanatic, named Paul,
> Never gets any honors at all.
> Since his Christian first name
> Was mainly to blame,
> He changed it, one morning, to "Saul."

FANNY (n) 1. A female name that has disappeared from use for the same reason that explains the demise of "Dick and "Peter"."
> Three couples stood in line waiting to enter Heaven. Saint Peter rejected the first couple, saying to the husband: "You're obsessed with money! Why, you call your wife "Penny." He then

rejected the second couple, telling the husband: "You're addicted to alcohol! Why, you call your wife "Marguerite."

Observing this, the husband next in line said to his wife: "I guess we may as well leave, Fanny."

2. Euphemism for that part of the human anatomy that holds up underwear. Several synonyms are in wide use among different classes of the population. "Posterior" is employed by ladies, "buttocks", by doctors, "gluteus maximus", by pedants, and "ass" by everyone else.

> Men won't indulge in, 'tis said,
> Women with fannies that spread.
> So girls, face the fact.
> Lose weight and contract
> If you want to be happily wed.

FAT (adj.) That part of a body's mass that affects its width rather than its height. In women, it tends to concentrate in the buttocks (gluteus maximus), while in men, it goes to the stomach (gluttonous maximus). In politicians of both sexes, it also goes to the skull, which is why they are often called, "fatheads".

Fat women have been cruelly ridiculed, as the following examples attest. They are offered with no enjoyment, merely to maintain the author's reputation for scholarship.

1. She is so fat that her husband has to drive his car to get on her good side.

2. She is so fat that she wakes up in sections.

3. She is so fat that when she hauls ass, she has to make two trips.

4. She is so fat that when she stepped on a talking scales, it said, "ouch!"

5. She is so fat that when she leaves the lake after a swim, she leaves a ring around it.

> Said a buxom young lady, named Kate,
> When accused of outweighing her date:
> "I'm not fat. That's a lie"
> (As she reached for the pie)
> "I am merely too short for my weight."

FATHER (n) A man who, having cast his seed on accessible ground, is given cause to regret that it was fertile. A priest in the Roman Catholic church is called, "Father,"
because, in earlier times, so many children in the congregation resembled him.

Years ago, there were priests not so pure,
Who said sex was a cross to endure.
When they preached, from the parable,
About seed on soil, arable,
There were crops in the pews, I am sure.

FATUOUS (adj.) Identifying words or deeds that issue from a fathead.

A fatuous father in France
Insisted his son take up dance.
The kid was so fat,
On his first entrechat
His belly propelled him to Nantes.

FAX (n) A type of telephone communication that avoids backtalk.

I.

That Elmer was shy no one can deny.
He shies from most intimate acts.
When he went to propose to his lady friend, Rose,
He popped her the question by fax.

II.

Some said he was crazy, but Joe was just lazy.
He was most decidedly lax.
When Doctor Van Buren requested some urine,
Joe sent it by soaking a fax.

FEEBLE (adj.) Lacking strength or on the verge of collapse, e.g., the national economy.

"You are old, Mother Gilliam," she said with a smile,
"And are now most uncommonly frail.
"So, why do you sharpen your foot with a file
"And use it as if it's a nail?"

"In my youth," Mother Gilliam replied to her daughter,
"I could stand with no trouble at all.
"But now that I'm feeble, I teeter and totter,
"So I anchor myself to the wall."

FEEDBACK (n) The reaction of some babies to strained carrots.

FEMALE (n) Formerly spelled "feemale" to signify that a man must pay a penalty for companionship, the spelling was altered during the reign of the first feminist, Queen Elizabeth I, who believed it too openly mercenary. The bonds of matrimony were substituted and men have been paying a much higher price ever since.

> A beautiful hooker, named Bea,
> Married a miser from Brea.
> Now, he's fit to be tied.
> When he beds with his bride,
> From habit, she charges a fee.

FEMINIST (n) A liberated female who asserts women's rights and is opposed by a repressed conservative who asserts their wrongs.

> A feminist leader, named Fay,
> Assembled her sisters to say:
> "Make men join our fight;
> "Shun sex every night!"
> So they went and had sex every day.

FETISH (n) An overpowering attraction for a person or thing, as in these examples:

1. A Democrat, for a new tax;
2. A Republican, for a new weapon system;
3. A Mexican, for the U.S. border;
4. A young man, for a young woman in her cups;
5. A middle-aged man, for a young woman out of her cups;
6. An old man, for a toilet;
7. A young woman, for a diamond ring;
8. A middle-aged woman, for a rich man with poor vision;
9. An old woman, for an old man on enough Viagra to avoid peeing on the bathroom floor.

FIBRILLATE (v) To tell a lie after midnight.

FIGHTING (n) A human trait that explains why shedding blood is more common than donating it.

> "It's not how big the dog in the fight is that counts,
> but how big the fight in the dog."
> > President Theodore Roosevelt

FILIBUSTER (n) A process by which members of the U.S. Senate talk a Bill to death. The techniques employed are the same as those used to put audiences to sleep during a political speech. This is the basis for the modern adage: "The tongue is mightier than the pen, the sword, and NoDoz."
"In Congress, when all is said and done, more is said than done."

FINESSE 1. (adj.) Possessing a skill so masterful that a difficult
objective is achieved, as in the following examples:

    1. Your fist is applied to another man's nose in a way that
persuade him his nose was to blame.

    2. You serve broccoli to your kids as a dessert and they
believe you.

    3. When you are being chased out of town by a mob, you
convince onlookers that you are leading a parade.

    4. You break wind in an elevator and convince the other
passengers that the elevator is to blame.

    2. (v) A tactic in Bridge that enables a player to win with
a comparatively weak hand.

    The late playwright and wit, George Kaufman, was a passionate
Bridge player who played weekly at New York's Algonquin Hotel.
Missing a fourth player, one day, an acquaintance was invited to
sit in as Kaufman's partner. As the game progressed, Kaufman grew
increasingly irate as his partner repeatedly trumped his high
cards and nullified each attempted finesse. Finally, the man
excused himself, saying he had to go to the toilet.

    "Well," commented Kaufman, sourly, "for the first time,
today, I'll know what you're holding in your hand."

FISSION (n) A split-up of a nuclear unit that produces an
explosion, extreme heat, a period of instability, and new
relationships (see DIVORCE, supra.).

      A nuclear scientist, Titian,
      Exploded himself to perdition.
      All they found was his note;
      Of himself, not a mote.
      What he wrote in the note was, "Gone fission."

FLASHBACK (n) (men) A memory of a sexual event that never happened.
(women) A memory of a shopping event that should have happened.

FLATTERY (n) Your description of another in terms that you would
wish to be described, both of you lying.

      "Flattery's the food of fools!"
      "So said the ancient schools.
      "But, now and then your men of wit
      "Will condescend to take a bit."

FLATULENCE (n) Unsavory gas produced in the digestive tract and emitted whenever the blame can plausibly be fixed on another. Called "farting" by the unpretentious, it is enjoyed by all, but acknowledged by none. Venters typically blame a release on a dog, cat, child, or any other inarticulate source within the launching range.

Should a defenseless scapegoat be unavailable when the bomb explodes,   these deceivers are not above indicting, trying, and condemning, another human being in the room. Lovers of baked beans seem to be the most successful in passing blame for the passed, and past, gas (probably because they are the most practiced). The most common technique is to fix the target with an accusatory eye, while screwing up the face, sniffing the air, and shaking the head, slightly.

> I went to the Archbishop's tea
> And left as ashamed as can be.
> His flatulence, abdominal,
> Was simply phenomenal,
> But, the others all thought it was me.

FLOOD (n) A water supply that knows no bounds, as a matter of course.

> "Except that streets are quiet, there is not much good to say about a flood."
> Mark Twain

FLORIDA (n) The appendix on America's body politic and, therefore, highly susceptible to such electoral infections as hanging chads, black myopia, disappearing ballots, and legislators getting sugar from people raising cane.

> Florida elections are wretched;
> With cheating and fraud they're imbued.
> Republican votes are all counted,
> While Democrat votes are eschewed.

FLORIST (n) A person who deals in dollars and scents.

FLY (n) A zippered access to male plumbing with an excruciating tendency to pinch the pipe.

> "Oh, Lord, will you please tell me why
> "I never can keep my pants dry?

"Why, whenever I zip,
"Is there always a drip
"That falls on the front of my fly?"

FOIBLE (n) The name men give to their infidelities and women to
their extravagances. For people in the Bronx, it is what a cat
spits up.
"While it's true that my foible is very enjoyable,"
Said philandering Fillmore from Maine.
"My wife, Kathleen Crimmin, doesn't like to screw women,
"So, why should the creature complain?"

FOLLOWER (n) Someone with the courage of another's conviction.
Said a Christian Right marcher from Pine,
As he followed his mate with a sign,
"I am strongly pro-life,
"Out of fear of my wife,
"And the life I am pro about's mine."

FOOL (n) Anyone who disagrees with your opinions.
More maxims have been written on this subject than on any
other, including love. This should be no surprise, since there are
so many more fools than lovers in the world. Following are several
instructive examples:
1. "Nothing is fool-proof to a determined fool".
2. "Fools rush in after their stockbrokers get out".
3. "Experience is a harsh teacher, but fools will learn from
no other."
4. "'Habit' is the name fools give to their mistakes."
5. "Fools and their money are soon parted,
"Leaving their heirs brokenhearted."

FOOTBALL (n) A business in which twenty-four grown men chase an
inflated pig's bladder in a field and try to hurt each other.
Said a father, named Jackson Sewell,
Sending his son off to school:
"Get all of the learnin'
"You need to be earnin',
"Especially 'bout football and pool."

FOREPLAY (n) The first scene in a disappearing act, at the end of
which a man vanishes.
"My romance with Ted is over and dead,"

85

Sobbed Sylvia Sharp to friend Dawn.
"His passion's so strong and our foreplay so long
"That when I am coming, he's gone."

FOREVER (adj.) Until something better turns up.
"I want to live forever. So far, so good."
David Letterman

FORGETFUL (adj.) A failure of memory that can range from a)
normal to b) pathological. In a man, these extremes are best
illustrated by a) forgetting to zip up his fly, and b) forgetting
to zip it down.

FORGETFULNESS (n) A type of mental illness that chiefly afflicts
sons and husbands, rendering them unable to remember anniversaries,
birthdays, and household chores.
Peggy Centurious is utterly furious,
When her husband neglects household trashes.
"I'm forgetful," claims he. "Your damn lazy," cries she,
"'Cause you never forget poker bashes."

FORNICATION (n) The only sin that cannot be committed by a
married person.
A dating young couple, Alsatian,
Went picnicking on a vacation,
Fire ants in their pants
Caused a wild mating dance,
Which looked like obscene fornication.
Students in a class on Family Law were asked by the professor
to explain the difference between adultery and fornication. One
student raised his hand and said: "Professor, there's no difference
between them. I've tried them both and they're the same thing."

FORTUITOUS (adj.) Occurring by accident rather than by design, as
when a pickpocket's hand gets caught in your pocket or a campaign
solicitor takes "no" for an answer.
Said Pickpocket Paul, for his plea:
"I'm not guilty, your honor, not me.
"'Twas the crowd, I am sure,
"Forced my hand to detour,
"And it caused the fortuity."

FOSSIL (n) Any old relic, whose age is relative to the observer:

1. (paleontologist) Anyone older than 100,000 years.

2. (anthropologist) Anyone older than 5,000 years.

3. (teenager) Anyone older than 40 years.

An 82 year old man was being urged by his broker to invest in long-term government bonds. "Why should I put my money in long-term anything?" replied the old fellow. "At my age, I don't even buy ripe bananas."

This same fellow was given the address of a brothel by his two sons, who urged him to visit the place for a good time. When the madam opened the front door and heard what he wanted, she took a long look at him and said, "brother, you've had it!" He looked startled and responded, "I have? Then, how much do I owe you?"

FOX (n) 1. An animal with a bushy tail that is hunted by men using dogs.

2. An attractive woman with a fetching tail who is hunted by men used to dogs.

Q. What is the difference between a fox and a dog?

A. Five martinis.

FOX HUNT (n) "The unspeakable chasing the inedible."
Ambrose Bierce

FREAK (n) A person or event uncommon in nature, as in these examples: 1. A truthful politician; 2. A humble judge; 3. A physician who makes house calls; 4. A reasonable attorney fee; 5. An honest tax return, and 6. A charity that pays more to its beneficiaries than to its administrators.

A freakish young fellow from Kent
Had a neck so long that it bent.
To take up the slack,
He bent his head back
And instead of coming, he went.

FREE (n) Having no price and, therefore, no value. This axiom explains why some things, thought free, are really not. For example, applying the definition to what has come to be called, "free love," one sees that it is a misnomer. It has keen value to the man and the woman pays a great price.

Said Hillary Hymond, about her new diamond,
"I owe it to many free kisses.
"But, when Tom wanted more, I said 'you can't score

"'Until you have made me your misses.'"
"Nothing is more expensive than a woman who is free for the evening."

Henny Youngman

FREEWAY (n) A highway designed to avoid everything interesting.
> On a freeway near Brea, A father-to be
> Shouted "911" into his cell phone.
> His wife sadly smiled, delivered her child,
> Then treated her husband, now prone.

FRENCH HORN (n) A wind instrument with the inclinations of a mutineer, in that it is prone to produce sounds never intended by either the composer or the player.
> A careless French Hornist, named Hartz,
> Blew clinkers in Brahms solo parts.
> The rest of the brass
> Shoved the horn up his ass
> And now he plays Strauss when he farts.

FRIEND (n) Someone who is always there for you as long as you never need him.
> "Oh Lord, protect me from my friend.
> "'Gainst enemies, I can myself defend."

Saint Augustine

I
> A famished old farmer from Fungher
> Borrowed food from a friend out of hunger.
> Since he owed him his life,
> He repaid with his wife,
> Then married a woman much younger.

II
> That old friends are best, is proved by this test.
> That, knowing your faults, none repines.
> And further, it's true, you know their faults, too.
> You're all rascals, but nobody minds.

FRIVOLOUS (adj.) Behavior that evinces only a slight regard for a serious subject, as in these examples:

1. Your wife laughs when she sees you naked.
2. Your son charged his bail bond on your credit card.
3. Your daughter took an air mattress with her on a heavy date.
4. Your employer gave you a raise that   is less than the increase in your parking fee.
5. Your elderly parent just gave all her assets to her

favorite charity.

> A frivolous farmer, Fred Foats,
> Vexed his family with odorous goats.
> His spouse, Spruce, ceased sewing,
> His sow, Sue, ceased growing,
> And his son, Sid, started sowing wild oats.

FROG (n) The animal with the shortest sex life. He hops on, hops off, then croaks.

> "Can you sound like a frog?" asked young Doak,
> To his grandfather, puffing a smoke.
> "Grandma said we'll all go,
> "Flying to Orlando,
> "Whenever you finally croak."

FUNERAL (n) A ceremony that enables family and friends to mourn the deceased's passing, enemies, to confirm it, and the proprietor, to profit by it.

Three married men were discussing the subjects of death when one asked the others: "what would you like people to say about you when they saw your corpse at the funeral home? I know I'd want them to say that I was a good husband and father."

A second man said, "as for me, I'd want them to say that I had a successful career."

The third man thought for a moment, then said: "I'd want them to say, 'look, he's moving!'"

FUSION (n) A physical phenomenon in which two unstable bodies tightly interlock, releasing enormous quantities of energy that results in a spent rod and extreme heat.
See INTERCOURSE

G

GALL BLADDER (n) An organ of the body whose principal function is to produce stones which, when stuck in a duct, teach men a better appreciation of childbirth.

GARAGE SALE (n) A business enterprise in which old junk of the seller becomes new junk of the buyer, neither of whom has any use for it.

GARLIC (n) A member of the onion family that is prized for a characteristic that promotes privacy. When displayed, it is said to repel vampires. When eaten, it repels everybody.

GAS (n) A hydro-carbon compound that is lighter than air and can be found in the bellies of the Earth, cows, and bean eaters everywhere.

> Said a flatulent fellow from Mass,
> Who markets his product of gas:
> "I don't mind the meter
> "That's next to my peter,
> "Half as much as the pipe up my ass."

GENDER (n) The classification of living things as either male or female according to their differences. In the case of men and women, the major difference is that while a woman wants a man to satisfy her every need, a man wants every woman to satisfy his one need.

GENES (n) Chemical compounds present in all living cells that control their development and dictate the physical and mental traits inherited by descendants. We should all celebrate the heroism of certain men who voluntarily remove themselves from the gene pool so human progress is not retarded. Following are three true examples of this self-sacrifice:

1. (Manitoba, Canada) A 31 year old telephone night watchman, Edward Baker, was killed on Christmas morning from an over-exposure to microwave radiation. He was trying to keep warm by watching television and drinking beer directly in front of a large microwave relay dish while on duty on Christmas eve. He had reportedly told a co-worker that it was the only way he could keep warm during nights when the temperature often reached minus forty degrees.

Microwaves can heat water molecules within human tissue in the same way that they heat food in microwave ovens. For his Christmas shift, Baker reportedly brought a twelve pack of beer and a plastic lawn chair, which he positioned directly in line with the strongest microwave beam.

2. (Moscow, Russia) A drunken security guard asked a colleague at the Moscow bank they were guarding to stab his

bulletproof vest to see if it would protect him against a knife attack. It failed the test and the 25 year-old guard died of a heart wound.

3. In FRANCE, Jacques LeFevrier left nothing to chance when he decided to commit suicide. He stood at the top of a tall cliff and tied a noose around his neck. He tied the other end of the rope to a large rock. He drank some poison and set fire to his clothes. He even tried to shoot himself at the last moment. He jumped and fired the pistol. The bullet missed him completely and cut through the rope above him. Free of the threat of hanging, he plunged into the sea. The sudden dunking extinguished the flames and made him vomit the poison.

He was dragged out of the water by a kind fisherman and was taken to a hospital, where he died of hypothermia.

GENEALOGY (N) The study of ancestral history by which we can identify past and present occupants of our family tree. A thorough study will lead honest people to conclude that the best of their families are not in trees at all, but underground.

> Said Christopher Klein, "my family tree's fine.
> "With the main trunk, I'm delighted.
> "But Martha, my wife, is the bane of my life,
> "For her branches are terribly blighted."

GENEROSITY (n) The impulse to give to others what we wish they had given to us earlier. When a man is said to be "generous to a fault," it is usually his fault he is generous to.

GENETICS (n) The branch of science that seeks to explain why men are so vulnerable to disease and are quarrelsome, violent, promiscuous, and unprincipled. According to the eminent geneticist, Dr. M. Brio, the answer is the same as the question-- "Y".

> A genetic fence kept Neanderthal gents
> From multiplying, 'tis said.
> 'Twas their butt-ugly face that foredoomed their race;
> They couldn't get women in bed.

GENITAL (n)   A sexually active non-Jew.

GENOME (n) A biological project designed to identify and evaluate the characteristics of Genes. When it is over, new projects will be undertaken to do the same for Harold, Herman,

Hermione, and so on, through Zoe.

> A doctoral phenom, involved in the Genome,
> Finished counting the genes in son, Sherm.

> Imagine his shock when the kid's total stock
> Was less than a typical worm.

GERM (n) The most prolific and dominant life form on Earth. If, as theologians contend, God is the image of His greatest creation, then He can be seen only under a microscope.

> "A mighty creature is the germ,
> "Though smaller than the pachyderm.
> "A childish whim by which it pleases
> "God to give us all diseases."
> Ogden Nash

GERONTOLOGIST (n) A medical specialist who studies why old people die.

> Said an elderly patient, Bill Licted,
> "I've a long lease on life; it's predicted."
> Said gerontologist, Art,
> "From your medical chart,
> "It appears that you'll soon be evicted."

GESTALT (n) Psycho-analysis without a couch.

> Said Gestaltist, Doc Eleanor Vores,
> "Tell me your troubles and sores."
> So, her patient, Jean Pate,
> Spoke for two hours straight,
> 'Til she heard Doctor Eleanor's snores.

GINGIVITIS (n) A gum condition that enables people to remove their teeth at will.

> Said a woman, named Grace, with two teeth in her face,
> "My bicuspids fell out in a heap.
> "Since the day I was weaned, all the teeth that I cleaned
> "Were the two that I wanted to keep."

GLOBAL WARMING (n) 1. What happens to a woman's chest during foreplay.

2. A planetary phenomenon that industry scientists attribute to gasses from cows and environmentalists.

> "There were so many candles on my last birthday cake that the

EPA cited me for contributing to global warming."
                    Rodney Dangerfield

GOLDEN RULE (n) A classic maxim expressed in these different
ways by Capitalists, Socialists, Democrats, and Republicans:
    "Do unto others before they do unto you." (Capitalist)
    "Those who have the gold, rule." (Socialist)
    "Do unto others what you want them to do unto you, first."
(Democrat)
    "Do unto others only after everything has been done unto you."
(Republican)

GOLF (n) A sport engaged in by round white men who pursue round
white balls into round black holes in a roundabout manner. Its
lasting popularity is probably due to the fact that it is the only
game in which the poorest player gets the most for his money.
    Weekend golfers exhibit some common traits, most important
of which are: 1. An inability to add correctly; 2. A partiality
for playing rough; 3. A tendency to lose their balls; 4. A marked
preference for the 19th hole over all others, and 5. An
irresistible urge to shout "fore" to golfers far beyond their
reach.
        "Golf is a way to ruin a good walk."
                Sir Walter Scott
        A newly wed wife in Penrub
        Confessed to her golf-loving hub:
        "I'm a hooker," wailed she.
        "Not to worry," soothed he.
        "Move your hands to the left on the club."

GOP (n) An acronym that identifies the Republican Party and
means "Grand Old Party", to them, "Guardian Of Privilege", to
Independents, and "Guilty On Principle", to Democrats.
        Said Martin, a merchant from Hazeltine:
        "GOP doctrine is also mine.
        "Of the poor, our view
        "Is similar to
        "A hydrant, seen by a canine."

GORILLA (N) Largest member of Homo Sapiens and a relative of Man,
its vegetarian diet and pacific traits place it a rung higher
on the evolutionary ladder. Proof of a superior intelligence
lies in the fact that humans provide him with free food and

housing for a life of leisure, then pay again to view his
idleness.

GOVERNOR (n) 1. An inanimate component of a motor that limits its
speed, efficiency, and work product.
    2. A partially-animate component of State government, whose
purpose and effect is the same as that in a motor.

GRANDCHILD (n) As the name denotes, a member of one of the better
classes of children. The blessings grandparents derive are
significant.   The child's visits are brief, her love is deep, she
rarely gives them the benefit of her inexperience, and there is no
legal liability attaching.
    Said a girl, name of Terrence, as she left her grandparents,
    "I wish mom and dad loved like you."
    Then she pocketed money, jars of jelly and honey,
    And candy bars more than a few.

GRANDFATHER (n) A man young in heart, but old everywhere else,
whose best days are behind him and best nights are when his trips
to the toilet are three or less and he shoots straight.
    "I want to die in my sleep like my grandfather did, not
yelling and screaming like his airline passengers did."
                George Carlin
        Cried rickety Grandfather, Blunder,
        "I am over the hill and no wonder."
        Said his Granddaughter, Sue,
        "It seems to me true
        "That it's best to be over than under."

GRAND JURY (n) A panel of lay persons in each State's criminal
justice system. Its sworn duty is to indict, for a later trial,
only defendants who appear guilty based on the prosecutor's
evidence.   Since the panel's only legal advisor
on questions of guilt is the prosecutor and only proof of guild is
considered, an indictment is rarely denied.
    A Grand Juror, a Hoosier, asked the judge to excuse her
    Because she was deaf in one ear.
    "Your request is denied," the jurist replied,
    "Just one side of each case will you hear."

GRATITUDE (n) An emotion which, like virginity in a

young woman, is often expected and rarely encountered. According to surveys, homeless recipients of charitable gifts are the least grateful--probably because only the donors get a worthwhile shelter.

"I thank you from my bottom to my heart."
George Szell (Retiring Czech conductor of the Cleveland Symphony, responding to a standing ovation)
> Tim Smith was imbued with profound gratitude
> Toward his wife for producing a son.
> But, the feeling soon failed. Every night the kid wailed
> And cleaning his ass was no fun.

GRAVE (n) 1. A place in the ground where a deceased loved one is put pending either his ascension to Heaven or assumption by worms, depending on his faith.

2. (adj.) The demeanor of the same relative when his death was imminent, as he weighed the likelihood of either fate.
"The only difference between a rut and a grave is the depth."
Herb Shriner

GRAVITY (n) A natural force that causes an older man's penis to fall toward the floor. Young men are able to neutralize this force, with the result that it is often their trousers that fall.

GREETING CARD (n) A vehicle for sending another a message of warmth, heat, or ice, depending on the relationship. Here are examples of the last type:

1. "Congratulations on your wedding day. Too bad nobody likes your wife."

2. "I've always wanted to have somebody to hold, somebody to love, and somebody to kiss. But, after meeting you, I've changed my mind."

3. "I must admit that you brought religion into my life. I never believed in Hell until I met you."

4. "As this fine day goes by, I think to myself how lucky it is that you're not here to ruin it for me."

5. "If I only get one gift for Christmas, I hope it's your sister."

6. "As you grow older, Mom, I think of all the things you have given me--like the need for therapy."

7. "Thanks for being a part of my life. I never knew what evil was before you came into it."

GRIFFIN (n) A mythological animal, half of which is an eagle and the other half a lion. The creature is all but extinct in America, with the Reverend Jerry Folwell the only living member. Half of him is a baboon and the other half an ass.

"Will you crawl a little faster,"
Said the griffin to the snail?
"There's a pit bull close behind me
"That is lunching on my tail."
(Apologies to Lewis Carroll)

GRIM (adj.) A severe demeanor, in reaction to a threat or challenge, as when:
1. You received an IRS bill when you expected a refund.
2. A young spouse is leaving on a trip.
3. An old spouse is returning from a trip.
　　The cell of a monk, Brother Tim,
　　Smelled so bad that it made his life grim.
　　He searched for the source
　　And discovered, of course,
　　That the smell was all coming from him.

GRIZZLY (n) A large carnivorous animal that roams throughout Yellowstone and Montana, making the lives of hikers and ranchers unbearable.
　　Two hunters suddenly confronted a grizzly on a mountain trail. Fleeing as fast as their legs would move, one abruptly sat and began replacing his hunting boots with running shoes.
　　"Are you crazy?" demanded his friend. "You can't outrun that bear."
　　"I don't have to," replied the other. "I just have to outrun you."
　　A bloodthirsty bear is the grizzly
　　Whose exploits are perfectly grisly
　　If you hunt him, be sure
　　That your life, you insure;
　　'Cause the one who'll be slaughtered is thee.

GROTESQUE (adj.) Having a face that not even a mother can love.
　　Said a beautiful lady from Ransom,
　　When asked why she married a man some
　　Thought simply grotesque:
　　"I looked in his desk
　　"And saw that his assets were handsome."

GRUNGY (adj.) Slovenly, therefore attractive to young people.
>A fat, sloppy, fellow from Dungee
>Was beloved for being so grungy.
>He lived with a dash
>And died with a splash,
>When his weight proved too great for the bungy.

GUARDIAN (n) In law, one who guards the property of another, called "beneficiary", and enlarges it until it is sufficient to pay his fees.
>Say Uncle Sam's nephews and nieces:
>"We're pleased that your love never ceases.
>"But, while guarding your masses
>"From Missiles and gasses,
>"You are taxing our asses to pieces."

GUN (n) A hunter's phallic symbol, a robber's key, a self-help substitute for divorce, and the means for a permanent end to a temporary quarrel between drinking buddies.
>   1.
>Said an eminent sportsman, named Dunne,
>After killing a doe with his gun:
>"It is not that I'm cruel
>"Or a bloodthirsty fool.
>"It's that shooting things dead is such fun."
>   2.
>When a NRA son purchased a gun,
>He vowed that, no crime, would he brook.
>So, three cats lost their life, he wounded his wife,
>But, not once did he threaten a crook.

GYPSY (n)A member of an itinerant population from Eastern Europe, many of whom are believed to possess psychic powers. This consists mainly of an ability to recognize a fool when they see him and prove the proverb by parting him from his money.
>Said a sheepish young man from Poughkipsie,
>When asked why he married a gypsy,
>"She has a good head,
>"She is active in bed,
>"And she kept me continually tipsy."

H

HABIT (n) (1)   "A shackle for the free."
                                    Ambrose Bierce
It is repetitive behavior so ingrained that any deviation
produces discomfort, as in these examples:

1. During a speech, a political candidate says something nice
about his opponent.

2. A merchant stocked-up on a loss leader article on sale
below her cost.

3. A challenger for political office disclosed something good
the incumbent did during his term.

4. A college student decided not to cheat on an examination
and was the only failure.

5. A slumlord failed to pay his fire insurance premium before
dropping a lighted cigarette into the wastepaper bin.

(2) A costume worn by Catholic nuns, which they are said
to inhabit.

When Sister Virginia retired, Father Michael asked if he might
kiss her goodbye. "Why yes, father," the nun replied, "but, don't
get into the habit."

HACKER (n) A rat with a mouse under his control, whose byte herz
worse because he infects systems with a virus that is caching.

A hacker, named West, claims that he is the best.
"At wiping out drives, I'm a whiz."
Then, his mouse's sudden jerk stopped the guy's wicked
                              work.
Seems the hard drive he wiped out was his.

HALF (adj.) Less or more than you want, depending on whether
pleasure or pain is measured. Outside of these, the significance
of halfness is relative to the subject, as in these cases:

1. (optimist) "The glass is half full."
2. (pessimist) "The glass is half empty."
3. (cost accountant) "There is twice as much glass than is
   necessary."
4. (government bureaucrat) "Fill up small glasses and throw
   all the large glasses away."
5. (Pentagon procurement officer) "Fill up the glass and keep
   it full or we'll only get small glasses."

HALLMARK CARD (n) A printed message that addresses someone's anniversary, birthday, wedding, or death. A good example of this last category is the card W.C. Fields sent after the death of the much-despised Hollywood producer, Irving Thalberg. Field's "sympathy" card was delivered during a memorial church service attended by a large crowd. It read: "As I have always said, just give the public what it wants and it will show up."

Many affecting sentiments have not yet made it into print, among which are the following examples:

1. "We've been friends for a long time. Let's say we call it quits."

2. "I'm so miserable without you, it's almost like you're here."

3. "Your friends and I want to do something special for you on your birthday, so we're having you put to sleep."

4. "Congratulations on your wedding. I wonder if you know that the service was performed by a pedophile?"

5. "Thanks for bringing religion into my life. I didn't believe in Hell until I met you."

HAMBURGER (n) commonly called, "ground meat," because it often tastes so much like soil amendment, it is said to have been named after an elderly resident of Hamburg, Germany. The old fellow accidentally strayed within range of French cannon during the Napoleonic invasion of 1809.

When his remains were later discovered on the battlefield, A French officer is reported to have said, "oh, there's a Hamburger."

HAMLET (n) 1. A small pig.

2. The name of one of Shakespeare's bloodiest villain, whose mayhem litters the stage with corpses. In order of achievement, he (1) murders his sweetheart's father, (2) induces her madness, (3) drives her to commit suicide, (4) is an accessory to his mother's murder, (5) kills his dead sweetheart's brother in a duel, (6) murders his uncle, and (7) abets his own murder.

At the end of this famous romp, with his victims littering the stage like cigarette butts and gore up to his eyeballs, the Prince of Denmark's best friend, Horatio (surely, the thickest blockhead in all of English theater--oblivious, as he is, to the imminent violence that surrounds him), recites one of the best satirical lines in all of the Bard's plays: "Goodnight, sweet Prince, may flights of angels sing thee to thy rest."

HAND (n) That part of a son or daughter's anatomy that is most often extended toward a parent. If contact is made, it is called a "touching", while if there is no contact, it is called a "touch." Although the frequency of the former is inversely related to the age of the child, the frequency of the latter (and the addition of a second hand) is directly related to it.

"May God hold you in the palm of His hand and not squeeze."
(Irish Prayer)

HANGOVER (n) A morning ailment caused by heavy drinking the night before. Classic symptoms often include a headache, upset stomach, empty wallet, and the inability to recall the name of the woman sleeping on the bed. It is sometimes called "the wrath of grapes," in honor of John Steinbeck.

HAPPINESS (n) A temporary mental disease that causes inappropriate smiles, loss of memory about past suffering, the inability to foresee future misery, and a compulsion to sing off key. A state of happiness resembles the State of Delaware in that almost as soon as you are in it, you are out of it again.

"I didn't know what happiness was until I got married and then, it was too late."
George Carlin

A certain young man in Cape Cod
Now seeks happiness only in God.
Last year, on two dares,
He jumped down some stairs
And fatally injured his rod.

HARLEQUIN (adj.) A type of romance novel that examines the human condition from the waist down.

HARLOT (n) A woman who works for back wages.

HARPSICHORD (n) A piano with laryngitis.

The celebrated British conductor, Sir Thomas Beecham, once described the instrument as "sounding like two pigeons copulating on a tin roof."

HEADLINE (n) The kernel of a story, preceding its chaff.

Here are several actual kernels harvested from American newspapers during the past year:

1. "Include Your Children When Baking Cookies"
2. "Police Begin Campaign To Run Down Jaywalkers"

3. "Drunk Gets Four Months In Violin Case"
5. "Iraqi Head Seeks Arms"
6. "Is There A Ring Of Debris Around Uranus?"
7. "Prostitutes Appeal To Pope"
8. "Panda Mating Fails; Veterinarian Takes Over"
9. "Teachers Strike Idle Kids"
10. "Plane Too Close To Ground, Crash Probers Told"
11. "Juvenile Court To Try Shooting Defendant"

HEALTH CLUB (n) A place where, if you exercise there regularly, you will die in good physical condition.

"I was a member of a health club for three years, at a cost of $400, and never lost a pound. Apparently, you have to show up."
David Letterman

HEART (n) The only organ in the human body that can break solely by emotion.

"The heart knows reasons that reason does not know."
William Shakes Spear

HEAVEN (n) 1. A place where the police are British, the cooks are French, the mechanics are German, love affairs are supervised by Italians, and everything is administered by the Swiss.

2. A post-mortem paradise to which only good Christians can gain entry. Room and board are free, the climate is controlled, work is not required, and neither the IRS nor bill collectors have access. The awe and ecstasy concerning it are inexplicable, since we have something comparable to it in America, called "prison."

HELL (n) A place in the afterlife where your friends will be pleased to see you. There, the cooks are British, the mechanics are French, the police are German, love affairs are supervised by the Swiss, and everything is administered by the Italians.

"Do you know there's a Hell, Mrs. Kerry?"
Asked the priest of a convert in Derry.
"I never believed
"Hell existed," she grieved,
"Until I got married to Harry."

HEREDITY (n) A scientific theory on the basis of which biologists blame parents for the defects in their children. This opinion is disputed by sociologists, who blame the environment; by fundamentalists, who blame Adam; by teachers, who blame school boards; by democrats, who blame republicans; by republicans, who blame increases in the minimum wage, and by children, who agree with the biologists.

David brought home his report card and his father exploded when he saw the 'D's'.

"How do you explain these terrible grades?" he demanded.

"Well," the boy replied, "I guess it must be either heredity or the environment."

HERO (n) "A person who is unaware of all the contingencies."
        Thomas Hardy
      "Charge and be heroes!" cried Major Moncriv.
      "It's your duty to country, your lives now to give."
      When they charged, he was queried
      For the reason he tarried.
      He replied, with a smile, "it's my duty to live."

HIKING (n) A type of walk that is not on the level.
      An ardent young fellow in Maine
      Hiked many rough miles to his Jane.
      Exhausted, he kissed her,
      Returned with a blister,
      And said, "it ain't worth all the pain."

HILLBILLY (n) A mountain resident in the Mid-Atlantic States who speaks a language that resembles English. Because the idiom is often confusing to outsiders, here are several common expressions and their translations:

1. "As welcome as a skunk at a picnic" (not welcome)

2. "Tighter than bark on a tree" (a miser)

3. "He thinks the sun comes up just to hear him crow" (a conceited fellow).

4. "Her mouth has ten tongues" (a gabby woman).

5. "Just because a chicken has wings doesn't mean it can fly" (don't assume anything).

6. "He looks like the dog's been hiding him under the porch" (he's not handsome).

7. "They ate supper before they said grace" (sex before marriage).

HIRSUTE (adj.) One whose crowning glory covers her entire body. This definition was traced back to 16th Century England. At that

time, the word was spelled, "hersuit",
in euphemistic reference to the thick covering of body hair that
many women of the day displayed. It is thought that Lady Godiva
was one of these.

> Lady Godiva, 'tis said,
> Rode nude, though a lady well bred.
> But, her bod wasn't bare;
> It was covered with hair
> And some of it grew on her head.

HISPANIC (n) A member of an ethnic class that settled Mexico
centuries ago and now unsettles California.

> A wily Hispanic, Jose,
> Slips into the U.S. each May.
> He's going from Leon,
> Where his dad is a peon,
> To his law firm in Santa Fe.

HISTORY (n) A type of fiction in which past events are
portrayed according to the bias of the publisher. Thus, Napoleon's
1812 invasion of Russia is portrayed as either a noble
expedition to liberate an enslaved people, or as a bloodthirsty
caprice by a military madman--depending on whether it was published
in Paris or Moskow.

> A critic, named Pree, tells, quite cynically,
> How Hitler will someday be painted.
> "Given the pap about Genghis and Nap,
> "Adolf will come across sainted."

HMO (n) An acronym meaning "health maintenance organization," it
is widely believed that the first word refers to the health of
patients. This is a mistake. It actually refers to the financial
health of the organization, which the company makes every effort to
maintain.

Here are the definitions of several other acronyms that are

frequently used in the industry and, as often, misunderstood:

1. "ASAP" (how soon patients are sued when they are late
paying their hospital bill)

2. "PDQ" (how quickly doctors are expected to
finish treating their patients)

3. "CPR" (a treatment that is provided only to insured
patients)

Since finding an inexpensive HMO is often a challenge, here
are several features that indicate a really cheap one:

1. Breast examinations are conducted at Hooters.

2. Directions to the facility begin with: "take a left inside the trailer park".

3. Tongue depressors have the lingering taste of fudgesickles.

4. The proctologist is a part-time operator for the local Roto-Rooter franchise.

5. The primary care doctor is wearing the trousers you gave to Goodwill, last year.

6. The only "wholly Covered" procedure is cremation.

7. Syringes are returns from the local needle exchange program.

8. Instead of Viagra, patients are prescribed a popsicle stick and duct tape.

HOMELESS (adj.) Free of the duty to make mortgage or rent payments. Out of compassion, society restricts this benefit to the poor.

"I am homeless," said she, "and as poor as can be;
"I am black and a pitiful sight."
"My advice," counseled he, "I give you for free.
"Get a job and try to look white."

HONEYMOON (n) A nuptial event that jump-starts the couple into a lifetime of debt. The custom has radically changed over the years, as the following history attests:

1. (pre-1930) A one night event at a relative's house, during which the couple shared a bed for the first time (cost-0).
(1930 to 1970) A one week event at a resort, during which the couple had intercourse for the first time (cost-$1,500, cash, and one baby).

3. (1970 to 1990) A one week event at a resort, during which the couple has intercourse without birth control measures for the first time (cost-$3,000, paid by their parents, and one baby).

4. (1990 to 2000) A four day event at the nearest Disney park, during which the couple is too tired for intercourse, for the first time (cost-$1,500, charged to a parent's credit card).

5. (2000 to ?) A one night event at a relative's home, during which the couple does not have intercourse for the first time (cost-0).

HOPE (n) First in a sequence of five emotions, followed by "expectation", "anticipation", "realization", and "disappointment".

"Why don't you get married," asked dad of his son?
"You have lived all your life in this house.
"And now that you've reached a mature forty-one,

"It is time you recruited a spouse."
"I had hoped for a wife," said the son, very portly,
Giving dad an affectionate smile,
"But, no woman I've met will agree to support me
"In your very generous style."
                    2.
A dealer in pottery put cash in the lottery;
Winning the pot was his hope.
As the drawing was made, he fervently prayed,
But, the answer from God was a "nope!"

HORROR (n) A strong, negative, emotion that can be expected in the following situations:

1. (middle-aged woman) Upon seeing her face for the first time after a corneal transplant procedure.

2. (small boy) After being told he must kiss a girl at a birthday party.

3. (small girl) After being told she must kiss her bewhiskered grandfather.

4. (new father) After being told he must share diaper-changing duties.

5. (young woman) After being told the condom broke.

6. (old man) After being assigned to play bridge with three old women at a senior center.

7. (old woman) After being told she must live with her daughter-in-law.

8. (nun) after being told that she is pregnant.

9. (priest) After being served with an arrest warrant by a former altar boy.

HORTICULTURE (n) A branch of the Arts designed for prostitutes.
"You can lead a horticulture, but you can't make her think."
                    Dorothy Parker

HOUSE GUEST (n) An overnight visitor who resembles a fish after three days; he stinks!

HOUSE RULES (n) Separate standards of conduct guaranteed to improve home life for both men and women. With the caveat that they have not yet received the stamp of approval by Good Housekeeping or Consumer Reports, the most important rules are provided here:
                    MEN'S RULES FOR WOMEN

1. Learn to work the toilet seat. If it's up, put it down. We need it up, you need it down. You don't hear us complaining when we find it down.

2. Shopping is not a sport and, no, we're never going to think of it that way.

3. Crying because we say, "no", is unfair.

4. Ask for what you want. Subtle, or even obvious, hints will not work. Just tell us so we know what to say "no" to.

5. "Yes" and "no", without more, are acceptable answers to almost every question.

6. Tell us about your problem only if you want help solving it. That's what we do. If you want sympathy, tell it to your girl friends. That's what they are for.

7. Anything we said six months ago is inadmissible in arguments, today. In fact, anything we say becomes null and void after seven days.

8. If you think you're fat, you probably are. Don't ask me. If I say "yes", you're insulted and if I say "no", you'll insult me.

9. You can either ask me to do something or tell me how you want it done, not both. If you already know how best to do it, then do it yourself.

10. Whenever possible, please say whatever you have to say during commercials.

11. If it itches, I'm going to scratch. That's what we do.

12. If I ask what is wrong and you say, "nothing", I will act as if nothing is wrong. I know you are lying, but it's just not worth the hassle.

13. If you ask a question you don't want an answer to, expect to get an answer you don't want to hear.

14. You have enough clothes and too many shoes.

15. Stop complaining that we are not in shape. Round is a shape.

WOMEN'S RULES FOR MEN

1. When you go to the toilet, keep your eyes on the target, aim for it, and don't try to play a tune.

2. Shopping is therapy. It may keep me from killing you.

3. If ever I cry in front of you and you smile, protect yourself.

4. Don't tell me what you want. Let me surprise you with something you don't want.

5. "No" is almost never an acceptable answer.

6. If I ask you to help me solve a problem, I do it to make

you feel important. For a problem I cannot solve myself, I will ask somebody competent.

7. Whatever you said in the past will be remembered and is fair game in a new argument.

8. Yawning is permitted, so long as you conceal the need to have your teeth cleaned.

9. Since only you snore, wait until I'm asleep before you follow.

10. Whenever you have to clear your throat, it is not necessary to do it from the toes up.

11. When you know nothing about the topic being discussed, it is better to be silent and appear stupid than to open your mouth and remove any doubt.

12. If you have to tell a lie, make it one we can respect you for, not one we can see through quickly.

HUMAN (n) "The only species on Earth that can blush and has cause to."
Mark Twain

HUMBLE (adj.) The chief trait of someone suffering from an inferiority complex. Few experiences are more humbling than those that follow:

1. Your dog gets upset when you blow in his face, but sticks his head out the car window whenever you drive him anywhere.

2. An attractive woman reacts to your smile by looking you over and laughing.

3. During a business meting, you are the one asked to go for sandwiches.

4. You are asked to be the "before" person in a health and fitness campaign by your employer.

"Don't try so hard to be humble. You're not that great."
Steve Allen
A man asked a psychiatrist if he could cure his inferiority complex. After subjecting the man to a battery of tests, the doctor told the patient that he could completely cure him for two hundred dollars, whereupon the man eagerly handed over the money and awaited the treatment.

"My cure," the psychiatrist said, "is to tell you that you have no inferiority complex at all. You really are inferior."

HUMOR (n) A type of communication that tickles one's funny bone by stealth. Surprise and human foibles are common characteristics and are illustrated by the following stories:

1. (surprise) The Lone Ranger wakened Tonto, one night, at their campsite and asked him to look up and say what he saw. "I see thousands of stars," the Indian replied. "What does that mean to you?" asked his companion. Tonto thought for a moment, then replied, "astronomically, it means there are millions of galaxies with billions of star systems; astrologically, it means that cancer is on the cusp of Capricorn, and meteorologically, it means that tomorrow will be a fine day. Is that what you meant?"

"No, you dumb ass," retorted the Lone Ranger, "it means that somebody's stolen our tent."

2. (foible) Convinced that his wife was growing deaf, her husband crept up behind her, one evening, as she was reading the newspaper. When ten feet behind her, he said, "Martha, can you hear me?", in a normal tone. There was no answer.

He then approached to within five feet and repeated the question, with the same result. Finally, he stood just behind her chair and said, "can you hear me, now?"

Without turning her head, his wife replied. "For the third time, yes."

HUNTER (n) A person who kills animals for the fun of it, then mounts their heads over his fireplace because they are so beautiful.

> A deadly young hunter, named Dow,
> Fills farmers with fear in Fort Howe.
> His unerring aim
> Brings down animals, tame.
> He has trophied six pigs and a cow.

HURRICANE (n) Satan's gift to the building trades and God's penance on the insurance industry. The phenomenon causes a widespread tropical depression, both meteorological and psychological, and is so-called because of its effect on stalks of sugar cane, causing them to hurry out of sight.

> Said God to the Devil, "it's vile that you revel
> "At a hurricane's awful destruction."
> Answered Satan, unmiffed, "It is such a great gift
> "To all of my friends in construction."

HUSBAND (n) Derived from "animal husbandry", the term denotes a man whose only functions (like other domesticated animals) are breeding and work. Wives greet their husbands' every opinions with instinctive skepticism. Sometimes, it is based on their thought that "if he was stupid enough to marry me, he's too stupid to have a worthwhile opinion." At other times, a husband's opinion is questioned because of the conviction that his breeding organ requires so much of his blood supply that too little is left for his brain.

This disdainful attitude raises a nagging question that female sociologists have been debating for years. If a husband stated an opinion in the middle of a forest, with no one else around to hear, would he still be wrong?

"My husband is like a loaf of bread. He often rises late, usually is puffed-up, is a big crumb, falls to pieces at the slightest pressure, is easily spoiled, and must be buttered-up to be enjoyable."
                    Martha Raye

HYPOCHONDRIA (n) The fear of excessive medical bills. Not so many years ago, it was deemed a minor mental disease and treated as a neurosis. Then, after many treatments and additional bills, psychiatrists were elated to find that the neurosis had deepened into a psychosis that now could be treated with drugs.

Today, the standard treatment for the ailment has taken a radical turn. Modern research has established that excessive medical bills are the norm and the treatment center has shifted from a psychiatrist's couch to Ralph Nader's desk.

HYPOCRISY (n) The tribute vice pays to virtue.

HYPOCRITE (n) One who expresses your opinion, then acts on his own. He is distinguishable from a "convert," who expresses his opinion, then acts on yours. Both are different from a Christian fundamentalist, who has no opinion not based on the Bible and acts foolish.

> Said a keen college dean at UC,
> "I am no hypocritical she.
> "Though opinions I speak
> "Tend to change every week,
> "I'm just seeking the ones best for me."

HYPOTHETICAL (adj.) An assumed reality beloved by politicians, lawyers and divines, in which none of the assumptions need to be true so long as the desired conclusion logically follows. Here are some common   fallacies:

1. (business) "Present and anticipated future revenues, less current expenses, result in current profit."
2. (wife) "My husband loves me too much to be unfaithful, even though menopause has made me frigid."
3. (husband) "If I had a heart attack when my wife was about to leave for her hairdresser appointment, she would ignore the appointment and take care of me."
4. (Republican) "If income taxes were reduced for me and others like me, the nation would be better off.
5. (Democrat) "If income taxes were increased on those who make more than me, the nation would be better off."
6. (Libertarian) "If there were no income taxes, the nation would be better off and I could move my family to Canada, where we would get free medical care."
7. (Socialist) "If all income was collected as taxes and paid out to the most deserving, the nation would be better off and so would my friends and me."
8. (Communist) "If nobody had money with which to pay taxes, the nation would be better off because there would soon be no fat children."

When the high school-age son asked his father to explain the difference between "hypothetical" and "real", dad told him to ask his mother and older sister if each would go to bed with the bachelor next door for one million dollars. The son returned after asking the question of the two women and reported that both had said, "yes."

"Well, then," said the father, "there's your answer. Hypothetically, we're millionaires, but in reality, we're living with two prostitutes."

HYSTERECTOMY (n) An operation that makes a woman inconceivable.

I

I AM (pro+verb) The shortest sentence in the English language, it is often contrasted with the longest sentence, "I do".
IDEOLOGY (n) Our deepest, most profound and enduring, convictions on life's most important issues--subject to

change without notice whenever we discover them to be looney.

> The Reverend William McFay
> Is an ideologue, people say.
> He rants against lust
> And girls showing bust,
> But, enjoys every two on display.

IDIOT (n) (1. (genetic) The product of a sperm that was injured while winning the race.

2. (environmental) The result of over-exposure to television radiation.

> "I am not a complete idiot. Some parts are missing."
> > George Carlin
> When Charlie was young, his praises were sung;
> He was bright and no sort of an idiot.
> But, now that he's twenty, his parents weep plenty,
> For the TV has made him a videot.

IGLOO (n) An hemispheric icehouse often used as a temporary residence by natives of the far North. When it is so occupied, it is irresistible to polar bears, who find it hard and crunchy on the outside, while moist and meaty on the inside. Mathematicians call the ratio of its diameter to the circumference its "Eskimo pi".

IGNORANCE (n) A grace God has bestowed on Mankind, enabling us to believe in Heaven and Hell, the gratitude of our children, that loans will be repaid, and that politics will be reformed in our lifetime. The most blessed among us are convinced they know everything. At this, those of us can scoff who really do.

> "Nothing in the world is more dangerous than sincere ignorance and conscientious stupidity."
> > Martin Luther King

IMBECILE (n) An acquaintance whose opinions are contrary to yours or a stranger who beats you to the last parking space.

> Said a staffer for candidate Mike Kimm,
> Who is running for Congress in Pikeham,
> "He's imbecilic, I know,
> "But, our surveys all show
> "That most of our voters are like him."

ILLITERATE (n) A person who does not get the full benefit of alphabet soup.

111

"One who does not read is no better off than one who cannot read."
(Sign posted at the San Diego Main Library)

IMMIGRANTS (n) All the people who have ever occupied the United States, save only its native Americans, who have not so much occupied the land as fertilized it.

IMPEDIMENT (n) Anything that hinders us from getting what we want and deserve, as in these true-life examples:

1. A lisp that results in her boyfriend hearing her say, "I want to get weighed."

2. A sound body, that prevents him from using a handicap parking placard.

3. A living parent, who disqualifies her from attending an orphan's picnic.

4. An ethics rule that limits the plaintiff's lawyer to pocket just one-third of the settlement as his fee.

Said a crook to the city detective,
"Disability Acts are protective.
"My impediment, large,
"Should win my discharge.
"For my morals are clearly defective."

IMPOSSIBLE (adj.) Insufficiently rewarding. Following are examples of the concept:

1. (boy) To kiss a girl, an old woman, or a bearded man.

2. (girl) To kiss a boy, an old woman, or a bearded man.

3. (Republican) To pay income taxes without a complaint.

4. (aspiring actress) To encourage the advances of a man with neither money nor influence.

5. (lawyer) To submit a fee bill that accurately reflects the worth of the services to the client.

"We do the difficult every day; the impossible takes a while longer."
(Lobby motto of the Lincoln Electric Company, in Cleveland)

"I've saved her from sin," cried Minister Lynne,
Of his beautiful daughter, named Bea.
"Her chastity lock is as strong as a rock;
"An impossible pick," gloated he
(Unaware that the girl had a key).

IMPOTENCY (n) A condition that leaves a man depressed.
A Detroit man was simultaneously sued for divorce, on the

ground of impotency, and for child support, on the ground of paternity. he lost both cases after jury trials. The appellate court upheld the results, holding that each jury was free to draw its own conclusions from the same facts. Thus have our courts emancipated themselves from consistency, to the greater glory of justice in America.

IMPOTENT (adj.) The ability of many older men to maintain their penis at quarter-staff, permanently.

(1)

A husband wore his new shoes into the kitchen to show them off to his wife. "Do you see anything new?" he asked, proudly. She looked him up and down and said "no."

Irritated, he went to the bedroom, removed all his clothes except the shoes, and returned to the kitchen. "Now do you see anything new?" She looked him up and down, again, and said, "no, it's still pointing at the floor."

"It's admiring my new shoes," exploded the husband, in exasperation. "Well," replied his wife, "I wish you had bought a new belt, instead."

(2)

A man of eighty-five was arrested for getting fresh with several female residents at a retirement home and charged with Aggravated Assault. When the case came on for trial, the judge dismissed it, saying that "an assault with a dead weapon is no crime".

IMPREGNABLE (adj.) Denotes a married woman whose memories of her last pregnancy are still fresh.

INCOMPETENT (adj.) Not the way you would do things.
　　　Said the pilot, quite sore, to his navigator,
　　　When their plane lost the way to White Sands,
　　　"You are nice, in the main, but to me it is plain
　　　"That you can't find your ass with both hands."

INCONTINENT (adj.) Unable to control one's bladder within the continent.
　　　When Al travels and wets his bed rental,
　　　His wife thinks the problem is mental.
　　　But, he says, "I am rational.
　　　"My leak's international,
　　　"So, my problem is incontinental."

INDECISION (n) A mental state that consists of a hesitation to choose among available alternatives until only the worst one is

113

left.

"He who hesitates is last."
Dorothy Parker (paraphrasing Poor Richard's proverb)

INDEPENDENT 1. (adj.) Possessing the courage to ignore the advice

of others and make one's own mistakes.
     2. (n) A member of the largest political party in America
who, like a falling leaf, believes he acts according to his free
will. The truth is that, as the leaf is controlled by gravity and
wind, the "Independent" is controlled by the conflicting "spin"
issuing from the Democrat and Republican camps.

INDIAN (n) America's original landlord, whose tenants had no
lease, paid no rent, laid waste to the premises, enlarged their
holdings at will, and in a switch of legal norms, evicted the
landlord for trying to share occupancy.
     Said the Indian chief, to Major Moncrief,
     "We can live as brothers, both free."
     Said Moncrief, "do you try and I'll send my reply
     "By bullet, at Wounded Knee."

INDICTMENT (n) A legal mechanism by which prosecutors inform the
trial jury that a "grand" jury has already convicted the defendant
of the same charge. The former customarily hear of this just
before the judge instructs them that they" must presume the
defendant to be innocent."
     Arrested was young Harry Sueter
     For hacking the courthouse computer.
     Said the techless judge, "son,
     "Tell me how it is done
     And I'll make you the court's own tech-tutor."

INDIGENOUS (adj.) Native to the country. American Indians were
indigenous on the land of the early colonies. Soon, most were
under it.

INFATUATION (n) An excessive and irrational affection
for another, i.e., to be in love. It literally means to become
foolish, which demonstrates how rooted in actual experience is
our language.

INFLUENZA (n) One of China's two principal exports to the United
States. The second one are toys that shatter, contain lead, and

cannot be assembled without an engineering degree or a small child.

It's time for Christmas, time for snow;
Holly wreathes and mistletoe;
Useless gifts   and soaring bills,
Time for influenza chills.
But, keep the faith and do not rue it;
With any luck, you'll live right through it.

INJUNCTION (n) A court order that either directs the defendant
to do that which the plaintiff wants done, to refrain from doing
that which the defendant wants to do, or to pay lawyer fees--which
neither of them wants to do.

A Taiwanese fellow in Huncshun
Sued his wife and obtained an injunction.
She was ordered to sew,
Clean, cook, launder, and mow,
On a finding of spousal dysfunction.

INSANITY (n) The only mental disease that parents acquire from
their children.

"You are acting so strange," the young man said;
"There's a murderous rage in your face.
"When I ask you for money, why did you get red
"And kick me all over the place?"
"In your childhood," the father replied to his son,
"Giving you change made me glad.
"But, now that you've recently turned forty-one,
"Your filial touch drives me mad."

INSPIRATION (n) What many men mistake for creativity and many
women confuse with enthusiasm.

INSTANT(n) The shortest interval of time between two related
events. The examples that follow are familiar to all of us:

1. The interval between the traffic signal changing to green
and the horn of the car behind you;

2. The interval between the discovery of a new pork barrel and
the adoption of a tax to fill it;

3. The interval between the expression of your opinion and its
contradiction by your spouse;

4. The interval between a one cent increase in
the price of a barrel of oil and a ten cent increase in the price

of a gallon of gasoline.

Said a mom to her son, "do your chores this instant!"
So, he left in a run and was soon quite distant.

INSURANCE (n) A form of gambling in which the players are
persuaded that they are beating the house. If reason ruled, the
profit the house garners would convince the players that Russian
roulette provides better odds.

INTEMPERATE (adj.) 1. (motorist) Consuming more alcohol than
MADD
allows or (pedestrian) consuming more alcohol than gravity allows.
2. Overreacting emotionally to trivial annoyances, such as:
shoplifting where you don't shop; sex in a car driving nowhere near
you; arson-caused destruction of a neighborhood eyesore, and
making an unjust profit at the expense of your broker.

Said Texas Jim Stoker, of a player at poker,
"This game, his intemperance disgraces.
"Because he's defeated, he claims that I cheated;
"But five kings do beat his four aces."

INTERMINABLE (adj.) Indifferent to the passage of time, as in these
examples:
--A young woman, talking about her children;
--A middle-aged woman, "putting her face on";
--A young man, trying to make a conquest;
--A middle-aged man, talking about his conquests;
--A campaigning politician, identifying the things he will do
if elected;
--An incumbent politician, explaining why he did not do any of
the things he promised during the campaign;
--A lawyer, justifying a large fee bill;
--A televangelist, explaining why God wants a generous
donation.

INTERNET (n) The electronic dump of the information age, filled
with trash, trivia, porn, blood, con, and an occasional bauble that
wide-hipped cyber junkies spend their lives mining.

A celibate monk was an internet wonk,
Who Searched for hot sex on the grid.
He saw on his screen what he thought was obscene,
But, he couldn't believe what they did.

INTERNIST (n) A medical doctor who is different from an interne
only by a) having forgotten everything he learned in medical school

and (b) having an annual income of more than $300,000.

INTERPRETER (n) A linguist who expresses his own ideas as if they were coming from the mouth of another.

In his epochal work revealing the many distortions of history caused by interpreter errors (often prompted by a wish to make the speakers seem more profound than they were), Professor A. P. Nutt points out that life would have been profoundly altered had statements by powerful World leaders been accurately translated. We are grateful to the professor for these persuasive examples:

1. (what the interpreter said) During his disastrous retreat from Moscow, in 1812, Napoleon was quoted as saying, "Every soldier should fight for his country!" As a consequence, thousands of French soldiers were killed fighting in retreat.

(what he actually said) According to Professor Nutt, what Napoleon really said was, "Every soldier should run for his country!" This misinterpretation explains why Napoleon reached Paris months ahead of his surviving troops.

2. (what the interpreter said) In a speech that launched the Second World War, Hitler was quoted as demanding "lebensraum". This was translated as, "living space for my people."

(what he really said) According to our authority, Hitler was merely complaining about the lack of a living room in his Berlin apartment.

3. (what the interpreter said) In a 1960 incident at the United Nations, Soviet Premier, Khrushchev, pounded his shoe on a conference table and was quoted as saying, "we will bury you!" This action and quotation greatly intensified the arms race, to the near bankruptcy of Russia and the United States.

(what he really said) The truth is that Khrushchev was merely trying to kill a cockroach with his shoe. What he actually said was, "I will flatten you!"

4. (what the interpreter said) God was quoted by a Hebrew scholar as commanding, "love thy neighbor," and down through history, innumerable infidelities and divorces resulted.

(what He really said)
In Professor Nutt's correct translation, God actually commanded: "love thy neighbor, but not his wife."

5. (what the interpreter said) In his Sermon on the Mount, Jesus was quoted as saying: "Blessed are the meek, for they shall inherit the Earth." As a result, for two thousand years, meekness

117

has been touted as a Christian ideal, and bullies have prospered.

(what he really said) Thanks to our authority, we now know that what Jesus actually said was: "Blessed are the meek, for all they can inherit is earth."

INTROVERT (n) An exhibitionist turned inside out. Such a person is so preoccupied with herself that she cannot admire you, adequately.

> A virtuous introvert, Kate,
> Keeps herself in a virginal state
> By trusting to God
> And thinking how odd
> A man looks when trying to mate.

IRISH (n) A nationality that, when male, wants a drink and, when female, wants a birth control pill.

> "To be Irish is to know that sorrow is sure to come."
> Daniel Patrick Moynihan

IRONY (n) Truth masked by a variable sarcasm. As is illustrated by the following true stories, The effect can be either a) gentle, or b) cruel:

a) An eight year old boy was gazing at a flag-bedecked plaque on the church wall when the pastor came up and explained that it was to remember the men and women "who died in service." The boy thought that over a moment and then asked, "was it the eight-thirty or the ten o'clock service?"

b) Well saturated with brandy, Winston Churchill got into a heated argument with a society matron. "You, sir, are drunk!," she accused. "I may be drunk, madam," he replied, "but you're ugly and I'll be sober in the morning."

IRRESOLUTION (n) A basic instinct of timidity, which doubts good prospects, tranquilizes strong ambitions, is skeptical of fond hopes, and transforms bold imaginings into fancied pipedreams--with no sense of loss along the way.

> "If 'ifs' and 'buts'
> Were candy and nuts,
> We'd all have a Merry Christmas."
> anonymous doggerel

IRS (n) An acronym conventionally interpreted as the "Internal Revenue Service", but more commonly understood as the "Infernal

Robbery System". The two official slogans of this Federal agency are: (individuals) "We've got what it takes to take what you've got" and (corporations) "Just take it offshore and we'll tax people more."

ISOLATIONIST (n) Someone who buys his underwear from China, his cars from Japan, his jewelry from South Africa, his computer from Taiwan, his champagne from France, his software from Israel, invests in an international stock fund, and demands that the United States withdraw from the World Trade Organization.

> An isolationist touring Bali
> Had a burning desire to pee.
> But, he stoutly desisted
> Because he resisted
> Exporting his water for free.

ISSUE (n) 1. A cause of wrangling between lawyers as to who is right.

2. A cause of wrangling between nations as to who is wronged.

3. A failure of family planning.

ITCH (n) A physical desire to scratch some part of one's anatomy, the strength of which is directly proportional to its inaccessibility and the number of people in the room.

"He's a lucky son of a bitch who has a scratch for every itch."

> Ogden Nash
> A society matron in Dorsett
> Was esteemed by her blue-blooded horse set.
> But, she lost her high niche
> By scratching an itch
> In a place that was under her corset.

J

JACKASS (n) 1. A four-legged animal that brays a lot and appears stupid.

2. A two-legged animal that brags a lot and is stupid.

"Women first turn their men into sheep, then convince them

they are lions, all the while regarding them as jackasses."
                    Honore Balzac
    "You, sir, are the South end of a jackass heading North."
    President Harry Truman (in a letter to a music critic who
had panned the singing of Truman's daughter, Margaret.)
            A beautiful girl in Madras
            Has a perfectly wonderful ass.
            It's not rounded and pink,
            As you may, perhaps, think,
            But, is gray, has long ears, and eats grass.

JAR (v) To shake something or somebody, abruptly, as when a
husband sees his wife without her face on for the first time, or
the wife sees her husband without his clothes on, in daylight,
for the first time.
            There was a young man from Del Mar
            Who said, "I'm not handsome, by far.
            "But, my face, I don't mind it
            "Because I'm behind it.
            "It's those up in front that I jar."

JARGON (n)   A class of babble that is
understood only by those in the profession that dabble in it.
Its use is an ancient and honorable way to protect clients and
patients from knowing how trivial their problem is and how costly
resolving it is going to be for them.
    Because lawyers have been, since the Middle Ages, the most
zealous in keeping the specifics of their drafting, litigation,
and billing, practices secret, Legal jargon is the most common of
all. It is so voluminous that its own dictionary is required--
bearing the evil-sounding name, "The Black Law Dictionary").
    Since it happens that your editor has long been a member of
this secret society of lawyers, he has reproduced some of their
jargon, here, at considerable risk to himself:
    1. "memoranda" Written exchanges between opposing lawyers at
a cost to their clients of up to one dollar per word, without
disclosing to the latter that nothing in the writings advanced
either client's case an inch.
    2. "brief" The intentionally-facetious name given lengthy
research documents filed with a court in connection with a
pending litigation. Court rules typically limit each brief to
thirty pages, the lawyers bill their clients for fifty and the
judges read ten.

3. "True Bill" A fee bill that is accurate.

4. "adversary" The lawyer's client.

5. "Bench" An enclosed and elevated seat that enables the judge to doze and kick her shoes off during a trial, unobserved.

6. "bar" Where the lawyers go after each court session.

7. "fee simple" A fee bill, before it has been multiplied by two and submitted to the client.

8. "fee tail" A fee paid by a female client in another currency.

9. "hung jury" A jury that had to be disciplined for a bad verdict.

JEALOUS (adj.) 1. Conscious that another is superior to you.

2. "Unduly concerned about the preservation of that which can only be lost if not worth keeping."
> Ambrose I　ᴄe
> Because she was jealous, Samantha was zealous
> To catch Tom and Mary in bed.
> But, to her surprise (scarcely trusting her eyes),
> She caught him with Larry, instead.

JEANS (n) A type of casual trousers favored by young men and women because of its characteristic tight crotch. Fellows blessed with abundance in that region believe the bulge signifies an enticing virility, while many women seem to believe that it proclaims their sex. Both are deceived. The bulge attracts homosexuals, repels women, and raises the wearer's voice half an octave. Young women, in turn, should reflect that if the upper half of their body does not prove their sex, the lower half will surely be disregarded.

JERK 1. (v) To quickly wrench and propel a body away.

2. (n) a wretch, who quickly repels everybody away.

The first sense is what you do when the second sense offends your good sense.
> "It's a lie!" said the Governor's clerk,
> To the charge that her boss is a jerk.
> "He's just soft to the touch
> "Of leeches and such.
> "Without him, I'd never find work."

JESTER (n) One who is adept in making others laugh. In former times, he was known as a "fool" and served as one of the king's

counselors. But, when the nobility came to realize that the
king was more foolish than his fool, the office was closed down.
In America, the position is held by the current Secretary of
Defense, who is a fool in the clinical sense.

JEWSHARP (n) An instrument for torturing music. The operator
holds it between gritted teeth and tries to brush it away into
the audience, whose teeth are gnashing.

JILT (v) To renege on an engagement to marry and spare the
other person a lifetime of regret.

> A fickle fellow, named Oley,
> Jilted a pious girl, wholly.
> When she learned what he'd done,
> She grabbed up a gun
> And used it to make Oley, holey.

JOGGING (n) A type of running that gets you nowhere, inflicts
long-term damage to your knee joints, threatens a heart attack
that may kill you, and is most enthusiastically advocated by
people who don't know you nor have any concern for your health.
Some experts say that every mile you jog adds 5 minutes to your
life expectancy. So, this will enable you to spend 6 extra
months in a nursing home, at $5,000 a month.

"The only reason I took up jogging was so I could hear heavy
breathing, again."
>> George Carlin

"I had to give up jogging because my thighs kept rubbing
together and set my pantyhose on fire."
>> Kate Sprague

JOKE (n) A form of therapy that endeavors to tickle a funny
bone without striking a raw nerve.

> It's wise to laugh at funny jokes,
> To show your wit's not numb.
> But, it's charity to laugh a bit
> When the jokes are really dumb.

A Sunday School teacher asked her class of children to stand
if they wanted to enter Heaven when they died. All stood but
Matt. "Don't you want to go to Heaven, Mathew?" she asked.
"Sure I do," he replied, "but, not if these kids are going, too."
JOSEPH SMITH (n) Said to be "the father of the Mormons" (or, at
least, a good many of them), this energetic prophet of the church

is primarily responsible for so many people named "Smith" crowding every corner of America. A leading Mormon obstetrician, Dr. I.M Potent, attributed this phenomenon to efficiency. "Every one of the prophet's sperm hit its target," he explained.

JOURNALIST (n) 1. Someone who gathers facts and rumors, then prints the rumors.
> Said a prize-winning journalist, Heine,
> When his tongue had been loosened by wine,
> "I never am lax
> "About just printing facts,
> "Unless the story is mine."

2. (n) A dead reporter, revised and expurgated.
> Dead journalist, Pete, appalled by the heat,
> Demanded to go some place higher.
> Said Satan, "I fear that I must keep you here.
> "You're my only professional liar."

JUDGE (n) 1. A lawyer who placed his political bets, wisely, and was willing to wait to win.

2. A courtroom fixture who looks down on everybody, faces backwards in the worship of precedent, wears black to match his mood and heart, and has fog on the brain, jargon on the tongue, a club in his hand, and hemorrhoids in his ass.
> A Federal judge in Latrobe
> Wears nothing under his robe.
> This nudity act
> Is explained by the fact
> That there's nothing in his frontal lobe.

JUNGLE (n) An area where wild beasts are responsible for killing and maiming people. The most feared places are in the Amazon basin, Kenya, Borneo, and Washington, D.C..

JURISPRUDENCE (n) The kind of prudence that is practiced by courts throughout America. It chiefly consists in avoiding the appearance of haste by entertaining every procedural motion, granting every request for delay, never deciding even the simplest question, quickly, and never risking their health by working a forty-hour week.

JURY (n) A group of people who, with the help of lawyers, distinguish between truth and falsehood and act on the latter.

This result is inevitable since one lawyer always acts to
exaggerate the truth beyond belief, the other lawyer acts to
conceal it, and the judge acts in a way that encourages both.
Thus, the jury is left with only its prejudices to rely on.
    Said a typical juror, named Milt,
    "I'm a fair man and just to the hilt.
    "But, seeing he's black
    "And the rags on his back,
    "I'm inclined to believe in his guilt."

JUSTICE (n) A legal process embedded in the U.S. Constitution
and proclaimed in the Pledge of Allegiance, guaranteeing equal
protection under the law to all but minorities, undocumented
immigrants, homeless people, Al Qaeda suspects, Pro Choice
believers, and Democrats.

K

KARATE (n) A method of chopping wood for the fireplace when no
axe is handy. It is highly esteemed by orthopedic surgeons,
everywhere.
    A karate pro, Nick, thought he'd mastered the trick
    Of splitting a brick with his fist.
    He gave one a crack, then a terrible whack,
    Now his fingers attach to his wrist.
    A man bought a Pekinese to be his guard dog based on the store
owner's demonstration showing the dog's prowess with karate.
 When the store owner said: "karate--the chair", the animal broke
the chair into splinters. When he said, "karate--the cage", the
dog tore a metal cage apart.
    When the man returned home with the dog, he found his wife in
the kitchen. "I bought a guard dog that knows karate," he said,
proudly. "She looked at the tiny dog and said, scornfully,
"karate--my ass!"

KELP (n) A marine plant that provides no-rent housing to needy
creatures. That there is accommodation for all who seek it is

attributed to the absence of landlords, equal housing laws, rent regulation, zoning inspectors, restrictive covenants, bank financing, and real property lawyers.

The rubbery leaves of the plant are widely believed to have an aphrodisiac effect on humans when dried and consumed. In his acclaimed book, THE CAUSE OF HARDENING OF THE ARTERIES AND OTHER PARTS, the eminent scientist, Dr. I. M. Potent, confirms this opinion. In it, the precise mechanism and several side-effects are described in the following graphic excerpt:

"After kelp is consumed, digestive juices separate out the heavy metals and minerals (chiefly lead, zinc, aluminum, calcium and cement). These elements are introduced into the blood stream where, under the influence of gravity, they are deposited into the vas minimis. As more precipitates accumulate, the vas minimis expands into the vas profundus."

In another part of the book, Dr. Potent sounds this warning. "An overdose of kelp may produce two undesirable side-effects: (1) The subject will not be able to sleep on his stomach, and (2) he will excrete partially-hardened mineral water."

> A celibate monk, somewhat gay,
> Ate oodles of kelp from the bay.
> 'Til he ran from his cell,
> With a Hell of a yell,
> And eloped with two nuns the same day.

KILL (v) To take a small step toward population control by creating a vacancy without appointing a successor.

> It gives Heinz a thrill to maim and to kill
> Invaders driven by greed.
> So, he slays with his knife (it's the joy of his life)
> Every plant in his yard that's a weed.

KILT (n) A costume often worn by hairy-legged Scotchman, in America, and Americans in Scotland, to display their support for Darwin.

A lusty young Scotchman, in a kilt, took a nap under a shade tree near a girl's school. Two passing students saw him and one dared the other to lift the hem of the kilt to see whether the gossip was true. She did so and the two went on their way, giggling. When the young man woke, he felt something strange under the kilt. Looking under it he saw a blue hair ribbon tied around his gazoo and addressed it, thusly: "I dinna know what you've bin doin', but, whatever it was, you took first prize."

KINDNESS (n) Generosity paid to another and often repaid with an expired iou and lively solicitations.

KING (n) "A male person commonly known in America as a "crowned head", although he never wears a crown and has no head to speak of."
                    Ambrose Bierce

KISS (n) An unsanitary and dangerous juxtaposition of lips by two people for reasons either of tenderness or profit. Given the multitudes of bacteria and other pathogens laying in wait and ready to spring forth to multiply, Italy's recent law requiring an impermeable screen between two kisser's lips seems prudent. An unexpected byproduct of Italy's kissing policy has been a decline in its birthrate. Ever on the lookout for new population controls, Chinese leaders have done Italy one better by banning all kissing-- insulated or not. They seem to believe that it is, somehow, directly involved in procreation. To their vast chagrin, the birthrate has not markedly declined, although colds are way down.
        "Young lady, oh fly from a cad;
        "Treat him as though he's a curse.
        "To let a fool kiss you is bad.
        "To let a kiss fool you is worse."
                    Alexander Pope

KIN (n) Those who are pleased to inherit from you after your death, unless it pleased you to disinherit them beforehand.
        A mysterious affinity exists between relatives and fish. When they are in your house, both begin to stink after three days.
        Said Darwinian, Edward McKnight,
        When his hero was given a slight:
        "Just compare my son, Stew,
        "With the apes in a zoo
        "And you'll realize Darwin was right."

KITH (n) How lispers may express their affection.
        Judy went to the County Fair with Bruce, a young man she liked very much. After treating her to lunch and games, he asked several times what she wanted to do. Each time, she replied, "I want to get weighed." Puzzled, he took her three times to the electronic scales. When she requested the same thing, yet again, he drove her

home in disgust and dropped her off without a parting kiss.

When the girl entered the house, her mother asked her what kind of time she had at the fair. "Wowsy!" Judy replied.

KLEPTOMANIA (n) An exotic condition of the hands that causes objects to stick to their surfaces. Fortunately, it responds to treatment and whenever it worsens, sufferers merely take something for it.

> Said psychiatrist, Frank,
> To kleptomaniac, Hank.
> "Until you are cured,
> "My fee is assured.
> "I got you a job in a bank."

KNIGHT (n) Once a warrior honored by the British sovereign for his swordplay, today he is more likely to be a heavily-taxed movie producer renowned for his foreplay.

KNISH (n) A Jewish whore d'oeuvre that anyone can make with dough, sugar, spice, and plenty of heat.

> "If wishes and buts
> "Were knishes and nuts,
> "We'd all have a Happy Hanukkah."
> Mort Sahl

KORAN (n) A holy book which Moslems believe was inspired by God. This is hotly disputed by Christians, who claim the distinction for the Bible, by the Jews, who claim it for the Torah, by Buddhists, who claim it for the Gita, by Mormons, who claim it for the letters of Joseph Smith, by Southern Baptists, who claim it for the speeches of Martin Luther King, and by atheists everywhere, who worship Huckleberry Finn.

KOSHER (adj.) A Jewish food sanctified by a blessing and the absence of pork. Neither condition enhances the flavor, but they do enhance the price.

KU KLUX KLAN (n) An organization of Southern men with a color quirk. Whenever they look at a Black, they see red; they wrap themselves in white and turn yellow unless armed.

> A KKK marcher, named Peet,
> Was arrested for blocking a street.
> When he claimed that his plexus

Got caught on a Lexis,
All the officer said was, "tough sheet."

Count: 1186

L

LAGGARD (adj.) Moving very slowly, as in these examples:
1. A Tijuana funeral procession with only one set of jumper cables.
2. A drop in the price of gasoline after a drop in the price of oil.
3. The return of your change from a son who shopped for you.
4. Gratitude from a cousin for money you loaned him.
5. An apology from the IRS, for mistakenly assessing you a penalty.

LANDFILL (n) Civilization's cemetery, future historians' treasure trove, toxic ruin of well water, scavenger hunt for rats, employment for the unemployable, and the despair of recycling advocates.

LAND MINE (n) A device that hurts the world market for shoes.
Chinese companies fatten on land mines that flatten
Foreign people in numbers fantastic.
That is business acumen, For the whole human ruin
Boosts exports of feet made of plastic.

LAPHORISM (n) An amusing aphorism, as in the following examples:
1. A lot of money is tainted. It taint mine and it taint yours.
2. A boiled egg in the morning is hard to beat.
3. A shotgun wedding is a case of wife or death.
4. A man needs a mistress just to break the monogamy.
5. A hangover is the wrath of grapes.
6. Dancing cheek to cheek is a form of floorplay.
7. When two egotists meet, it's an "I" for an "I".
8. A Will is a dead giveaway.
9. A chicken crossing the road is poultry in motion.

128

10. She had a boyfriend with a wooden leg, but she broke it off.

11. If you don't pay your exorcist, you get repossessed.

12. You're stuck with your debt if you can't budget.

13. Every calendar's days are numbered.

14. He broke into song because he couldn't find the key.

LATIN (n) A dead language presently employed only by the Vatican, lawyers, and language professors. The first group uses it to foster illusions, the second, to festoon their ignorance, and the third, to conceal it.

Here is an ancient maxim that has retained its value over many centuries:

"Nil legitimati non carborundum" ("don't let the bastards grind you down").

"The Latin language is quite dead,
"As dead as dead can be.
"The Romans killed it, it is said,
"But teachers still, the ashes spread
"And now it's killing me."
 Cathedral Latin high school doggerel
There was a young lawyer, named Rex,
With diminutive organs of sex.
When charged with exposure,
He said, with composure,
"De minimis non curat lex."
 ("The law does not regard trifles.")

LAUGH (v) To emit spasmodic noises in a way that expresses your joy, compresses your face, and depresses those who don't get the joke. Sometimes the joke is on you and you don't get it, as exemplified by this lament:

"I joined in the laughter and then, sometime after,
"Sought to find out who had quipped.
"I was wrong to pursue it, for soon I did rue it,
"When told that my fly was unzipped."

LAUGHTER (n) A physical response to incongruity that is uniquely human. The most pronounced symptom is a series of convulsive spasms that shake the body. This serves the same purpose as shaking a rug, i.e., to clean out accumulated debris left from being stepped on.

"He who laughs last, laughs best."

Poor Richard
"He who laughs, lasts."
Sophie Tucker
"He who laughs last, has a slower wit."
H. L. Mencken
"Laugh and the world laughs with you.
Cry and you cry alone.
For the sad old Earth
Has little of mirth
And troubles enough of its own."
Edgar Guest

LAUNDROMAT (n) The worst possible place for a man to meet his
future bride. If she cannot afford a washing machine, she
probably will not be able to support him.

LAXATIVE (n) A pharmaceutical product designed to make men
regular fellows and women come clean. Bad experiences have led
users to caution others not to take a sleeping pill at the same
time when retiring.

LAW (n) 1. The profession that is best Abel to
raise Cain with people and teach them to believe in Hell.
"There are tricks to all trades, but law is the only trade
of all tricks."
Mark Twain
Said the son of a farmer in Glined,
"Toward pursuing the law, I'm inclined."
"Go ahead and pursue it,"
Said his dad, "I won't rue it.
"But, don't catch the damn thing or I'll mind."
2. A rule adopted by government to regulate illegal conduct
so that only the correct people profit.

LAW SCHOOL (n) An academic institution that sharpens the mind
by narrowing it.
Will Rogers

LAWSUIT (n) A case in court that was a mere difference of
opinion before it was given to lawyers to settle.
LAWYER (n) A member at the Bar who, for a fee and sober or not,
will argue in court that the sun rises in the west and produce
ten expert witnesses to prove it. The reason they are said to

130

"practice" law is that, no matter how long they try, they never seem to get it right.

No profession has been more justifiably skewered throughout history nor been the object of so many accurate jokes. Here are examples of both renderings:

(historical) 1. "Cast lawyers onto a dunghill."

King James Bible, Old Testament

2. "First, we will get rid of all the lawyers."

Sir Thomas More, "Utopia"

3. "Why does the hearse horse snicker while carting a lawyer away?"

Carl Sandburg

(humor) 1. Q. "Why are lawyers buried twenty feet down in the ground instead of the traditional six feet?"

A. "Because deep down, lawyers are really good."

2. (client): "What is your fee?"

(lawyer) "One hundred dollars for the answers to three questions."

(client) "That's very steep, isn't it?"

(lawyer) "Yes, now what is your third question?"

3. Q. "Why does New Jersey have the most toxic waste dumps and California have the most lawyers?"

A. "Because New Jersey had the first choice."

Said an eminent lawyer, named Soke,
Who is known as a battling bloke,
"Never once do I bend!
"I will fight to the end!
"Or, at least, 'til my client is broke."

LEADER (n) The only person in any organization who can clearly see the direction that will benefit him most.

"Only the lead dog in the team gets a good view."

Robert Crandall (former CEO of American Airlines)

LEADERSHIP (n) 1. (military) The ability of an officer to persuade subordinates to go to a dangerous place and get there long before he does.

2. (corporate) The ability of a CEO to persuade the Board of Directors that money saved from downsizing should be added to his bonus.

"If you are leading and no one is following, you are just out for a walk."

Newspaper Editor, John Warren
A Highlander, Angus McTattle,
Followed his men into battle.
When his lagging brought gripes,
He played on his pipes,
Which induced all the foe to skedaddle.

LECTURE (n) "A magical process by which the notes of the professor become the notes of his students, without passing through the brains of either one."
Ambrose Bierce

LEGISLATURE (n) A body of elected representatives to the Federal and State governments. It is called a "body" because it emits a lot of gas as it works. This forces out many clods of

manure, called "Bills", because of their cost to taxpayers.
"As to the legislature, when all is said and done, more is said than done."
H.L. Mencken

LESBIAN (n) 1. A homosexual female, whose nature it is to be sexually aroused only by women.
2. Applying the same definition, a heterosexual male.
(1)
An erotic young fellow, named Hugh,
A lesbian, started to woo.
When she scorned him and said,
"I love women, in bed,"
He cried, "oh my God, I'm one, too!"

LIAR (n) Someone who speaks fiction. To help the reader identify the breed, here are several groups whose noses would grow like Pinocchio's if they were as responsive:
1. Those who say they never lie.
2. Anyone who says to you, "I'm not lying," during an argument.
3. Any woman over forty who volunteers her age.
4. Any man who estimates the number of his sexual conquests.
5. Any politician who promises to increase services while cutting taxes.

An elderly woman in Rye
Possessed a compulsion to lie.
She said she was twenty,

132

Though her body sagged plenty,
And married a sight-impaired guy.

LIBERAL (n) 1. A tenderized conservative.
2. Someone who is generous with the money of conservatives.
3. A conservative who has just gone on social security.
4. A Libertarian who has just lost her job.

(1)
Sam Hill is a gent with a liberal bent;
He will tax every shirt off your back.
"My object, you see," he says with some glee,
"Is to make sure there's nothing I lack."

(2)
(to be sung to the tune of "Home On The Range")
Oh, give me a home where the liberals roam;
Where the ACLU's always suing.
Where ever is heard the Sierra Club's word,
Causing Big Business hot stewing.
Want no home that is strange in the midst of my range,
Where conservatives rant, rage, and foam.
Where a right-winging crowd keeps lobbying loud
To export the homeless to Nome.

LIFE (n) 1. What happened to us after two adults acted with only sex on their minds.

Said a fun-loving Scotsman in Fife,
"I could hae such a wonderful life.
"With me drinkin' and jokin'
"With a woman provokin'
("As long as she isn't me wife!")

2. (n) The sum total of bad decisions and missed opportunities.

It's the set of sail and not the gale
That decides the course boats take.
And it's the paths we choose and don't refuse
That shape the lives we make.

"Few of us know the difference between making a living and making a life, and why do we celebrate the years that have been added to our lives and not deplore that no life has been added to the years?"

George Carlin

LIFE INSURANCE (n) The only form of gambling in which the winner never lives to enjoy the payoff.

Grumped a woman, named Maude, loving wife of her

Claude,
"Life insurers are crooks, you can bet.
"Their pledge is a lie! If I don't help Claude die
"I'll have paid in much more than I'll get."

LIFETIME (n) An interval in the space-time continuum during which parents are expected to support their children and after which, they can expect the latter's gratitude.

Unlike his friends, Alfred Sutch
Built up his estate very much.
Now, his friends' kids don't call
Their parents at all,
But, Al's kids are always in touch.

LIMERICK (n) A rhyming five line verse that tickles your ribald zone and lowdown funny bone. Limericks are featured in this work for the moral enlightenment of its readers and range from the profane through the mundane to the inane. Here are three stellar examples of the genre:

(1)

There was a young man with a hernia
Who said to his doctor, "gol dern ya.
"When you're fixin' to cut,
"Go right ahead, but,
"Don't mess with what don't concern ya."

(2)

A diner, while dining in Crewe,
Found a large mouse in his stew.
Said the waiter, "don't shout
"And wave it about,
"Or the rest will be wanting one, too."

(3)

A limerick is furtive and keen.
You must hold it in tight quarantine
Or it slips to the slums
And promptly becomes
Disorderly, rude, and obscene.

LISP (n) A speech defect that sometimes prevents the speaker from being understood.

When the girl told her boyfriend, named Tim
That she'd like to get "weighed" at the gym,
He complied, growing surly,

134

Then took her home early;
Which was, she said, "wowsey of him."

LITIGATION (n) Court action commenced by two or more lawyers to
prevent an early settlement of differences between their clients
until such time as adequate attorney fees have been incurred and
paid.

> Lawyers adore litigation,
> Where efforts at peace are ignored.
> Prolonging disputes in the nation;
> Producing fees few can afford.

LITTER (n) A type of garnish used to decorate the nation's
urban byways. Typically American, it serves a purpose somewhat
similar to that of parsley on a restaurant's dinner plate. While
the first makes the byway barely passable, the second makes the
dinner barely edible.

> Said a sign near the town of Albread:
> "$10 for littering, ahead."
> Jake scattered some trash,
> Then asked for the cash,
> But, they emptied his wallet, instead.

LOAN (n) 1. Money that banks rent to those who do not need it.
   2. Money advanced to a friend or acquaintance who, lacking
principle, has no interest in repaying it.
   3. Money advanced to a son or daughter, whose concept of the
transaction is spelled, "gift".

> Said a Son to his Dad, "lend an
>   ear.
> "I can make myself wealthy, this year.
> "Lend me five thousand bucks,
> "To corner corn shucks.
> "I will pay you back, fodder, don't fear."

LOATHSOME (adj.) Greatly deficient in compensating qualities,
e.g., an old man who is poor.

> "He is a loathsome, stinking, swine;
> "A vile, disgusting man.
> "He is rich and ninety-nine,
> "So I'll marry him if I can."

LOBBYIST (n) Someone who twists the arms of politicians,
greases their palms, weeps on their shoulders, schemes behind
their backs, and praises their shit--all for the sake of their
"ayes".

(1)

Said a lobbyist, Krause, when he lost in the House
On a Bill to turn tattle to tittle.
"It wasn't my touch or my pushing too much;
"My mistake was in paying too little."

(2)

A lobbyist for steel has client appeal
Because of his strange compensation.
His fees, so inflated, are inversely related
To the good that his laws do the nation.

LOGICAL (adj.) The ability to add two apples to two apples and not get four pears. It is bested only by common sense as the rarest trait among human beings.

"Someone who is logical is a nice contrast to the real world."

Steve Allen

LOOKS (n) What a look in a mirror sees.

Doctor (to a husband in the waiting room): "I don't like the looks of your wife."

Husband: "Neither do I, but she's a good cook and the kids love her."

LOTTERY (n) A form of gambling in which the odds of winning are worse than Las Vegas slots and better than Russian Roulette.

Said a lottery chief, William Dunn,
"I am having a great deal of fun.
"What is chiefly amusing;
"There's no chance of me losing,
"'Cause the chance of you winning is--none!"

LOVE (n) A distemper in the brain caused by a surplus of testosterone in men and optimism in women. It is the antidote for hate, the cure for indifference, the relief for loneliness, bread to the emotionally starved, water to souls on fire, and fire to souls asleep.

"Whereas love springs eternal in young men, in young women, it often becomes maternal in the Fall."

Margaret Moody

So I be written in the book of love,
I do not care about the book above.
Erase my name; or, write it as you will.
So I be written in the book of love
That all can see I care for Mankind, still.

Love's not put in the heart forever to stay.
It's not of much use 'til it's given away.

LUBRICATE (v) To apply something to rubbing parts for the purpose of reducing friction and facilitating the movement. Here are several examples of success:
1. An ear, to a wagging tongue.
2. A novice salesperson, to a slippery customer.
3. A redevelopment agency, to a skid row.
4. A deep-tissue massage, to a hula dancer.
5. A toilet, to loose bowels.
  A pushy old fellow, in Pine,
  Thinks grating on people is fine.
  "They owe me," says he,
  "Though they may not agree.
  "It's my rubbing that brings out their shine."

LUCK (n) 1. (bad) The explanation for our mistakes.
2. (good) "What happens when ability and preparation meet opportunity."
                Ambrose Bierce
Two domestic situations illustrate the difference between good and bad luck:
(good) A woman misses her ex-husband and is out of ammunition.
(bad) The same woman tries again after taking shooting lessons.
An optimist, Sledd, was hit on the head
  By a horseshoe that fell on her bonnet.
  As she tottered and bled, she cheerily said,
  "I'm in luck that a horse wasn't on it."

LUMBERMAN (n) A forest farmer who reaps, but rarely sows, depending on nature for his crops.
  "I think that trees, in any number,
  "Are most appealing when they're lumber."
    (Lumberman's reply to Joyce Kilmer)

LUST (n) The strongest appetite in a young man before it rises to his stomach in middle age.
  Said old Elmer Peevage, of a girl showing cleavage,
  "That once raised my lust all to heck.
  "But now, there's no stress when I look down her dress
  "And the only thing stiff is my neck."

137

LYRICS (n) The words of a song or opera. They are unintelligible in modern songs and traditional operas, but thrilling in such Twentieth-Century classics as the one that follows:

DARLING, I AM GROWING OLDER
(sung to the song of the same name)

I (husband)

"Darling, I am growing older,
"Silver threads among the brown.
"Both my feet have gotten colder
"And the hair has left my crown."

II (wife)

"Yes, my sweetheart, you're decrepit
"And your brain has turned to trash.
"Now, my love for you is tepid,
"So, I'm leaving with the cash."

III (husband)

"Fatty, leave and I won't hunger
"For the sight of your dyed locks.
"I will get a woman, younger,
"And enjoy my bonds and stocks."

IV (wife)

"Shithead! You're a boastful feller,
"But, I don't believe your dame
"Will stay with you whene'er I tell her
"That all you have is in my name."

V (husband)

"Darling, I am getting older,
"Silver threads on mostly skin.
"Put your head upon my shoulder
"And, a new life, let's begin."

VI (wife)

"Though, my sweetheart, you're decrepit
"And your brain has gone astray,
"Though my love for you is tepid,
"With you, dear, is where I'll stay."

M

MAN (n) Someone who looks funny, naked. For three thousand years, men dominated women and thought they were entitled to do so. But, in recent years--beginning with the advent of birth controls and credit cards--women have emerged as the superior sex. They live longer, have a greater share of private wealth, resist pain better, and despise football.

Scientists are beginning to answer some disturbing questions about men, among which the following reveal the basic helplessness of the sex:

1. (Q) Why is it necessary that at least one woman astronaut accompany the men on each mission?

(A) So somebody will be there to ask directions if they get lost.

2. (Q) What does a man mean when he refers to a seven course meal?

(A) One hot dog and a six pack.

3. (Q) How does a man help with housework?

(A) He lifts his legs while she vacuums.

4. (Q) How can a man be persuaded to do sit-ups?

(A) By placing the TV remote control between his feet.

MAD (1) (n) A mental aberration that prevents a sufferer from conforming to the customary standard of behavior, as in the following cases:

1. A lawyer, who does not bill his client for "phantom" work.

2. A funeral director, who tells a joke at a wake.

3. A preacher, who only asks for what his congregation can afford to give.

4. A politician, who voluntarily retracts a lie he told about his opponent.

(2) (adj.) Extreme anger, of the type usually found in a losing professional football team's fans and betrayed wives on a good day.

"You can tell the measure of a man by what makes him mad."
Samuel Pope

MAIDEN (n) An unmarried and unmarred member of the unfair sex.

"The genus has a wide geographic distribution, being found wherever sought and deplored wherever found. She is not altogether unpleasing to the eye nor, without her piano and her views, insupportable to the ear although, respecting comeliness, inferior

to a rainbow and, respecting that part of her that is audible,
beaten out of the field by the canary--which also is more
portable."

Ambrose Bierce

MALAPROPIST (n) One who employs words, creatively, thereby greatly
expanding their definitions and enriching our vocabulary.
Following are several true stories illustrating this growing art
form:

    1. (letter from a Minnesota Aunt to her Niece) "Your Uncle and
I were so happy to hear of your wedding and hope that you are
enjoying the same martial experiences that have kept the two of us
together over so many years."

    2. (letter from a German exchange student to her host family)
"I thank you very much for your hospitality and hope that some day
I can hospitalize you, too."

    3. (letter from a college sophomore to her parents) "You don't
need to worry about me getting into trouble on a date down here.
I want you to know that I'm impregnated."

MALEFACTOR (n) Originally pronounced with a broad "a" and in two
syllables, the word identifies the primary cause of human violence.
The female factor, called "femalefactor", explains why the species
still survives.

MALTHUSIAN (adj.) Pertaining to The doctrine of the famous
European economist, who called for strict limits on the World's
population to avoid mass starvation. Three of his most ardent
disciples were Napoleon, Stalin, and Hitler, but generals
everywhere and throughout history have been of the same mind.

    The chief opponents of population controls have been the
Catholic Popes, even though, ironically, the lowest per capita
birth rates have been, in recent years, within the Vatican State,
itself. Popes preach that it is a mortal sin to limit human
reproduction by artificial means, even in nations with the highest
rates of infant mortality. This view apparently stems from the
conviction that these children will get the care in Heaven that
they will not get from the pro-lifers on Earth.

MAN (n) A male human whose blood supply is insufficient to serve
the requirements of both his brain and penis, simultaneously. When
he is over seventy, it is insufficient for either one.

    Said God, when asked why, a man's   blood supply

140

Won't service both sex and deep thought,
"If he thought, while he's screwing, of just what he's
doing,
"He would never make kids as he ought."

MANNA (n) "A food miraculously given to the Israelites in the wilderness. When it was no longer supplied to them, they settled down and tilled the soil, fertilizing it with the bodies of the original occupants."
Ambrose Bierce

MANURE (n) A bovine mainstay of organic farming that fertilizes fruits and vegetables intended for human consumption. It supports the reverse of the old adage by proving that: "What goes out at one end is sure to come in at the other."
A wonderful thing is manure;
It's a boon though it smells so impure.
The horses and cows
Give it all for our plows
And they feel better, after, I'm sure.

MARDI GRAS (n) In New Orleans, an orgy of promiscuous sex, drunken revelry, and riotous parades--celebrating the beginning of Catholic Lent and abstinence.
Said Mardi Gras Phil, preparing his bill
For twelve hundred cases of liquor:
"To help you through Lent, Cajun Stew's Heaven-sent,
"But, juleps and highballs are quicker."

MARITAL (adj.) A Freudian misspelling of "martial". The two words illustrate how accurately language mirrors life.
Said a divorcee, Brea, when she got her decree,
"To living alone I am partial.
"Though my ex was a stud, life with him was a dud;
"His marital arts were all martial."

MARKETING (n) An indispensable part of any business that strives to sell a sow's ear as a silk purse. In practice, it often seems to customers to work in reverse.
During the 1960's, General Motors marketing officials were perplexed by the poor sales of its Chevrolet Nova line in Latin America. Belatedly, they learned that the name means "it doesn't go" in Spanish.

141

More recently, Coca Cola marketers had to find a new name for their product in China, after learning that the name means "bite the wax tadpole" in phonetic Mandarin Chinese.

MARRIAGE (n) 1. One way for a man to get his laundry done, free.

2. A prerequisite for a divorce.

3. A relationship ordained by God and dissolved by lawyers, proving that lawyers are more powerful than God.

Because ruinous divorces have become so common in America, several eminent thinkers advocate ending this plague by banning marriage, altogether. One benefit from this would be that prospective in-laws would become outlaws and need never be invited to your home to sponge and criticize the furnishings.

Among the best commentaries on the institution are those that follow--written, you might guess, by men:

1. The quickest way for a man to learn to remember his marriage anniversary is to forget it, once.

2. If it wasn't for marriage, women would go through life thinking they had no faults at all.

3. If you want your wife to pay undivided attention to what you say, talk in your sleep.

4. "(son) "How much does it cost to get married?"

(father) "I don't know, son. I'm still paying."

5. One nice thing about marriage is that it gets young people to bed at a decent hour.

Said a sorrowful woman, Claire Reed,
In whose flesh Cupid's shaft never buried:
"Twenty years, Saints above,
"I have never known love.
"For in all of that time, I've been married."

MARRY (v) To enter into a legal relationship in which the man assumes that he gets the right to have sex, often, and the woman assumes that she gets the right to be supported, indefinitely. Another assumption they both have is that a divorce will be easy to get if things do not work out. Only this last assumption is true.

"A man wants to possess a woman and must marry her to get it, while a woman wants to marry a man and must give him possession of her to get it."

Thomas Hardy

MARTYR (n) Someone who refuses to lie about his convictions in order to avoid punishment. At the present time, there are no martyrs, but plenty of liars.

MASSACHUSETTS (n) A Penobscot Indian word meaning "Land of the Kennedys".

MASSEUR (n) A person who rubs people the right way.
       A masseur, named Bob, works with zeal at his job.
       Does he loosen his clients? You betcher!
       Only one thing is wrong. Big Bob is so strong,
       When they leave, they go out on a stretcher.

MASS (n) The name given a sacred ceremony in the Catholic Church that indicates the size of the congregation that is put to sleep.

Before it was reformed during the last Century, the Mass was celebrated in Latin and the final collections were much larger than they has been ever since. That is because most people in the congregations did not understand that the priests' announcement, late in the service, "Ite missa est", meant "The mass is over." So, they stayed put and the collections were taken.

Now that English is spoken, the congregations are roused from slumber and sprint for the exits, leaving only the elderly, the hard-of-hearing, and the arthritic to contribute.

MASSACHUSETTS (n) An Algonquin Indian word meaning "Land of the Kennedys".

MATHEMATICIAN (n) An expert with numbers who expresses them in such a way that he can only be understood by another mathematician. Many are employed by the Federal government and specialize in narrow computations. If they are assigned to the Pentagon, for example, they   can only multiply, while   if they work for Health and Human Services, they are permitted only to subtract.

"A mathematician can tell that he is growing senile if, at first, he forgets his theorems, then he forgets to zip up, and finally, he forgets to zip down."
                    Mathematician Paul Erdos

MATERIAL (adj.) Having a physical existence rather than an invisible one. A good example is the difference between a wall socket and what emerges when you stick your finger in it.
       "Material things," said lawyer Snow,
       "Are fees I earn and what I see.
       "All other things folks claim to know
       "Are immaterial to me."

MAUSOLEUM (n) The final buffoonery of the rich.

MAXIM (n) A concise statement expressing an unforgettable truth that has been forgotten. It contains so few words that lawyers deem it unprofitable to use. Moreover, it expresses an idea so clearly that politicians shun it out of fear that they will be understood.

Here are several examples of History's most profound maxims:

1. Time wounds all heels.
2. Behind every successful man is a mother-in-law, pushing.
3. If moonlight becomes you, utter darkness will do even more.
4. A woman's word is never done.
5. If more men were self-starters, fewer women would have to be cranks.
6. Better to remain silent and appear a fool than to speak and remove all doubt.
7. If at first you don't succeed, don't try parachute-jumping.
8. "The trouble with winning a rat race is that, when it's over, you're still a rat."
     Lily Tomlin
9. It is better to be over the hill than under it.
10. If you live each day as though it will be your last, eventually, you will be right.

MAYHEM (n) Originally, the name of a Spring fertility dance in Scotland, during which maidens raised the hem of their skirts high in the air as they whirled, exposing skin never seen by their partners before. Over time, the word came to denote the scene that inevitably followed.

> When a lusty young Scot, Duncan Frye,
> Danced with busty and pert Nellie Bligh,
> She raised up her skirt,
> The provocative flirt,
> And his kilt lifted up in reply.

MECHANIC (n) Someone who keeps your car running until the warranty expires.

> A mechanic from Hyde was fit to be tied.
> Though he worked the car over so long;
> Tugged at it, tore, twisted and swore,
> He couldn't find anything wrong.

MEDDLER (n) Someone so indiscreet as to interfere with another's fraud.

MEDICAL TERM (n) A word or phrase that has a special meaning to medical personnel, as in these examples:
    1. "retired physician" A doctor who finally got it right and doesn't have to practice anymore.
    2. "barium" What doctors do with their mistakes.
    3. "nitrate" Cheaper than the day rate.
    4. "outpatient" A patient who has lost consciousness.
    5. "rectum" A procedure that damaged the patient's testicles.
    6. "tumor" Three problems, total.
    7. "GI series" A military procedure.

MEMORY (n) A kind of neural quicksand that allowed you to remember, yesterday, what you cannot accurately remember, today, and not at all, tomorrow.
    Due to a loss of brain cells, men and women over seventy have difficulty remembering anything that happened to them more than ten years earlier, except that women have perfect recall of their husbands' offenses whenever they occurred.
    A Chicago lawyer, on his way to a conference in San Francisco, stopped at an Indian reservation in South Dakota to see a Sioux reputed to have the best memory in the nation. After exchanging "how's", the lawyer asked the Indian what his favorite breakfast food was. "Eggs," the latter answered, promptly. Ten years later, on another trip West, the lawyer stopped to see the same Indian and greeted him with a "How." "Scrambled," the Indian replied.

MERGER (n) In business, the marriage of two strong companies to form one weak one. Its mathematical equation is expressed as $1 + 1 = .75$, with an automatic deduction of 1.25 that represents funds siphoned from the deal by security brokers, lawyers, and corporate executives.
    Here are several likely mergers to watch for:
    1. Fairchild Electronics and Honeywell. The new name will be: "Farewell Honeychild."
    2. Grey Poupon and Docker's Pants. The new name will be: "Poupon Pants".
    3. Honeywell, Ibasco Marts, and Home Oil. The new name will be: "Honey I'M Home."
    4. Three M and Goodyear. The new name will be: "MMM Good".

5. W.R. Grace, Fuller Brush, Mary Kay, and Hale business Systems. The new name will be: "Hale Mary Fuller Grace".

METEOROLOGIST (n) A quasi-prophet who has nothing to do with meteors, predicts the weather in terms of whether, substitutes a radar screen for a crystal ball, and is most accurate when his forecasts correspond with what he sees happening outside.

> Said meteorologist, Craining,
> His skeptical critics, disdaining:
> "Of computers and such,
> "I don't know very much.
> "But, I certainly know when it's raining."

MICHIGAN (n) A place where Ann Arbor lives and feeds Buckeyes to her Wolverines, on which they thrive. The State's Spartans, on the other hand, get indigestion from them.

> Oh, give me a Middle-West home
> Where lawyers, like cockroaches, roam.
> Where the Dems rarely thrive
> And Republicans strive
> To ship all their poor off to Nome.

MILITIA (n) Also known as the National Guard, it is an organization of civilians who avoid being shot at during hostilities by fighting looters and forest fires, instead. It is said that whatever testosterone deficiencies
there may be in male members are more than offset by levels in the females.

> A militiaman, Lime, carries guns all the time;
> They make him feel strong, he has said.
> But, his wife, who won't lie, tells her friends, with a
> > sigh,
> That he can't lift a thing in their bed.

MILLENNIUM (n) Either a thousand years of starvation, pestilence, wars, and genocide, or a thousand years of human progress and development --depending on whether you are listening to an historian or geneticist.

> Says famous biologist, Krennium,
> On the fate of wildlife this millennium:
> "Any species you choose,
> "Except those in zoos;
> "There's only extinction for any of them."

146

MILLIONAIRE (n) Someone who has either a million
U.S. dollars and is rich, or a million Mexican pesos and is poor.
The majority of Americans spend like they are rich and save like
they are poor, while a large minority can afford to do neither.

"He has become a millionaire and, in the process, has
acquired all the virtues I dislike and none of the vices I
admire."

Winston Churchill, of Lord Beaverbrook

MIND (n) Father of thought and child of the brain, it is the only
part of a human being that has no weight and knows it. This being
so, giving people a piece of your mind will probably result in you
needing it more than they do.

"Great minds follow ideas, average minds follow events, and
small minds follow emotions. That is why so many small minds rule
nations."

Winston Churchill

MINISTER (n) Chief cleric in a Protestant church who practices
what he preaches (when he has a wife to get it right).

A buxom believer, Miss Sloan,
Goes home with the minister, alone.
As she says, "I aspire
"To sing in the choir,
"And he's checking my chest for its tone."

MIRACLE (n) A condition that is unprecedented in nature and
human experience. Here are several examples that demonstrate the
rarity:

1. "The Star Spangled Banner"
sung on key.

2. An honest billing from a military contractor.

3. A humble Japanese businessman.

4. A modest Federal judge.

5. Truth in a political speech.

6. Humor in a Baptist sermon.

A young woman was examined by an Obstetrician. After the
tests, the doctor reported that she and her husband would soon
have a child.

"Impossible!," protested the woman, "I'm not married."
After re-examining the laboratory results, the doctor reported that she
and her boy friend would have a child in five months.

"Ridiculous!," exploded the patient. "I haven't had sex

with a man in over a year."

The confounded physician agreed to evaluate the tests a third time. When he returned to the waiting room, he crossed to a window and stood looking off into the distance. After several minutes of silence, the woman asked him, impatiently, "why are you looking out that window?"

"Why," he said, "the last time something like this happened, three wise men came out of the East. I don't want to miss them, this time."

MISANTHROPE (n) Someone who bases his opinions about human beings entirely on television commercials.

> Said an old misanthrope from Dundee,
> "I dislike every human I see.
> "But, there's one I despise
> "Who cheats, brags, and lies.
> "That contemptible fellow is me."

MISER (n) A person who gives others no more than they deserve.
> Said a tight-fisted father from Kaiser,
> Who his sons vilify as a miser,
> "To counter their leeching,
> "I'm constantly preaching
> "That doing with nothing is wiser."

MISFORTUNE (n) The kind of fortune that never misses.
> "If you can smile at your misfortune, you have somebody in mind to blame for it."
>> Dorothy Parker
> Said a newly-wed beauty, named Honey,
> "My marital state is not funny.
> "My misfortune, to tell,
> "Was seducing too well
> "A big-spending man with no money."

MISSPELL (v) To write, creatively.
> "It's a damn small mind that can spell a word only one way."
>> President Andrew Jackson

MISTAKE (n) Conduct that, unintentionally, benefits another or injures you.
> "Learn from the mistakes of others. You won't live long enough to make them all yourself."

H. L. Mencken
"Experience is the name man gives to his mistakes."
Ambrose Bierce
Louie the dip gave the judge righteous lip
When his sentencing came on the docket.
"A mistake!" said he, loud; "I was squeezed by the
crowd
"And my hand stuck in some fella's pocket."

MISTRESS (n) Formerly, a woman who is married, now, one who is
marred.   When a woman in Dallas accused her
husband of keeping a mistress, he denied everything and promised
never to see her again.
    (Q) "What is the difference between a mistress and a   married
woman?"
    (A) "Night and day."
Abigail Van Buren

MODEL (n) A perfectly proportioned young woman who displays
clothes that were designed for her, then sold for a ridiculous
figure.
    A furious female, Fran Fetter,
    Returned her new dress with this letter:
    "This gown that I bought
    "Is not what I thought.
    "When I saw it displayed, it looked better."

MODERATE (n) Someone whose "middle of the road" position
exposes him to sideswipes from both the right and left.
    On matters of sin, young Timothy Chin
    Is a moderate sort of a sir.
    While is church cites him text, his girl is quite vexed
    Unless he goes sinning with her.

MODEST (adj.) Concealment of flesh under the prompting of virtue.
    A modest streetwalker, named Trude
    Refuses to pose in the nude.
    When the artist complains,
    She tartly explains
    That showing her navel is lewd.

MODESTY (n) The chief trait of homely women. While they always
strive to keep their parts, private. beautiful women often flaunt
their private parts in public.
    "Nothing becomes a man so much as modesty."
Alexander Pope
    "Nothing becomes a man so much as money."
Mae West (correcting Pope)

MOMENT (n) A variable interval of time that ranges from the prolonged (e.g., senior moment), to the brief (e.g., a moment of silence), to the instantaneous (e.g., a moment of contrition).

"Every moment spent mourning what we have lost is a lost moment that could have been spent appreciating what we have left."
Jack Lemmon

MONEY (n) A commodity that is of no benefit to us until we part with it.

"Try not to become a man of money, but a man of value."
Albert Einstein (advice to a young student)

MONEY (n) 1. A commodity that has no value until it is parted with.

2. A current of exchange among people. In the case of parent and child, the current flows to the child in exchange for ingratitude. Both flows increase in proportion to the latter's age.

(son in college) "No mon, no fun, your son."
(reply) "Too bad, so sad, your dad."
"While money isn't everything, it keeps the kids in touch."
Bumper-sticker seen in California

MONGREL (n) A member of the animal kingdom whose family tree was pollinated, haphazardly, producing assorted fruits and nuts.

An Australian legislator of mixed ancestry, named Ian MacKenzie, was once described in this way:

"He's Scotch-Irish, which creates a big problem. Half of him wants a drink and the other half won't pay for it."

MONKEY (n) A relative of Man whose evolution has been so retarded that it has not yet learned to lie, cheat, steal, or kill others of its kind for religious reasons.

Three monkeys sat in a coconut tree
Discussing things that are known to be.
Said one to the others: "Now listen, you two,
"There's a rumor around that can't be true;
"That man evolved from our noble race.
"The very idea is a great disgrace.
"Here are several things we monkeys won't do.
"Go drinking, nights, and get in a stew;
"Or use a gun or club or knife
"To take another monkey's life.

"Yes, Man descended, the ornery cuss,
"But, brothers, he didn't descend from us."

MONOPOLY (n) Control of a market by one entity to the exclusion of competitors who wish to penetrate it. In the context of human relationships, this is called "marriage".

MONY (s) A suffix common to words that describe a predictable sequence in marital relationships, i.e., "harmony", "matrimony", "acrimony", and "alimony".

MORALS (n) Ethical rules that guide the conduct of others so as to protect your right to pleasure, profit, and peace of mind.
Several examples of this benevolent standard readily come to mind:
   1. A man wants his wife to be chaste and his girl friend to be chased.
   2. A retailer wants his wholesaler to be honest and his customers to be gullible.
   3. A physician wants her malpractice insurer to be frugal and her patients to be forgiving.
   4. A lobbyist wants a Senator to be bribable and his bribe deniable.
   The Earl of Sandwich, an 18th Century wit and dandy, was confronted by a rival at a dress ball:
   "You, sir," bellowed the assailant, "will either die on the gallows or of the pox."
   "That will depend on which I embrace," calmly replied the Earl, "your morals or your mistress."

MORMON (n) A Christian denomination once pitied for its practice of polygamy. The practice died out, as did its male practitioners--from exhaustion.
   In the old Mormon Church, men were blessed.
   But, their evenings were fearfully stressed.
   Their multiple wives
   Led them tiring lives;
   Too much bouncing in bed to get rest.

MORON (n) 1. Someone who thinks that "rock and roll" refers to a boat and that "hung jury" identifies a jury that was punished for a bad verdict.
   2. Someone who contradicts your opinions.
   A California State Senator was trying to change a flat tire

151

late one evening, across from the Riverside County institution for the mentally challenged when 2 of the 5 lug nuts rolled into a nearby ditch. After searching in vain for twenty minutes, a young man approached from the facility and asked the despairing politician what was wrong. On hearing the problem, he mounted the spare tire, using the remaining lug nuts at the ten, two, and six, positions.

Learning that his rescuer was an inmate of the institution, the amazed Senator asked: "How in the world did you think of that?"

"I may be a moron," the other replied, "but I'm not stupid."

MORTAL (adj.) Having a short life, as with human beings or their remorse for sinning. The antonym, "immortal", applies only to God, who will live for as long as a clergy exists, or a person with imagination.

The Catholic Church candidly identifies its most serious sins as "mortal" and guarantees their brevity by an expungement process predicated on the sinner confessing the sin and donating to his parish building fund. Thus freed from guilt, he is free to commit the same sin, again.

> Said the papacy's expert, Bartel,
> "The fate of non-Catholics is fell.
> "When they pass through death's portal,
> "They become quite immortal,
> "By living forever in Hell."

MORTGAGE (n) A legal instrument vital to the Free Enterprise System, by which a bank can seize real property for a fraction of its true value, evict the owner, and sell it for a profit .
The word derives from French and literally means "death pledge," once again demonstrating how closely language mirrors life.

> A mortgagee bank loaned a mortgagor, Frank,
> Ten thousand, his home to improve.
> When Sally, his mate, made two payments late,
> It then gave him ten days to move.

MOSES (n) A famous leader of the Jewish people during Biblical times, his most celebrated action would be illegal in America. He parted the Red Sea without first preparing an Environmental Impact Statement.

Moses to God: "Now, let me get this straight. You're going to give all the oil to the Moslems and we have to cut off the tips of our what?"

152

MOSQUITO (n) A creature God has placed on Earth to help us accept death when it finally comes.

> A sleeping Bill Leto, from uptown Toledo,
> In a dream, saw his girl bite his peter.
> Crying "son of a bitch," from a terrible itch,
> He saw it weren't her but a skeeter.

MOTHER (n) A woman who once made a mistake. Her maternal history consists of one sleepless night, nine months of deformity, eighteen years of drudgery, and a lifetime of ingratitude. She is primarily responsible for keeping children on the straight and narrow path until they are old enough to blame her for what they missed.

She is renowned for teaching children many important things, among which are the following:

1. (about hypocrisy) "If I've told you once, I've told you a million times--don't exaggerate!"

2. (about the circle of life) "I brought you into this world and I can take you out of it, again."

3. (about behavior modification) "Stop acting like your father!"

4. (about envy) "There are millions of less fortunate children in this world who don't have wonderful parents like you do!"

5. (to appreciate a job well done) "If you're going to kill each other, do it outside.   I just finished cleaning!"

6.   (about religion)   "You better pray that will come out of the carpet."

7.   (about time travel) "If you don't straighten up, I'm going to knock you into the middle of next week!"

8. (about logic) "Because I said so, that's why."

9.   (about foresight) "Make sure you wear clean underwear in case you're in an accident."

10.   (about irony) "Keep laughing and I'll give you something to cry about."

11. (the science of osmosis) "Shut your mouth and eat your supper!"

12. (about stamina) "You'll sit there three days, if necessary, until all that spinach is eaten."

> There was a young mother from Bray
> Whose life grew more frantic each day.
> 'Til she fled to a zoo,
> Where there's nothing to do,
> And lives with a zebra, named Ray.

MOTORCYCLE (n) A vehicle designed for the profit of brain
surgeons, the despair of parents, the irritation of automobile drivers, and
the
enjoyment of the mentally impaired.

> A feminine biker in Maine
> Falls often, with serious pain.
> It isn't hot flashes
> That cause all her crashes.
> She suffers from air on the brain.

MOUNTAINEER (n) A rock climber whose favorite hymn is, "Nearer,
My God, To
Thee." If the approach is near enough, God is likely to lift the climber all
the
way up.

> Said a comely young climber, named Gert,
> Who climbs in a very short skirt,
> "I know that it's bold
> "And awfully cold,
> "But, it keeps men below more alert."

MOUSE (n) The de facto owner of all real estate in America. To those
skeptics
among you who require proof, here it is:

a) He has the run of all buildings without needing a key.

b)   He is not restricted to a toilet stall when he needs to relieve
himself.

c) He has the right to copulate where and when he pleases, so long as
it
pleases him to do it right.

d) His mate never makes him carry trash out to the curb; humans do it.

e) He never makes a mortgage, rent, insurance, or tax payment.

f) A lawyer was not needed to draw up title documents.

> Hickory, dickory, dock.
> Two mice ran up a clock.
> The clock struck one
> (Just for the fun)
> And sent him into shock."

MOUTH (n) The major outlet of the brain. In humans, it is large enough
to accommodate the owner's foot and far enough to allow him to put it
there.

> "When you put your foot in your mouth, do not make a meal of it."
> Sarah Bellum

MULE (n) An animal with a foghorn at one end, a manure spigot at the other, and four reminders of man's mortality underneath.

"There is no special wisdom in the second kick of a mule."
Senator Ernest Hollings

MUMMY (n) An Egyptian corpse spared digestion by worms so it can be looted by museums. The result has been widespread starvation among
worms and explains why Egypt is now mostly sand.

Cried archeologist, Strummy,
At a crypt in a pyramid's tummy,
"I was left, when just four,
"At an orphanage door.
"Now, at last, I have found my lost mummy."

MUSCLE (n) Part of the human anatomy that men strains to display and women strive to conceal.

"A man will seldom indulge in
A woman whose muscles are bulgin."
Ogden Nash

MUSHROOM (n) A fungus that is a metaphor for a Congressman. It is always kept in the dark; manure is repeatedly dumped on it; sometimes it is poisonous, and it is regularly cut off and sent packing.

MUSIC (n) Aural sex, in which the effects of aids are confined to the ears.

MYSTIC (n) One whose colon is stuffed from sitting, whose loins are stuffed into a diaper, whose stomach is stuffed with vegetables, whose throat is stuffed with prayer, and whose head is stuffed with nonsense.

One of the mort celebrated of the species, Mahatma Ghandi, sat in prayer most of the day, lived meagerly on sour goat's milk, and had bad breath because of his diet. When he died, the headline in the New Delhi Times read: "The super calloused fragile mystic expired with halitosis."

A Bengalese mystic took a powerful physic,
Constipated from sitting all day.
During the night, it worked with such might
That he jetted off down to Bombay.

NAKED (adj.) Deprived of protective camouflage, as in "he told the naked truth."

"'Clothes make the man', is a true maxim. I have never known a naked man who was able to cheat anybody."
Mark Twain

NAME (n) The label on a person or thing. Applied to the former, It comprises at least two components, called the "Christian" and "family" names. These classifications automatically excludes 90% of the world's population, who are either infidels or have no family.
> Helen Beloit found love in Detroit
> And decided to marry Tom Bedd.
> But her passion soon thawed when her father guffawed
> At her marital name, "Helen Bedd".

NAME CALLING (n) A type of verbal exchange during which the names of "mother", God", and body parts, are frequently heard, but never the names of the participants, themselves.
"Never wrestle a pig. You both get dirty and the pig likes it."
Will Rogers

NARCISSISM (n) A condition that enables you to see yourself as others should see you. It is distinguishable from other conditions of affection, such as love of a spouse, called "conjugation"; love of one's children, called "apparent"; love of moon gazing, called "lunacy" and love of a neighbor, called "adultery".

In one of Aesop's fables, a dog with a bone in his mouth admired his reflection in a pond after a fox had praised him. At the other's suggestion, he opened his mouth to display his teeth and lost the bone to the wily fox. The morals of this story are: 1) Admire yourself as much as you want, but keep your mouth shut about it; 2) If someone praises you, it is probably because she wants something you have.

NARCISSIST (n) Someone who thinks better of herself than of you.
> Said Timothy Snow to a girl who said "no,"
> "That I'm homely and fat, I allow.
> "Still, predicting my fate, I will make a good mate
> "For I'll never look worse than right now."

NATIVE AMERICAN (n) Bottom layer in America's melting pot, right
next to the heat. White settlers found them a fertile heathen race
and converted them to--fertilizer!
>"Past methods were crude," said Timothy Drood,
>Of the Bureau of Indian Affairs.
>"But now, we're much slicker. With gaming and liquor,
>"They are totally free of all cares."

NATURAL RESOURCES (n) Riches that Nature endows us all with.
She
is especially generous to the elderly, who have silver in their
hair, gold in their teeth, water on their knees, lead in their
feet, fiber in their brains, calcium in their joints, and gas in
their colons.

NECTAR (n) Favorite beverage of the Gods, who selfishly concealed
the recipe from mortals. Nevertheless, Scottish distillers
believe they are bottling the main ingredient.
>Juno drank nectar that didn't affect her
>And spurned mighty Jupiter's charms.
>When he gave her scotch, straight, she just couldn't wait
>To fall in the big fellow's arms.

NEIGHBOR (n) "One whom we are commanded to love as ourselves and
who does all that he can to make us disobedient."
>Ambrose Bierce

NEGOTIATE (v) To engage in a settlement process by which you
will get less than you demand and more than you deserve.
>Said a famous tort lawyer, Dundee,
>Showing how all his wealth came to be:
>"I negotiate, reasonably,
>"So they pay the claim, seasonably,
>"Then take 50% as my fee."

NEOLOGISM (n) A word that enters a language in much the same way
that a baby enters the world--ugly, misshapen, and unique. English
is the delivery room for so many verbal monstrosities, from
hyphenated splicing to foreign mutations, that some implacable
abortionists advocate neologicide.
>(1)
>English, like sex, is certain to vex,
>By altering much as we age.

Most neologisms are damned solecisms
That goad any purist to rage.

(2)

Of the new words, accursed, those with hyphens are worst,
A lexicographical test.
Don't say "caring in-laws," but say "meddling outlaws";
The whole words are clearest and best.

(3)

Don't say, "I'm sixty-four," but "I'm forty and more,"
The dash links are foolish and trite.
So let's quickly out-siphon the contaminant hyphen
From our word-pool and hide it from sight.

NEPOTISM (n) Originally, a radical French philosophy whose core principle rejected use of marijuana. It has since emigrated to the United States, in a rotated form, and now promotes the employment of pothead relatives in the name of family values.

NEUROSIS (n) Called a "mental condition" by psychiatrists and "worry" by everybody else, it can be cured by the former. After months of treatment, it often develops into a mental illness, called a "psychosis". This condition responds to shock therapy, which is administered in the form of the psychiatrist's bill.

Although much has been written to explain the difference between a neurosis and a psychosis, it is really quite simple. A neurotic builds a castle in the air while a psychotic lives in it, paying rent to the psychiatrist who moved him in.

NEUTER (v) To unload a male's procreative weapon so it cannot become a pop-gun.

A potent old Mormon, named Pree,
Was neutered at seventy-three.
He was fit to be tied
When he learned his wives lied,
"'Twas neutral she said I would be."

NEUTRALIZE (v) To take the teeth out of an adversary's bite. According to one expert, Dr. Dee Bates, the best way to neutralize an opponent on any issue is to appear to agree with her. This persuades her that she must be wrong.

NEWS (n) Information too recent to be propaganda, too indiscriminate to be a press release, and too biased to be true.

It is classified as either "good news" (e.g., an economic forecast from the White House) or "bad news" (e.g., any television news.

The following story proves that the difference between the two may be slight:

A doctor called his patient, saying he had good and bad news, and asked which he wanted to hear, first.

"Give me the good news," replied the patient.

"The good news is that you have one full month to live," the doctor said.

"Why, that's terrible!" the other replied. "What can the bad news be?"

"I should have told you last month," said the doctor.

NEWSCASTER (n) One who puts his mouth where his money is.

> Said a newscaster, Brett Dirk, of his boss at the
> network,
> "He demands I get stories and views.
> "It's so very unfair! I'm an actor on air
> "And know nothing at all about news."

NIMBY (n) An acronym meaning "not in my back yard." It is popular among modern suburbanites as a rallying cry of opposition to everything from halfway houses to fire houses, detention centers to dementia centers. Politicians understand that the targets are inner-city residents, who correctly hear it as "nimbyby" ("not in my back yard but in yours").

> Community leaders in Greered,
> Protested an orphanage they feared.
> "Nimby! nimby!", they shouted.
> Staff and children were routed.
> At that, all the neighborhood cheered.

NOBLEMAN (n) (monarchical) A member of the ruling class that often competed with the king for control of the country. Noblemen could be distinguished from commoners only by the color of their blood, which is why kings shed it so often.

(Modern) A man distinguishable by his lofty principles, selfless ideals, and gracious manners. Owing to these high standards, he is now extinct.

NOISE (n) What, to the ears, is smoke to the eyes, manure to the nose, cod liver oil to the mouth, and pain to the ass. It is sound run riot and the surest sign of a civilized society.

NOMINATION (n) In American politics, selection of the candidate most willing to pander to the biggest donors.

NONSENSE (n) The mode of expression preferred by television producers and best illustrated by their hit shows. Its language consists mainly of one-syllable words, such as "f..." and "sh..," together with others whose meaning has been altered to fit current tastes, such as "gay" and "straight."

In poetry, the verse of Lewis Carroll is better known and more loved than that of Walt Whitman. Who among us has not thrilled to the following lunatic lines:

> "The time has come," the walrus said,
> "To talk of many things:
> "Of shiips and shores an sealing wax;
> "Of cabbages and kings;
> "And why the sea is boiling hot,
> "And whether pigs have wings."

NON-VOTER (n) A member of the majority political party. This person has elected not to elect any one of the ballot candidates for one of the following reasons:

1. He once voted for Richard Nixon and fears he might make a similar mistake.

2. No candidate on the ballot has positions as wacky as his own.

3. The only candidate on the ballot he likes resembles himself and he knows what a shmuck that is.

4. He delayed too long casting his ballot while he waited for a better offer from one of the candidates.

5. He would have voted if he could have, but the ballot was entirely in English.

> Said a non-voter, Tess, in awful distress,
> "My failure to vote was a curse.
> "Phil Watson, a fool, lost by one vote to Poole,
> "Whose I Q's substantially worse."

NORMAL (adj.) Having the same eccentricities as you.

> Said the judge to defendant McKee,
> Turning down his insanity plea:

"My opinion, most formal,
"Is that you are quite normal.
"You're as proud, rude, and surly, as me."

NORTH CAROLINA (n) The part of Caroline that houses her brains and
heart. The lower part, called "South Carolina", houses her
intestines and is subject to indigestion, chronic flatulence and
constipation.

"Let our song, 'Dixie' play," old Carolinians say,
"We revere that Johnnie Reb sound."
They are still very sore that the South lost the war,
And the best of them sleep underground.

NOSE (n) The "oldfactory organ" in classical anatomy (the "d" has
since been dropped to aid pronunciation), it was so called because
safety inspectors discovered that old factories have a distinctive
smell that varies according to age and that this organ could be
relied on to tell when repairs were necessary.

In Her infinite wisdom, the creator placed the nose out
in front of the rest of the face for two important reasons: 1. to
smell perspired fearin one's enemy or oneself, so as to trigger the
fight or flight response, and 2. to stick into other people's
affairs.

"There's a man with a nose and wherever he goes
People run in a panic and shout:
'No cotton have we for our ears, if so be,
'He blows that interminus snout.'
So, the people applied for injunction. 'Denied!'
Said the judge. 'The defendant's prefixtion,
'Whatever it portends, appears to transcend
'The bounds of   this court's jurisdiction.'"
                Ambrose Bierce

NOSTALGIA (n) A type of brain disease marked by a selective
amnesia. This, in turn, produces the delusion that some past
condition or event was enjoyable. It is this distemper that
explains why so many women have more than one child and so many men
remarry.

NOTICE (n) A type of advertisement that is created by amateurs
and, therefore, is rarely noticed. One sub-type
has grown in popularity over the years. Posted on church bulletin
boards, it often contains much unintended humor--as in the
following examples:

1. "Everyone attending the Bible Study class is invited to
have tea and cookies with the Pastor after the B.S."

2. "The low-esteem support group will meet next Thursday at 7:00 P.M. They are requested to use the back door."

3. "Our retiring Pastor will preach his last sermon, next Sunday, after which the church choir will sing "Thank God From Whom All Blessings Flow'.""

4. "Our Eighth Graders will give a performance of Shakespeare's 'Hamlet', next Saturday at 4 P.M. All parishioners are encouraged to attend this tragedy."

5. "A potluck supper will be given at the parish hall, next Thursday night. Prayer and medication will follow."

6. "A Boston Baked Beans dinner will be provided at the church hall next Tuesday evening. Music will follow."

7. "At the service, next Sunday, the sermon topic will be 'What is Hell?' Come early and listen to our choir practice."

8. "Our Weight Watchers group will meet, next Wednesday night, in the basement meeting room. They should enter through the large double doors at the rear of the building."

NOTORIETY (n) 1. A reputation for villainy based mostly on facts.

2. Fame, before the editing.

The tendency of fame to slide into notoriety is graphically expressed in the following pearls:

1. "It's the tallest nail that gets hammered, first."
Japanese proverb

2. "The higher the monkey climbs, the more his ass is exposed."
Jack Welch (former General Electric CEO)

NOVEL (n) A book of fiction whose quality is somewhere between the opinions stated on the book jacket and those expressed by critics. Among the latter, perhaps Samuel Johnson, H.L. Mencken, and Dorothy Parker, had the sharpest wit--as what follows attests:

1. When the son of a friend of Johnson asked him to read his new novel, the great man complied and sent back this note: "I found your novel both good and original. Unfortunately, the part that is good is not original and the part that is original is not good."

2. After reading a novel he was asked to review in the Baltimore Sun, Mencken wrote: "The best time to read this book is at night, preferably with the lights out."

3. Writing about a novel in the New Yorker magazine, Dorothy Parker summed it up in two sentences. "This book should not be set aside, lightly. It should be pitched out with violence."

NOVICE (n) Someone who is ready to give others the benefit of his inexperience.

A novice priest gave his first sermon and, afterward, asked his pastor for a critique. "You were very nervous," replied the superior. "Why don't you sip a little vodka before your sermon, next Sunday, to relax yourself."

On the following Sunday, the novice remembered the advice, gulped down a half glass of spirits, and was wonderfully fluent.

After the Mass, he asked the pastor how he had done. "Better," said the latter, "but there are a few things that need to be straightened out.:

"First, there are ten Commandments, not twelve, and twelve Disciples, not ten;

"Second, David slew Goliath; he did not kick the shit out of him;

"Third, we do not refer to Jesus Christ as 'the late J.C.';

"Fourth, next Sunday, there will be a taffy-pulling contest at Saint Peter's, not a peter-pulling contest at Saint Taffy's;

"Finally, the Father, Son, and the Holy Ghost, are not to be referred to as 'Big Daddy, Junior, and the Spook'."

NUN (n) A female functionary in the Catholic church whose title (spelled in accordance with Latin)   emphasizes her vow of chastity. She is proclaims to be the "bride of Christ", which makes the latter a bigger polygamist than Brigham Young. In recent years, the number of applicants for the vocation has steadily dwindled, suggesting that the spelling of the job title may soon be changed to "none".

Sister Agatha retired after 30 years of teaching in the parish school, Father Timothy asked if he could give her a hug and kiss. "Why, yes, Father," the nun replied, "so long as you don't get into the habit."

NURSE (n) A health professional trained to save patients from their doctors and HMO's. As Florence Nightingale III points out in her forthcoming book, "How Sick Is Our Health System?", the Hypocritic Oath orders doctors to "Do no Harm"--and they do--while the laws of all fifty States order HMO's to "Pay Just Claims"--and they don't.

A raunchy old surgeon, named Berce,
Employed a voluptuous nurse.
One day, while excising,

He saw her breasts rising
And his patient went home in a hearse.

NURSING (n) A profession in which many practitioners do what physicians do, for doodoo wages.
> A virtuous nurse in Devore
> Was seduced by a doctor, named gore.
> Complaining of rape,
> She got it on tape;
> The poor thing's not poor anymore.

NURSERY RHYME (n) Verse so awful that it is fit only for children. The following examples of the genre are especially memorable:

(1)
> Mary, Mary, quite contrary,
> How do your pimples grow?
> "From oily pores and running sores,
> "And blackheads all in a row."

(2)
> "Jack, be nimble! Jack, be quick!
> "Jack jumped over the candlestick.
> He jumped so low and moved so slow
> That both his buns are charred and glow.

(3)
> Hickory dickory dock;
> Two mice ran up the clock.
> The clock struck one (just for the fun)
> And sent him into shock.

(4)
> Little Miss Muffit sat on her tuffit
> And fell through the hole in the seat.
> Along came a spider, who slid down beside her
> And said,"can that smell be my feet?"

(5)
> Little Jack Horner sat in a corner,
> Drinking a beer for his thirst.
> He was chugging it, nice, when out jumped two mice,
> Saying, "we were drinking here first."

OBESE (adj.) A weight condition that leaves a woman disfigured and a man rebutted. It is exemplified by a man unable to reach his fly and by a woman who must weigh herself on truck scales.
"I don't have to get in shape. Round is a shape."
Rodney Dangerfield
(1)
An obese Texas man, name of Matt,
Has a willie that's hidden by fat.
So, he tied a long string
To the secretive thing
And reels it out this way and that.
(2)
Said a girl, quite obese, of her rival, Therese,
"She's been mocking my size thirty eight.
"I'm as fat as can be, but I'm better then she,
"'Cause she's ugly and I can lose weight."

OBITUARY (n) The published report of the death of a sinner that describes a saint and is unrecognizable to those who knew him best.
"I wake up each morning and gather my wits,
"Then I pick up the paper and read the obits.
"If I don't see my name, then I know I'm not dead.
"So I eat a good breakfast and go back to bed."

OCEAN (n) "A body of water occupying about two-thirds of a world made for man, who has no gills."
Ambrose Bierce

OCCULT (n) The metaphysical source of all explanations of phenomena that cannot be explained by science, as in these examples:
1. The parents of a young woman discovered a handsome young man in their daughter's bed, early one morning. She explained that she had taken a frog to bed the night before and when she woke, the frog had been miraculously transformed.
2. A wife discovered an earring on the back seat of her husband's car. He took it, thanked her, and promptly attached it to his ear, explaining that he had purchased it to look "cool" and it must have fallen from the bag.

3. A Kentucky farmer was arrested for making 160 proof whiskey at his still. He promptly fell on his knees and thanked God, explaining that he had been distilling pure water when God performed this second miracle.

OCTOGENARIAN (n) One who has outlived her enemies and the fear of being sent to prison by the IRS.

"The biggest problem for a younger woman who marries a man in his eighties is that she will soon feel old-age creeping up on her."

Groucho Marx

A couple in their eighties celebrated their fiftieth wedding anniversary by staying in the same hotel room where they had spent their wedding night. He had just slipped off to sleep when he was awakened by his wife's sobbing. "What's wrong, Mabel," he asked? "You're just heartless," she complained. "You've forgotten that when we were in bed together, just like this, fifty years ago, you leaned over and nibbled on my ear." Without a word, he got out of bed and headed for the bathroom. "Where are you going?" she asked. "To get my teeth," he replied.

Gerontologists maintain that exercise is good for this age group, but this author respectfully disagrees. He knows of a woman in her eighties who walked five miles every day since she was seventy. Now, nobody knows where she is.

On his eightieth birthday, a Michigan man's son and grandson treated him to a visit by a local hooker. She took the old man into a bedroom, saying she was going to give him "supersex."

He mulled that over for a while, then said, "if it's all the same to you, I think I'll take the soup."

ODOMETER (n) An automotive device designed to show the owner that his warranties have expired. Some used-car dealers misuse it in the same way that some middle-age women misuse the calendar--by turning it back.

ODOR (n) Fragrance, from the opposite perspective.
There's a certain small fellow in Kennebunk,
Of whom people said that he "really stunk".
Though his odor was frightful,
One found it delightful.
That one was--you guessed it--another skunk!

166

OEDIPUS (n) An ancient Greek monarch who knew his mother better than most men know theirs.

Two Jewish mothers were discussing their sons. "I just feel terrible," said one. "My son, Sidney's psychiatrist says he has an Oedipus Complex." "Oh, Oedipus shmedipus," scoffed the other, "Why should you care so long as he loves his mother?"

> Poor Oedipus Rex had trouble with sex,
> Every woman he met left him numb.
> When he finally scored with a gal he adored,
> She turned out to be his lost mum.

OFFAL (n) The remains of an animal carcass after it has matured under the sun, been seasoned by flies, and tenderized by worms. It is highly prized by fast-food restaurants for its flavor and price.

> thought Ted, who had fainted, from meat that was
>   tainted,
> "It must have been offal," he reasoned.
> But, thought his dog, Treasure, who ate it with
>   pleasure,
> "I think it was perfectly seasoned."

OFFSPRING (n) 1. Literally, a defect in a mattress that produces an ultra-springiness in the lower section.
2. The natural consequence of "1".

OFFSPRUNG (n) Children who have left the family home.

OIL (n) A combustible hydrocarbon that makes both motor vehicles and environmentalists fume.

"If peanut oil comes from peanuts and olive oil comes from olives, where does baby oil come from?"
                         Lily Tomlin

OLD (adj.) Seasoned or spoiled by many years, depending on your age.

The late British actor, James Mason, enjoyed telling the story of an encounter with a female fan when he was in his 70's. As she approached him, staring intently at his face, her expression changed from doubt, through suspicion, to certainty. Clutching his arm, she asked: "Aren't you the former James Mason?"

You know you are old when any of the following applies:
1. It takes you two tries to walk over a speed bump.
2. When you wink at a pretty girl, she laughs.
3. You get out of breath walking down a flight of stairs.
4. When you sit down to eat your breakfast cereal, you hear a snap, crackle, and pop, but you haven't poured the milk, yet.
5. After you get onto a dance floor, you need a push to get started.
6. The tooth fairy wants a discount for quantity.
7. Your ears go up when you hear a laxative commercial on television, but nothing moves when Viagra is pitched.
8. Joggers pass when you are driving your car.
9. Your birthday candles are cited by EPA for contributing to global warming.
10. You wonder why everybody is starting to mumble.
11. Your underwear is creeping up on you and you enjoy it.
12. People at the airport tell you that you have to check in your bags and you're not carrying any.
13. Your life insurance company sends you a free calendar, one month at a time.
14. Your easy chair has more power options than your car does.
15. You have to look both ways before crossing your living-room.
16. Your social security card has only three digits.
17. It takes you all night to do what you used to do all night.

> "Come, grow old with me. The best is yet to be;
> "The last of life for which the first was made."
> > Alfred Lord Tennyson
> "Come, grow old and be incontinent with me.
> "The last of life for which Depends are made.
> "My limbs all quiver, cirrhosis has my liver,
> "And soon, all memory of you will fade."
> > (parody of Tennyson)

OLFACTORY (adj.) Pertaining to the sense of smell, recent studies prove that a dog's olfactory ability is thirty times keener than Man's. This makes the smell of cabbage cooking, unwashed gardening clothes, a gay's aftershave lotion, a bachelor's kitchen, and a baby's diaper, cruelty to dogs. Each constitutes a prosecutable offense, a source of new business for lawyers, and an affront to animal rightists--who believe that "dog" should be spelled backward and treated accordingly.

 Said an old garlic eater in Vail,
 "I know that my breath turns folks pale.
 "But my smell, I don't mind it,
 "Because I'm behind it.
 "It's those up ahead that I nail."

OMEN (n) A sign that something will happen, if it does happen. If it does not happen, then it was a prediction and, if it cannot possibly happen, it probably is a plank in a political party's platform.

ONCE (adj.) One too many

ONCOMING (adj.) Although meaning the same as "coming", it is preferred by teachers seeking tenure, composers who link it with "tide", and the many lawyers who charge by the syllable.

 If an outgoing personality is an extravert, then an oncoming personality must hit on himself.

 An elderly Ohio man was driving North on the I-71 freeway when he got a cell call from his wife. "Are you alright?" she asked. "Of course," he replied, "why are you asking?" "Well," she said, "I'm watching the news on TV and they're talking about a car on I-71 going the wrong way in the Southbound lanes." "Yes, I know," he informed her, "There are quite a few of them. I see a lot of oncoming headlights."

OPERA (n) A form of musical theater in which no actor speaks, few can act, and many die on stage too slowly. The audience does not speak, either. It snores.

OPINION (n) A conclusion the accuracy of which is directly proportional to the promotion of your interests and inversely proportional to the furtherance of opposing ones.

 If the opinion is expressed by a professional "expert witness", the accuracy is inversely related to the amount you had to pay him to express it. Finally, if the expert was hired by your opponent, a little research will usually uncover past instances when he expressed the opposite conclusion for another payer. Judas Iscariot founded this profession and is the model all present members emulate.

 "When I want your opinion, I'll give it to you."
  Archie, to his wife, in "All In The Family"

OPINIONATED (adj.) Stubbornly adhering to opinions contrary to yours.

OPPORTUNIST (n) One who exploits another before you can.

OPPORTUNITY (n) 1. The moment when your success or a rival's failure is possible.
    2. What results when prayer combines with connivance.
    Said an alpinist, Leek, as he climbed toward the peak:
    "My opportunity's near."
    Said his rival, Fignewt, as he yanked on Leek's boot,
    "My opportunity's here!"

OPTIMIST (n) 1. A person with a bad memory.
today, despite knowing that today was worse than yesterday.
Victims of this malady can be identified by any one of the
following reactions:
    1. Whenever they smell flowers, they look about for a wedding.
    2. They call horseshit fertilizer and use it on their garden.
    3. Whenever there is flatulence at the dinner table, they congratulate the perpetrator on feeling better.
    4. When a teenage daughter tells them that she missed a period, they believe it is a punctuation mistake.
    "The only thing worse than a young pessimist is an old optimist."
> Voltaire
> (1)
> Said an optimist boy, who was digging with joy,
> Into a pile of manure:
> "With all this horse shit, I don't doubt it a bit;
> "There's a pony down here I am sure."
> (2)
> Grumped a grouchy old woman from Nile,
> With a grin on her face all the while,
> "My life's a bad joke.
> "Because of a stroke,
> "I am cursed with this idiot smile."

OPTOMETRIST (n) A professional who helps people see that they do not need an ophthalmologist.

Said irked patient, Wes, to optometrist, Les,
"Your fees are as high as a hill.
"While my vision is perky, on one thing it's murky;
"I can't see me paying your bill."

ORGAN (n) A device for producing sounds that sometimes resemble music. For centuries, it has been closely associated with churches because its bass notes are believed to duplicate the sound of God, snoring. Most contemporary parishioners do not favor it, preferring to do their own snoring.

ORGY (n) The name given a college fraternity party.
Reverend Porgy, caught in an orgy,
Was shocked to see women in bed.
After seeing the fun, he called nine one one.
"Send police in the morning," he said.

ORTHODONTIST (n) A type of dentist who straightens your teeth for a good bite, then sends you a bill with a better one, thereby vastly improving his smile.
Said an orthodontist, named Lisa,
After straightening the tower of Pisa:
"I braced it on Naples,
"Secured it with staples,
"And charged all my fees on their Visa."

OTTOMAN (n) A fixture that supports heels (see MARRIAGE).
While some experts trace the word back to the Ottoman Empire, the revered German philologist, Dr. Hans Offel, is convinced that it was named after a Munich sausage maker, Otto Mann. According to this theory, Mann designed a padded piece of furniture so he could rest his legs on something soft while his wife cleaned under them. The invention caught on in Germany and soon spread throughout the world, to wherever husbands loaf.

OUCH (n) The first word spoken by children with older brothers.

OUNCE (n) What one loses, in fat, after ten hours of strenuous exercise and regains after one piece of pie. Based on Ben Franklin's proverb, two ounces of prevention are better than sixteen ounces of cure. If so, then it is far better to prevent a Republican from becoming President than have to cure the disorders that will follow.

OUTGO (n) A monetary flow that is subject to a special law of hydraulics that causes it to moves with twice the speed of the opposite flow, called "income."

"If your outgo exceeds your income, your upkeep will be your downfall."

Fred Allen

Said a hard-working fellow from Kent,
To his wife, on the money she spent,
"Our outgoing flow
"Tops our incoming so,
"That our credit has got out and went."

OUTHOUSE (n) In America's rural past, an outdoor site where old Sears catalogues were stored, flies and spiders nurtured, farmers mooned, and offal collected. The smell was offal, too.

Samuel Chin emigrated to California, where he started farming and became an ardent patriot of his adopted country. When his three sons came, he steeped them in stories of George Washington and other early heroes. One night, someone pushed the outhouse into an adjacent gully. Next morning , the father lined up his sons and demanded to know which one did the nasty deed. Finally, after tears and threats, the eldest son confessed, whereupon the father bent him over his leg and spanked him hard and long.

After his punishment, The boy tearfully complained, "why did you spank me when you told us that George Washington's father praised him for admitting that he chopped down a cherry tree?"

"George Washington's father not in cherry tree at the time," Samuel replied.

OUTLAW (n) Someone on the outs with his in-laws.

Young Timothy Heft was accused of Grand Theft,
Though police deemed the case a grand bother.
All he did was get sweet on a girl down the street
And steal her away from her father.

OVA (n) At an end; done with.

OVATION (n) In earlier times, a ceremony during which the audience threw eggs at a performer. Nowadays, audiences throw their hands together to demonstrate that they hold no eggs. Many people regret the loss of the old custom.

"The only sound reason for a standing ovation is so the audience can adjust its underwear."

Sir Winston Churchill

OXYMORON (n) Two consecutive words that are contradictory, as in "honest politician." The word derives from a neurological condition marked by a deficiency of oxygen to the brain. Over time, "oxygen moron" contracted into the present form and sufferers have tended to become editors, preachers, politicians, and lawyers. Here is a list of notable examples culled from a week's worth of editorials, sermons, speeches, and legal briefs:

1. "ethical lawyer;
2. "Soft Rock";
3. "negative growth";
4. "Defense Department";
5. "common sense";
6. "progressive tax";
7. "fair sex";
8. "reasonable man";
9. "angelic child;"
10. "compassionate conservative".

OZONE (n) A gas that contains too much oxygen for breathing, just enough to kill bacteria in drinking water, and causes industrialists and environmentalists to hyperventilate about "the hole."

Ozone rises to the heavens and somewhere there it stops.
It spreads into a layer, as though birds were using mops.
Then, hydrocarbon gasses, spewed out by industry,
Reduced the ozone layer by simple chemistry.
"You must stop these hurtful gasses," the EPA decreed.
"But then," producers cried, "our revenues will bleed.
"Our profits will have holes in them and they will go right
                    through."
But, EPA stood its ground and said, "the ozone has holes,
                    too."

PACIFIST (n) A person who lets others fight to protect his principles at the expense of their principal.
> For pacifists, reason is might
> And warring never is right.
> But, when fighting is done
> And benefits won,
> They share in the spoils with delight.

PACKAGE (n) A parcel that usually contains less than meets the eye.
> "He who is all wrapped up in himself makes a small package."
> Confucius

PANDER (v) Catering to a base appetite of another to satisfy your nobler appetite for profit.
> Said an expert, Doc Gander, "I never will pander
> "To your client to earn a fat fee.
> "But, for the right pay, I can honestly say,
> "With his views, I am sure to agree."

PANIC (n) 1. The effect sight of a mouse has on a woman.
> 2. The effect sight of a woman has on a mouse.
> "If you have kept your head while all around you are losing theirs, maybe you're missing something."
> Reverend William Boland
> Sue's in a great panic; her action is manic.
> A mouse has appeared on her floor.
> Both tremble in fright; both start-up in flight.
> Together, both run out the door.

PARADOX (n) 1. Two doxes.
> 2. An insoluble problem, as in these examples:
> 1. How can a man fall into a woman's arms without falling into her clutches?
> 2. How can a parent give a teenager $20 to buy a $15 item and get change back?
> 3. How can an engaged girl get advice from her mother on baking a cake without getting a lecture on sex?
> 4. How can a politician hold a news conference without revealing his I Q?
> 5. How can a woman say, "I do," without committing herself to a lifetime doing everything?

PARANOIA (n) Worry about being victimized, after the condition has been treated by a psychiatrist and his bill has arrived.

> Snapped an NRA member, named Hank,
> When accused of being a crank,
> "According to Freud,
> "I am not paranoid."
> Then he drove himself off in his tank.

PARANOID (n) Someone who best knows what she deserves.

> "Paranoids have enemies, too."
> Jay Lenno

PARKERISM (n) An acerbic retort of the celebrated and feared wit, Dorothy Parker. Here are several that justify the opinions:

1. A society matron with whom Parker was feuding sent her this note: "I am having a dinner party, next Saturday, but you are not invited! I cannot bear fools."

DP returned the note with this postscript: "Obviously, your mother could."

2. "I would rather have a bottle in front of me than to have a frontal lobotomy." (Note to a friend, who was trying to persuade her to give up drinking.)

3. Informed by a colleague at the New Yorker magazine that Calvin Coolidge had just died, she asked: "How could they tell?"

4. Writing in the New Yorker about a Debutante's Ball, she said: "If all those attractive young ladies were laid end to end, I wouldn't be at all surprised."

5. In a review of a play starring the young Katherine Hepburn, Parker wrote: "Miss Hepburn ran the gamut of emotions from "a" to "B".

6. In a review of the play "Cleopatra", starring Gloria Swanson, DP wrote: In the first scene, "Miss Swanson, as Cleopatra, rode the royal barge down the Nile to Thebes, where it promptly sank."

7. When she and Clare Booth Luce, with whom she was feuding, accidentally arrived together at the revolving front door of New York's Algonquin Hotel, Luce invited Parker to enter first, saying, "Age before beauty, my dear." Parker complied and, as the other woman came through the door, said: "Pearls before swine, my love."

8. "Men never make passes
    At girls who wear glasses."
    (Reply to a friend, who asked why she was not married.)

9. "You can lead a horticulture, but you can't make her think."

PATHETIC (adj.) A condition in one person that elicits pity in another. Here are several true-life examples:
1. A pregnant woman, to a lesbian.
2. A pregnant woman, to a new mother.
3. The husband of a pregnant woman, to a married man with a vasectomy.
4. The husband of a woman who is conceiving a child in his absence, to the man helping her.
5. The wife of a celebrity, to the wife of another celebrity.

PATHOLOGIST (n) A specialist in performing autopsies, the purpose of which is to disprove that the death was caused by malpractice.
Said pathologist Dove, from his autopsy of
Pompous old Senator Gray:
"Cause of death, without question, was acute indigestion;
"From eating his words every day."

PATIENT (n) A client for medical services, so-named because of the long wait he must endure before the doctor will see him.

pedophile
PATRIOT (n) 1. Someone who embraces his country as passionately as he does his mistress, risking his health with both. Here are several unforgettable utterances that have been forgotten by everyone but American Legion historians and middle-school children:
1. (Nathan Hale, American spy during the Revolutionary War) "I regret that I have but one life to give for my country." (So did the British, who were quite ready to hang him as often as his lives permitted.)
2. (Stephen Decatur, American naval officer) "My country, may she always be right, but, my country right or wrong." (Responding to unpatriotic Libyans, who objected to his butchery of hundreds of civilians while chasing Barbary Coast pirates.)
3. (Charles Wilson, former General Motors Chairman and U.S. Secretary of Defense) "What is good for General Motors is good for America." (Unpatriotic skeptics at the time reasoned that, while making more polluting automobiles might be good for America's economy, it was not so good for America's lungs.)
A patriot, General Speers,
Inspired his soldiers to cheers.

"You must go there and fight
("Never mind if it's right"),
"As for me, I'll support you from here."
2. A person who defends his country's right to be wrong.
A patriot, Pete, proclaims with some heat:
"The USA is the best!"
When asked about violence, he lapsed into silence,
Then, angrily drew on the pest.

PEDAGOGUE (n) ("Ped"--from the Latin, meaning "foot") A teacher
who moves about in class to avoid having to answer questions.
Said an old pedagogue, in Girard,
"I constantly move, though it's hard.
"But, the last time I tarried,
"I damn near was buried
"Under symbols of student regard."

PEDOPHILE (n) From the Latin, someone with an abnormal love for
children or feet, depending on whether he is a pederast or
podiatrist. Both compulsions can be controlled by the same
procedure, called a "pedicure."
I think that priestly pedophile
Would lose their yen for juveniles
If Rome would let them marry misses
And let off steam with legal kisses.

PELICAN (n) A water bird with a goiter and an indiscriminate
appetite.
Praises are heard for the Pelican bird;
His life's ecological toil.
He holds in his beak rotting fish from last week,
Beer bottles, used condoms, in oil.

PENAL (adj.) Pertaining to the penis, as implied in the term
"penal servitude", which refers to marriage. Many States, like
California, have a "Penal Code", which identifies and describes
various crimes committed by that organ.

PENIS (n) A male organ that functions alternatively with the
brain. Recent research has found that the average man has enough
blood for either his brain or penis to function, but not both
simultaneously.

177

Experience tells us that the organ has a personality of its
own. It is
either
upstanding or downcast, depending on whether its owner is sixteen
or sixty.

There was a young lawyer, named Rex,
With diminutive organs of sex.
When charged with exposure,
He said, with composure,
"De minimis non curat lex."
("The law does not regard trifles.")

PENITENTIARY (n) A place where criminal penitents gather to
reflect on their past antisocial conduct and pray for future
guidance so that they will never again be caught.

PENSIVE (adj.) A state of sad reflection evoked by memories of
missed opportunities to better ourselves and batter our enemies.

Following are several examples guaranteed to elicit moist
eyes and an aching heart:

1. An opportunity to tell a boss where he should go before he
goes there.

2. A chance to tell your former wife that if she had any
taste, she never would have married you.

3. An opportunity to refute the general opinion that you are
stupid by becoming a stock day trader.

4. A chance to get in the last word during an argument with
your spouse, thereby starting another argument.

Said a wife to her spouse, newly wed,
When he asked, "why so pensive?" in bed.
"I can't sleep a wink
"Whenever I think
"That I could have wed Larry, instead."

PENTAGON (n) An enormous building in Washington, D.C.,
whose only beneficial function is to prove the theory that a vacuum
expands indefinitely, to the limits of its enclosure.

Some Pentagon generals seek
Pleasure in scaring the meek.
But, their brains are so fuddled;
Their planning so muddled;
Thank God those they bully are weak.

178

PERFECT (adj.) A condition of sublime purity that is limited to elected officials, corporate executives, college deans, and admirers of this lexicon.

"I am truly quite perfect," a CEO said,
"Neither foolish, nor selfish, nor crass."
"He is right", said another, an AFL head,
"The man's, truly, a quite perfect ass!"

PERFECTIONIST (n) Someone who never makes a mistake about trifles. If it is a man, he is bound to be a bachelor. If it is a woman, she will be the proverbial "Miss Right," whose first name is "Always."

"I am not a perfectionist, but my parents were."
Will Rogers

PERIODONTIST (n) Second in a sequence of four dental practitioners who will, thanks to modern specializations, separately charge you for working on a troubled tooth. The first in the series is the Dentist, who excavates part of the tooth in such a way that it cannot be filled. Next comes the Periodontist, who gums up the exterior of the tooth to prepare it for the accomplice that follows. Next, comes the Endontist, who roots around inside the tooth to preserve it. Last is the Oral Surgeon, who pulls it.

PERIPATETIC (adj.) A mobile teaching style that saves college professors from questions they cannot answer.

A peripatetic professor's athletic;
He moves on so fast that he's blurred.
Whenever a student asks a question imprudent,
He's too far away to be heard.

PERSIAN (adj.) A type of rug that is featured in many "going out of business" sales. A customer need never hurry there, since the sale will continue for several years.

Said a Persian rug dealer in Spears,
"I have 'Closing Now' signs, but no fears.
"The business won't fail,
"For my 'Lost Our Lease' sale
"Has lasted for twenty five years."

PERVERT (n) A woman who seduces a man's wife, a man who seduces the husband, or anyone who seduces both at the same time.

A certain young man from Wilkes Barre
On the mouth, kissed a male star.
When charged with perversion,
He offered this version,
"I was giving the hunk CPR."

PESSIMIST (n) An optimist with experience. While an optimist
believes this is the best of all possible worlds, a pessimist knows
he is right.
"If you need money, borrow it from a pessimist. He doesn't
expect you to repay it."
　　　　　Steve Allen
　　　Said pessimist, Gary, to optimist, Mary,
　　　"If we wed, my demise I foresee."
　　　Said she, with a smile and no little guile,
　　　"With that prophecy, I agree."

PHILANTHROPIST (n) A person who does good for others for no worse
reason than that it does good for her.
　　　Proclaimed a philanthropist, Bea,
　　　"My motive is not charity.
　　　"When I do good for others,
　　　"It's furthers my druthers,
　　　"Which are solely to do good for me."

PHOBIA (N) An irrational fear, as in the following everyday
examples:
　　　1. Auntiephobia (fear of maiden aunts).
　　　2. Dogdophobia (fear of stepping on dog turd).
　　　3. Mipplophobia (fear of nursing an infant
with hard gums).
　　　3. Asseataphobia" (fear of falling through a toilet seat). 4.
　　　4. Iranaphobia (fear of Iranian used car dealers).
　　　5. Mommyphobia (fear of mothers with too many facelifts.
　　　6. Fartaphobia (fear of passing gas in public).
　　　For a phobic young fellow from Teare,
　　　Losing his pants was the fear.
　　　To relieve what he felt,
　　　He lengthened his belt,
　　　And fastened it to his right ear.

PHONEY (adj.) Referring to the spiel of a telephone solicitor.
　　　Said Senator Howard Maloney,

"I can't help that my speeches sound phony.
"My ideas, I am told,
"Are as precious as gold.
"But to many, they sound like baloney."

PHARAOHS (n) Royal leaders of the ancient Egyptians who preserved their bodies, gold jewelry, and precious gems, for the profit of grave robbers and museums. When a counselor warned one of them about the danger of looting, the latter is reported to have said, "tut-tut", which became the name he is known by, today.

A pharaoh admonished his daughter
To bathe as a pretty girl oughter.
But, he wasn't so glad
When she hollered, "hey, dad,
"You should see who I found in the water."

PHYSICS (n) A field of science that undertakes to explain things that are obvious in ways that make them obscure to all but physicists. Early in his career, Sir Isaac Newton was hit on the head by an apple and spent the rest of his life explaining, with gravity, gravity.

It took Albert Einstein a thousand double-sided manuscript pages to explain that an airplane passenger could prolong his life merely by walking down the aisle in the direction of the flight. His critics complain that he would have rendered a greater service to mankind if he had figured out when the same passenger was most likely to find an available toilet in economy class.

PIOUS (adj.) Having such heat for God that little warmth remains for people.

Baptists mortify God with their rants.
Moslems vex Him with fanatic chants.
Televangelists shock
By fleecing His flock.
Catholics finish Him off with their cants.

PIRATE (n) A criminal class active several centuries ago that robbed the public, looted cities, and fed innocent people to the sharks. Nowadays, they are called lawyers, politicians, and securities brokers.

There once was a pirate named Tate,
whose hornpipes were never first rate.

He fell on his cutlass,
Leaving him nutless,
And practically useless to date.

PIT BULL (n) A set of teeth to which a dog is attached. Once
it locks onto its prey, there is no power on Earth that can
loosen it hold--which makes it the nearest thing to an IRS
tax collector alive today.

PITTANCE (n) What is left of wages after the withholdings.

PITY (n) 1. What Republicans prefer to dispense among the poor.
    2. The only thing Democrats can afford to dispense.
    3. What Libertarians refuse to waste upon the poor.
    4. What Greens prefer to dispense among animals, on whose
habitats the poor often sponge.

PLACEBO (n) Pretended medication that is less harmful to patients
than the real thing. Both real and pretended medications are
administered by researchers during what is known as a "double
blind" study. It is called this because, after the study is
completed, neither positive results nor any remains of the
government money that funded it can be seen.
    Wailed a medical student, named Flo,
    Who conceived in a park gazebo:
    "It isn't my shame;
    "The pill is to blame.
    "I was given a damned placebo."

PLAGIARISM (n) Publishing as one's own the literary work of someone
who is dead and cannot sue.
    "Quoting one is plagiarism. Quoting many is research."
        H. L. Mencken

PLANNING (n) Preparing to take governmental action that is a)
excessive in concept; b) flawed in design; c) bloated in scope; d)
profligate in expenditure; e) obsolete when completed, and f)
hailed as a triumph when the costs are disclosed.

PLATITUDE (n) Words that rouse, expressing an idea that
sleeps. It is the raw material from which sermons, political
speeches, parental advice, and judicial decisions, are made.

PLATONIC (adj.) A relationship between a man and woman that used to be play for the former and tonic for the latter.
Nowadays, it is not necessarily in that order.

PLEASURE (n) The chief goal of a man's life. When a woman is intimately involved in it, she acts as goalie and imposes conditions.
   "The keener the pleasure, the more likely it is that you will live to regret it."
                    Will Rogers

POET   (n) Someone who rhymes with reason.
                    (1)
     Shaw's poems and plays are replete
     With toxic opinions not sweet.
     The words made him septic
     And greatly dyspeptic,
     From having so many to eat.
                    (2)
     "Most poets don't know it;
     "Their feet don't show it.
     They're stubby, like Bellows',
     Not lanky Longfellow's."
     (University of Michigan English Dept. doggerel)

POLAND (n) A nation whose past has been intermittently seared by invasions from Russia and whose present is continuously soured by jokes from the entire world. The following exemplifies the latter:
                    (1)
   "Bulletin from Warsaw: The worst air disaster in Poland's history occurred, yesterday, when a small passenger plane crashed into a cemetery outside Warsaw. Search and Rescue workers have recovered 837 bodies from the scene, thus far, and that number is expected to climb as they continue digging through the night."
                    (2)
   Q. "Why are the rest breaks of Polish workers limited to ten minutes?"
   A. "Any longer and they would have to be retrained."

POLEMIC (n) A form of academic combat that generates great heat, but no light; overwhelms the audience, not the enemy; wounds every combatant without (to their keen regret) killing anyone, and ends with no victor.

183

When teaching debating, Dobbs has a high rating;
Polemic opponents are buried.
"It's useful, besides," he warmly confides,
"After my students get married."

POLITICAL CANDIDATE (n) A person who has his tongue in your ear, his hand in your pocket, and his eyes and ears on other people.

Said political candidate, Lett,
"I have no positions, as yet.
"But, with survey results
"And expert consults,
"Soon I'll know what to think, I should bet."

POLITICAL PARTY (n) An association of people who are united by having the same screws loose. It is organized according to procedural rules first adopted by the Mad Hatter for his Tea Party.

One important rule requires a convention of party delegates, every four years, to select the Party's Presidential candidate. Since the candidate had already been chosen in State primary elections, another important rule

dictates that convention delegates (like the Dormouse in "Alice") must be steeped in drink, kept in the dark, and shift allegiance from one candidate to another as each one's dirty plate is exposed.

"It is easier to teach Democrats prudence than to teach Republicans compassion and it is easier to teach Republicans compassion than to teach politicians of both parties common sense."
James Farley

"I don't belong to an organized political party. I'm a Democrat."
Will Rogers

POLITICIAN (n) The used-car dealer of government. Both sell a commodity that does not run well, for an exorbitant price. There is one difference between them. The dealer's vehicle will sometimes get you where you want to go.

POLITICS (n) A type of consumer fraud in which bad government is sold for good money. Derived from the Greek prefix, "poly", meaning "many", and the suffix, "tics", referring to bloodsucking insects. the word shows how often language mirrors life.

"Politics is the conduct of public affairs for private advantage."
Ambrose Bierce

"How can politics be made simple in a nation that has over two hundred varieties of cheese?"

> Charles DeGaulle

> Anew college grad, Thomas Trent,
> Chose politics as his life's bent.
> His mom, for a modest fee,
> Got Tom a lobotomy
> And now, he's our Vice-President.

POLLUTION (n) The most abundant product in the civilized world and the only one that increases with population. In the interest of promoting a clean environment, here are the major pollutants and their primary causes:

1. (Air Pollution)Toxic speeches by environmentalists and their critics

2. (Water Pollution) Defecation by fish, marine mammals, and small children in swimming pools.

3. (Trash Pollution) Laws against poor people cherry picking from dumpsters and dumps.

> Said a corporate prexy, named Bland,
> When accused of polluting the land,
> "Our harm to the soil
> "Just makes my blood boil.
> "Still, our profits were certainly grand."

POPULAR (adj.) Liked by others for catering to their tastes, opinions, and pleasures.

> "No man is popular who only tells the truth about others."

> Socrates

> "If you want to be noticed, stand up. If you want to be heard, speak up. But, is you want to be popular, sit down and shut up."

> Hubert Humphrey

POPULIST (n) A politician who publicly endorses the will of his constituents as soon as he privately discovers what their won't is.

> A populist Mayor in the town of West Thayer
> Chased women with vigor and joy.
> But, when his gay givers exceeded straight livers,
> He claimed he'd been gay since a boy.

PORNOGRAPHY (n) The graphic depiction of sex so salacious as to be fit for viewing only by celibate clerics, repressed moralists, penile therapists, and hypocrites everywhere.

The defining standard varies from generation to generation according to the mores of the times. In 1880, sight of a woman's bare ankle was deemed racy, while in 1920, the view of her bare back on the beach was heart-stopping. Nowadays, Internet depictions of naked bodies coupling are so commonplace as to elicit yawns. In her authoritative new book on the subject, "The Porno Promise", Professor Dee Mented predicts that America will soon return to the 1880 fashion. This will undoubtedly be a good thing since, in many women, the ankle is their most attractive part.

> Fumed Father O'Horne, after viewing taped porn,
> "This filth is a sin and a crime."
> So indignant was he that, quite innocently,
> He played the tape through a fifth time.

POSTHUMOUS (adj.) Literally, "after topsoil", the word relates to an award after death has rendered the honoree speechless.

> They gallantly fell in Nam's bloody Hell,
> As our planes spoiled the soil with their bombs.
> Now all is forgiven; by death, they are shriven.
> Their posthumous selves feed the palms.

POTABLE (adj.) Suitable for smoking.

> A certain young farmer, named Sneed,
> Got wealthy by growing a weed.
> Said he, "it is notable
> "Because it is potable,
> "Just before it has quite gone to seed."

POTENCY (n) A condition that makes a man upstanding.

Medical science tells us that the mind influences a man's performance more than the body does. This validates the Chinese proverb: "He who thinks it is impossible to do should get out of the way of him who is doing it."

POWER (n) The result when energy is multiplied by time and applied to somebody weaker.

> "Power is the ultimate aphrodisiac."
> Henry Kissinger
> "Power corrupts and absolute power corrupts absolutely."
> Lord Acton
> "It is not wealth, but power, that all men crave."
> Bertrand Russell

"Flattery's the food of fools".
So say the ancient schools.
But nowadays, all those in power
Are eager to, this food, devour.

PRAGMATIST (n) Someone who believes that the ends justify the
means, that principles are interesting, but irrelevant, and that
ethical standards adapt to the needs of the moment.
　　Said our President, George, "I've consensus to forge
　　"and nothing will stand in my way.
　　"Don't cite me the facts. Just lower the tax
　　"On my wealthy supporters, then pray."

PRAY (v) The act of communicating a request
to God by the method least likely to reach Him. The assumption
that the creator of billions of galaxies is tuned in to human
beings, in a nondescript star system, surely is
one of the most absurd conceits of a narcissistic species. It is
on a par with the fantasy that we are made in Her image.
　　A salivate preacher in Bray
　　Juicily preaches away.
　　People duck down in fear
　　Whenever they hear,
　　"Fold your hands, bend your knees, and let's pray."

PRAYER (n) A petition to God for favors, made on bended knees in
so groveling a manner as to impugn His reputation for creative
genius. In consequence of the affront, relentless petitioners are
granted the gift of osteoarthritis.
　　University of Michigan professor, Charles Stevenson, was
teaching a class in Philosophy of Religion when a student
asked, "should I believe that my prayers will be answered?"
　　"Yes," replied Stevenson, "as long as you also believe that
the answer will be 'no'."
　　In California, a true believer prayed five hours a day, for
three weeks, asking God to make him a lottery jackpot winner.
But, when each week's winners were announced, he won nothing.
　　Finally, in despair, he fell on his knees in church and
lamented: "Lord, I don't understand why you ignore me. I tithe
to the Church, attend services twice a week, pray to you
constantly, and the only thing I have ever asked for myself is to
win the lottery. Why do you treat me this way?"
　　A deep, bass, voice boomed from the altar:
　　"Give me a break. Buy a ticket!"

187

PREACHER (n) Someone with a divine train of thought who lacks a terminal facility. He succeeds with his flock by putting his tongue in their ears, his hand in their pockets and his faith in their gullibility.

> A lazy young preacher, named Day,
> His flowers neglected to spray.
> But his wife, with aplomb,
> Bought a pesticide bomb
> And said to her spouse, "let us spray."

PREPARE (v) To lay the groundwork for a mistake.

PREPOSITION (n) A part of speech as to, when, why, and about which, grammarians, English teachers, and language mavens everywhere hotly debate. When he was England's Prime Minister, one of Winston Churchill's aides corrected a draft of a speech by eliminating a dangling preposition. When he saw the revision, Churchill restored the original phrasing and sent it back to the offender with this note: "This is the sort of damned nonsense I will not be a party to and which, in future, twice you should think."

On hearing a knock at the Pearly Gates, Saint Peter asked, "who is it?" "It is I," came the answer, causing Peter to exclaim, "oh, no, not another English teacher."

PRESIDENTIAL ELECTION (n) (2000) A contest between two named "none of the above" choices.

> After a thorough inspection,
> To both Gore and Bush, I've objection.
> Al's tongue isn't straight;
> George's brain, underweight,
> Has, so far, evaded detection.

PREVARICATOR (n) A liar with good manners.

> Said a lawyer in Southern Decatur,
> A consummate prevaricator,
> "Divorce claims I despise
> "But, thanks to my lies,
> "My wife doesn't know that I hate her."

PRIDE (n) Ego's costume, the splendor of which is inversely proportional to the wearer's worth.

"Pride is thrust on those who deserve it and ridicules those who do not."
Henry Fielding

PRIMAL SCREAM (n) The sound a man makes when caught in his zipper.

PRINCIPLE (n) An ethical rule of conduct that is so fundamental a part of each person's best nature that it may only be disregarded when it conflicts with his best interest.
"In matters of style, swim with the current. In matters of principle, stand like a rock."
Thomas Jefferson

PROCRASTINATE (v) "To put off until tomorrow the things that you put off until today."
Ambrose Bierce

PROCRASTINATION (n) (Note. The author intends to supply this definition at a later date.)
"The best labor-saving invention for today's work is tomorrow."
Charles Mendel

PROCREATION (n) God's plan for producing a human being without providing the means to care for it.
Right to Lifers say, with exaltation,
When promoting Third World procreation:
"Those souls have the right
"To alight from their flight.
"It's God's Will if they die of starvation."

PROFANITY (n) Words that sting and never snore,
But, often bring a need for more.
"We never really learn profanity until we learn to drive."
George Carlin

PROFESS (v) To work at a profession.
A hardworking streetwalker, Tess,
Was charged with soliciting Jess.
Said she, with a sigh,
"I can't help it if I
"Don't give it away, but profess."

189

PROFESSIONAL (n) Someone who performs a special skill for compensation.
>A newlywed prostitute, Flo,
>Makes her husband pay cash for each throw.
>As she says to her Rex,
>"Charging for sex
>"Is required because I'm a pro."

PROFLIGATE (n)(adj.) A person who wastes what you and I want.
>A Libertarian, Mott,
>Has sniffed out a Federal plot.
>"Its profligate mission
>"Is to drain our ambition,"
>Says he from the bridge of his yacht.

PROGNOSIS (n) A medical prediction concerning the future course of a patient's illness. It serves two functions. First, it determines how much time the patient has left to pay his doctor bills and second, it determines the maximum number of office visits that can be scheduled and paid for by his insurer and/or his estate.

(1)
>A medical doctor's prognosis was that his patient had six months to live. At the end of that period, the patient was still alive, but had not paid his bill. So, the doctor gave him six more months.

(2)
>"I have good news and bad news for you," a doctor told his patient. "Which do you want first?"
>"Oh, give me the good news," said the latter, apprehensively.
>"You have six full months to live," the doctor said.
>"That's good news?" gasped the horrified patient. "What's the bad news?"
>"I should have told you six months ago," replied the other.

PROGRESSIVE (n) A liberal, revised and edited for public consumption.

PROMISCUOUS (adj.) Possessing a catholic appetite, a Mormon rationale, a heathen conscience, and a bitch's instinct.
>An elderly Mormon in Ghent
>Is a very promiscuous gent.
>Of his kids, twenty-eight
>Can never live straight
>Because his old willie is bent.

PROPAGANDA (n) 1. Truth, altered to fit.
    2. Truth that supports the opinion of an enemy.
       Charged the Papal Inquisitor, Spurnful,
       Giving Galileo's rack a turn full:
       "You've denied Earth's centrality,
       "Proving your immorality,
       "By goring the Holy See's Bull."

PROSTATE (n) A male gland designed by God for the profit of
urologists. When enlarged, it makes a man unavoidable. Without
prompt treatment, it can cause incontinence or, if a sensitive
patient prefers it, death.
       An old Utah senator, Orrin Tate,
       Has the Guinness Book's most enlarged prostate.
       He's as fit as a fiddle
       And keen as a riddle,
    But it takes him two hours to urinate.

PROSTITUTE (n) A professional who lays down on the job.
       Though I know Sarah Smith is a whore,
       She looks like the lady next door.
       When I knocked at her bower,
       She kept me an hour
       And did things most ladies abhor.

PROSTRATE (adj.) To comply with gravity.
    A college freshman in a creative writing class wrote a short
story that contained this riveting passage: "She lost her balance
and fell down the stairs, where she lay prostitute on the floor."
    The professor corrected the mistake by crossing out
"prostitute" and substituting "prostrate", explaining the
distinction in this note at the bottom of the page:
"It is the difference between a fallen woman and a woman who
has merely fallen.   "

PROVERB (n) Common sense expressed concisely, hence precluded
from the lingo of lawyers, politicians, telemarketers, and clergy.
They cannot be concise about anything, lack sense, and deny they
are common.
    Benjamin Franklin was the most prolific creator of proverbs,
among which are these expressions of his genius:
    1. "Always put off until tomorrow the things you put off until
today."

2. "Time wounds all heels."
3. "To err is human, but it feels divine."
4. "It is better to have loved and lost--much better!"
5. "If at first you don't succeed, don't try rock climbing."
6. "All stings come to those who wait."
7. "Learn from the mistakes of others. You won't live long enough to make them all yourself."
8. "The worst part about giving people a piece of your mind is that you probably need it more than they do."
9. "A beautiful young person is an accident of nature, but a beautiful old person is a work of art."
10. "Where there is a will, there is a way. Where there is none, there is an alibi."

PSYCHIC (n) One who can read the mind of another and discover a dupe.

> At a séance, a widow named Gold
> Claimed her husband's voice sounded too old.
> Said the psychic, "don't fret.
> "That's his voice, you can bet.
> "It's just that I have a bad cold."

PSYCHOSIS (n) A mental disease, after the patient's depression has been treated by a psychiatrist and his bill submitted.

> Said a shrink to a patient named Dee,
> Who thought that her nose was a flea:
> "Your psychosis, I'll cure,
> "But, until I'm quite sure,
> "Don't blow the darn thing onto me."

PSYCHOTHERAPIST (n) A doctor who applies unregulated techniques to uncertain problems and gets unpredictable results for an unimaginable fee.

PSYCHOTIC (n) One who has a mental condition intermediate in severity between a neurotic and a psychopath. The neurotic builds castles in the air, the psychotic lives in them, and the psychopath burgles them.

PUBLIC (n) The people, collectively, for whose good fortune politicians used to sacrifice their pleasures. Nowadays, the people sacrifice their fortunes to politicians, whose pleasure it is to enjoy their good fortune.

"No one ever lost money by underestimating the intelligence of the American public."
H. L. Mencken

PUBLIC SPEAKING (n) A type of mass sleep therapy especially effective in churches, auditoriums, courtrooms, television sitcoms, and radio talk shows. By inserting their tongues into many ears and blowing in vast quantities of hot air, these therapists administer an anesthetic from which the patients are finally roused by a growing ache in their buttocks. This linkage of extremities has resulted in many people addressing practitioners as "buttheads."
"There are four B's in public speaking: B relevant, B interesting, B brief, and B seated."
Robert Ingersoll

PUN (n) Words on a play that sickle wrong tits. A good pun is said to be its own reword. What follows are some of the best payoffs:

1. To test the effects of weightlessness, NASA intends to send a group of cows on an upcoming shuttle mission. Officials call it "a herd shot around the world."

2. Frogs say: "it's fun time when you're having flies."

3. While members of a chess club waited to be seated at a popular restaurant, they argued over who among them was the best chess player. When the argument became heated, the manager ordered them to leave, saying: I can't stand chess nuts boasting in an open foyer."

4. The chief of an African tribe lived in a two-story grass house in which the thrones of his predecessors were stored on the second floor. One night, during a windstorm, the house collapsed, killing the chief and prompting the medicine man to proclaim: "People who live in grass houses should not store thrones."

5. A masseur gave special attention to the posteriors of his clients so that it was said of him: "no stern was left untoned."

6. When a fraternity member died from excessive drinking, the college president commented: "He put the quart before the hearse."

7. A dentist told his patient that the latter needed a new chrome dental plate to replace one that had been corroded by years eating hollandaise sauce. When the patient asked why it had to be made of chromium, the dentist replied: "There's no plate like chrome for the hollandaise."

8. A pharmaceutical researcher, in Africa, was shown a plant

193

with gigantic fronds and told that the leaf cured constipation.
Marveled the researcher: "With fronds like these, who needs
enemas?"

Q

QUACK (v) To make a noise like a quacking duck. This is as
precise a definition as any lexicographer can reasonably be
expected to make.
(n) A physician whose malpractice makes a perfect defendant.
A certain surgeon in Nyack
Leaves scars that wander and crack.
When the hospital staff
Meets him after a gaff
They walk like a duck and say "quack."

QUANTUM MECHANICS (n) A special theory of physics that
describes a subatomic world that changes with every attempt to
view it. Nobody fully understands the theory except, perhaps,
its discoverer, Dr. Neils Bohr, and cremation reduced him to even
smaller particles.
Modern physicists tell us that every human being is composed
of the same particles. From this, we are asked to believe that
there is no difference between a Democrat and a Republican--a
conclusion too absurd to discuss.
A wonderful world is the Quantum,
With zillions of particles, count 'em.
But, it bothers me much
that electrons and such
Don't behave like physicists want 'em.

QUAYLISM (n) A blooper by a celebrity that is so outrageous as
to disqualify the speaker from contributing to the human gene
pool. It is named after a former Vice-President, who set so
high a standard that, like the speed of light, it can be
approached but not equaled. Following are several examples that
lifted him to his present distinction:
1. "I was recently on a tour of Latin America. My only
regret is I didn't study Latin in school so I could converse with
these people."
2. "If we don't succeed, we run the risk of failure."

3. "Republicans understand the importance of bondage between mother and child."

4. "President Bush, Mrs. Bush, and my fellow astronauts."

5. "We don't want to go back to tomorrow. We want to go forward."

6. "I've made good judgments in the past. I've made good judgments in the future."

7. "What a waste it is not to have a mind. Yes, a mind is a terrible thing not to have."

QUARK (n) A subatomic particle, it is one of the smallest units of matter in the universe. Only slightly larger is a steak at a fast-food restaurant.

A physicist, Christopher Stark,
For twenty years, searched for a quark.
When he caught one last May,
He found, in dismay,
It was only a firefly's spark.

QUARREL (v) Oral combat in which tongues hurl missiles guided by the thalamus rather than the cerebrum. It is the only type of marital intercourse that increases over time.

"Why quarrel so, Wyatt?"
Asked the wife of her mate.
"If you just said, 'go buy it,'
"Our life would be great."

"I don't dare try it,"
He replied with some pique.
"If I did say, 'go buy it,'
"We'd be broke in a week."

QUEBEC (n) France's only remaining overseas colony.
Quebec's language is French; English speakers retrench.
Lingua Franca's the cultural balm.
Other provinces yell; Anglophiles there rebel.
How sweet it must be to Montcalm.

QUEEN (n) A woman in London or a man in West Hollywood.
Experts advise that if a man has a suspicion about his date, he should measure her/his upper arm. If it is between 15 to 17 inches, it is a woman. If it is less than 15 inches, you have a surprise ahead. Finally, if the measurement exceeds 17 inches, your date probably is an ape and you should avoid passionate embraces.

QUEER (adj./n) 1. A condition that is noteworthy because it is unusual, as in: "It is queer of him to wear a woman's clothes here in Salt Lake City."
    2. A condition that is not noteworthy because it is usual, as in: "He must be queer because he's wearing women's clothes here in West Hollywood."
    Friends thought him a fag when they saw Jack in drag.
    All were incredibly stressed.
    They were greatly relieved when they learned he received
    First prize in the Miss Bronx contest.

query (n) A question of special importance addressed to another, the answer to which may either be good, bad, indeterminate, or informative. Illustrating these alternatives are the following answers to the special question, "will you marry me?":
    1. (Good) "yes, but only if you let me keep my job".
    2. (indeterminate) "yes".
    3. (indeterminate) "no".
    4. (bad) "Yes, but only if you change several disgusting personal habits, first.
    5. (bad) "Yes, but only if you let mother move in with us."
    6. (informative) "Yes, because I understand this State will allow a lesbian to marry."
    Here are several important queries that, to this author's knowledge, have never been answered:
    1. "Why is it called 'menopause' when it only happens to women?"
    2. "If money doesn't grow on trees, why do banks have branches?"
    3. "Since pizza is round, why are pizza boxes square?"
    4. "Once you get to Heaven, are you stuck with the clothes you were buried in? What if you were cremated?"
    5. "What disease did 'cured ham' have?"
    6. "Why do people say they 'sleep like a baby' when babies only sleep for two hours, then wake up crying?"
    7. "If a deaf person has to go to court, is it still called a 'hearing'?"
    8. "Why are people who join Weight Watchers told to wear 'loose-fitting clothes' when, if they had any, they wouldn't need Weight Watchers?"
    9. "Why do brain cells come and go, but fat cells live forever?"
    10. "Since there is no eleven on our telephone dial, how are we supposed to call nine-eleven in an emergency?"

QUINTET (n) In opera, five characters searching for harmony, sung by five singers who have found it.

quirk (N) Behavior so aberrant that it suggests a physical or mental abnormality, as in these examples:

A physician who makes house calls; a lawyer who declines a fee he did not earn; a young man who resists an opportunity to seduce a pretty girl; a dentist who does not ask a question while working in your mouth; an IRS examiner who apologizes for his mistake; a boy who wipes his muddy shoes on the door mat before entering the house; a cleric of any denomination who obeys his vow of poverty, and a President who, during an election year, admits a mistake.

QUORUM (n) According to parliamentary law, the minimum number of committee members who must be present at a meeting to commit an official folly.

> Said the Chairman of Teetotalers, Inc.,
> To the motion of member, Bill Spink:
> "Since we now have a quorum,
> "We can, with decorum,
> "Adjourn to the bar for a drink."

QUOTABLE 1. (adj.) A statement worth repeating (see any entry in this work).

2. (n) Any statement that has been repeated at least twenty times and attributed to a celebrity, who never wrote or said it. Following are some notable quotables:

1. "If you miss your ex, take shooting lessons and try again."

2. "Nobody is much interested in how well you are doing until they first learn how much good you are doing."

3. "If everything is coming your way, you are probably in the wrong lane."

4. "From those who have much to give, much sympathy is expected."

5. "If you want to be heard, speak up; if you want to be seen, stand up, and if you want to be loved, sit down and shut up."

QUOTATION (n) A witty, profound, or historic, statement attributed to someone who wishes he really had said it.

When Whistler made a witty remark in his presence, Oscar

Wilde said, "I wish I had said that," to which Whistler replied, "you will, Oscar, you will."

Following are several quotations that may be apocryphal, but are not likely to be disavowed:

1. "The only time I ever got a four point in high school was when my blood-alcohol was tested."

George Carlin

2. "I live in my own little world. But, it's okay because they all know and like me here."

Lenny Bruce

3. "I saw this sign in a Chinese pet store: 'Buy one dog and get one flea.'"

Buddy Hackett

4. "If flying is so safe, why do they call an airport, 'the terminal'?"

Joan Rivers

5. "I don't believe in political jokes. I've seen too many of them get elected."

Will Rogers

6. "There are two sides to every divorce--the wife's and shithead's."

Marla Cooper

7. "It's so great to have found that one special person who you want to annoy the rest of your life."

Dorothy Parker

8. "Here is an example of the kind of deductive logic that is taught in colleges, today: '(syllogism 1) I am nobody; (syllogism 2) Nobody is perfect; (conclusion) I am perfect.'"

George Carlin

9. "The duration of a minute depends on which side of the bathroom door you're on."

Phyllis Diller

10. "Every time I walk into a Singles Bar I remember my mother's warning: 'Don't pick that up. You don't know where it's been.'"

Cathy O'Donnell

11. "The reason why women prefer to disrobe in front of men rather than in front of women is that, while women are judgmental, men are simply grateful."

Robert DeNiro

Said an author, intent, on his artistic bent,
"The opinions I state are profound.
"But, attribute I must, to men who are dust,
"Or the critics will say I'm unsound."

QUOTIENT (n) "A number showing how many times a sum of money belonging to one person is contained in the pocket of another (usually, as many times as it can be got there)."
Ambrose Bierce

R

RABBI (n) The spiritual leader of a Jewish synagogue. To do their chief honor, the congregation is sometimes called "the rabble."

    Said a rabbi, one Solomon Getter,
    To a Catholic friend, Father Hetter,
    "While doubtless you're right
    "That pork's a delight,
    "I find that a wife is much better."

RABBLE (n) 1. See RABBI
    2. A large group of people who oppose the local newspaper editor's opinion. It is distinguishable from a "crowd" by the fact that, in dealing with the latter, the police count heads rather than break them.

RACE (n) 1. A classification of the human species according to skin color, e.g.RAM, white, yellow, black. Whenever persons in the various classes have to deal with each other, they often see only red.
    2. A contest designed to see which competitor finishes last. This person is favored by our divine trainer, who said: "Blessed is the slowpoke, for he shall be first and the first, last."

RACK (n) An instrument of law enforcement widely used in the past to elicit confessions of crime from innocent people. In America, it was discarded when prosecutors realized they could achieve the same results by piling on felony charges and providing the defendants with unskilled lawyers.

RACKETEER (n) An entrepreneur without a legislative lobbyist.

RACONTEUR (n) One who is paid to relate other people's stories as his own.

RAILROAD (n) A mode of transportation chiefly used, nowadays, to move truck trailers and tramps.

ramshackle (adj.) One of the four most popular architectural styles in America (the other three are called "Dorkic," "Ironic," and "Myopic," respectively). Nearly 100% of public buildings in the nation's capitol fit one of these styles, excepting only the Pentagon, which has a style all its own, called "Idiotic". The name of this building sinks to the level of its style, for neither admirals nor generals seem aware that it has both a top and bottom side, making seven in all. Thus, it should be called, "Septicon."

RAP (n) An aural assault on our culture that is misrepresented as music by corporate merchandisers who hear only the chink of money paid by the half-deaf pre and post-pubescent that buy it. The word, itself, conveys the assailant's intention toward the listener's head.

> A bothersome fellow in Gap
> Used to constantly holler out rap.
> 'Til some folks, not as hip,
> Grabbed hold of his lip
> And stapled it over his yap.

RAPIER (n) A bladed instrument widely employed during the French Revolution to predict who would lose their heads in an emergency. The prediction usually came true.

During a recent post-Olympic rapier exhibition, the Bronze and Silver medalists displayed their finesse by slicing flies in halves, then in quarters, respectively. When the Gold medalist took his turn and sliced at another fly, the latter flew away apparently unscathed. As the audience began to jeer, the champion explained: "He can still fly, yes. But, he will never have children."

RAT (n) The least appreciated animal on the face of the Earth, even though their contributions to human health is priceless. We reward their services by feeding them lethal doses of toxic chemicals, cigarette emissions, artificial food coloring, women's cosmetics, hamburger meat and french fries, rock and roll music, and other known health hazards. Is it any wonder, then, that they refuse to stay and drown on a sinking ship?

> Rats are ill-treated, with scorn are they greeted;
> Their public relations, a mess!
> Like roaches and ferrets, disdain for their merits
> Is simply a case of bad press.

READ (v) The ability to see and comprehend writing in all its forms, including daily newspapers. To be able to devote hours to the latter medium, learning about wars, homicides, rapes, pedophiles, and corporate crimes, proves the superiority of mankind over the animal species. Further, it explains why dogs have no trouble sleeping.

"Those who do not read have no advantage over those who cannot do it."

Charles Lamb

REBUFF (v) A cold shoulder to hot pants. It is a woman's way to put down an unwelcome suitor without having to move more than her tongue and is illustrated in the following examples:

1. (man) "Is this seat available?"
(woman) "Yes, and if you sit in it, my seat will be available, too."

2. (man) "Haven't we met some place before?"
(woman) "Yes, and that's why I don't go there anymore."

3. (man) "If I saw you naked, I would die happy."
(woman) "Yes, and If I saw you naked, I would die laughing."

4. (man) "Shall we go to my place or your place?"
(woman) "Both places! You go to yours and I'll go to mine."

5. (man) "Want to go back to my place?"
(woman) "I don't know. Will two people fit under a rock?"

6. (man) "What's your telephone number?"
(woman) "It's in the book."
(man) "But, I don't know your name."
(woman) "It's in the book, too."

7. (man) "Your body to me is like a temple."
(woman) "Sorry, there are no services, today."

8. (man) I would go to the ends of the Earth for you."
(woman) "Yes, but would you stay there?"

RECIDIVIST (n) 1. A criminal repeat offender who, being worthier than a homeless vagrant, receives his room and board at the taxpayers' expense and under a renewable lease.

Said a four-time recidivist, Ray,
When asked why he backslides this way:
"In prison, rent's free;
"So are food and TV.
"While only those outside pay taxes."

2. A criminal who made the same mistakes, twice. He got caught and he accepted a public defender.

> A recidivist, Rex, is a victim of sex
> And has yielded again and again.
> Once again, he's distraught that his urge got him caught.
> He got married to wife number ten.

RECOUNT (n) In electoral politics, a second tally of votes cast that more nearly coincides with the forecast of the party in power.

> An incumbent Mayor in Goaders
> Lost the election to Soeders.
> But the recount, when booked,
> Gave him votes overlooked,
> Totaling more than the voters.

RECTUM (n) What happened to the boy's genitals when he tried to jump over a barbed-wire fence.

RECYCLE (v) To convert things that are superfluous into things that are unnecessary, at great public expense.

> A hard drinking Joe, age thirty or so,
> Tended recycling machines.
> One day, filled with gin, he fell in the bin
> And out came two boys in their teens.

REDNECK (n) Southern mountain men whose numbers are declining because their stepdaughters can outrun them. Their favorite exercises are hopping up and down in church, lifting a jug to their lips, spitting tobacco juice, and mopping the floor with their wives.

You know you belong to the class if any one of the following applies:

1. You are thrown out of the KKK as a bigot.
2. You think God looks like Hank Williams, Jr.
3. You drove back and forth to elementary school.
4. You consider dating a cousin to be "playing the field".
5. Your bicycle has a gun rack.
6. Going to the toilet in the middle of the night requires shoes and a flashlight.
7. Jack Daniels is on your list of the ten most admired men in America.
8. You think a seven course dinner is a six pack and chips.
9. Your sewage treatment is provided by pigs.

10. You refer to the fifth grade as "senior year".

11. Your dad walks you to school because you're both in the same grade.

12. Your wife tells you she's "game" and you shoot her.

13. You stare at a can of orange juice because it says "concentrate".

14. You think a Volvo is part of a woman's anatomy.

15. You think the last line of the Star Spangled Banner is "Gentlemen, start your engines".

REFORMER (n) Someone who strives to make a silk purse out of a sow's ear--while the ear is till attached.

> "I love reformers who are ready to take the first step, not those who theorize about the two hundred and first."
> > President Theodore Roosevelt
> > A famous reformer, Sir Hives,
> > Civilized cannibal lives.
> > Now, whenever they boil,
> > They use British oil
> > And garnish with Commonwealth chives.

REHAB (n) Treatment for quitters.

> "I have no sympathy for these people who say they can't quit smoking. Why, in my experience, there's nothing easier. I've done it at least twenty times."
> > Mark Twain

REGULAR (adj.) Occurring in a predictable order, as in the case of a Cleveland man who sought help from his doctor to correct a serious problem.

> "I have a bowel movement every morning of my life at eight-thirty," he told the physician.

> "That's no problem," replied the doctor. "I have many patients who would give a lot to be that regular."

> "You don't understand," complained the patient, "I don't get out of bed until nine."

RELATIVE (n) 1. Someone who is linked to you by family imposition, rather than by choice.

> > Said a straight-talking fellow, named Strauss,
> > To a visiting nephew, named Krause:
> > "All relations, I think,
> > "Like fish, start to stink

203

"After spending three days in my house."
   2. Linking two or more objects, usually in conjunction
with the word "to", as in the following example:
   "Their hands were active relative to each other's body; his
hand on her breast and her fist on his nose".
   A physicist, Oliver Bright,
   Learned to travel faster than light.
   He left home one day,
   In a relative way,
   And returned on the previous night.

RELATIVISM (n) A social philosophy much prized in America for its
central tenet that nothing is either bad or good unless polling
results say so. Following are several popular applications:
   1. (politics) Bad leaders are good, relative to their
opponents, who are worse.
   2. (justice) We must forgive our enemies, but only after we
execute them for the sake of public opinion.
   3. (religion) The Golden Rule relative to corporate
executives is: "Do Unto Others Before They Do Unto You."
   4. (business ethics) Stealing from your clients is wrong.
Cheat them, instead.
   "Don't steal your neighbor's chattel!
   "It's criminal and ill-bred.
   "To get it back, he'll battle.
   "So, take his wife, instead."

RELIGION (n) Superstition masquerading as realism.
   "My husband and I divorced over religion. He thought he was
God and I didn't."
                    Imogene West

REMARRIAGE (n) The triumph of optimism over experience.
   "A woman who remarries tries her luck. A man who remarries
risks his."
                    Oscar Wilde
   Several people were placing flowers at a grave when they saw
an heard a man at a nearby grave site who was prostrate with grief.
He was crying unrestrainedly and saying," Oh, why did you have to
die...I'll never get over it..God should not have taken you"..and
similar phrases. Finally, one of the spectators interrupted the
outpouring, saying, "I'm very sorry to disturb you. Is it your
wife or child you're grieving for?" "No," the other replied, "my
wife's first husband."

REPUBLICAN (n) One of the two great political parties in America. The other one is the Inaugural Ball.

The average Republican male has an American flag in his lapel, a woman under his thumb, fat beneath his belt, and money on his mind. The average Republican female, on the other hand, has a Bible in one hand, a credit card in the other, tranquilizers in her purse, and nothing on her mind.

> A Republican boss, from Lorain,
> Succumbed to political strain.
> Friends found him dead drunk,
> With an elephant's trunk,
> Trying to fax it to Maine.

REPULSIVE (adj.) Approximating the attraction of manure.

> Said she, so impulsive, "your figure's repulsive.
> "God played me a terrible prank."
> Said he, with a sneer, "'Tweren't my bod hooked you, dear,
> "'Twas the figure you saw at my bank."

REPUTATION (n) Gossip about a person that is put through a laundering process that extracts the dirt, then spreads it.

> Said a damsel, named Anne, from a town near Spokane:
> "Since my reputation's at stake,
> "I do all that I can, when I sleep with a man,
> "To make sure that he doesn't awake."

RESOURCEFUL (adj.) The ability to achieve a difficult result, as, for example, when a starlet achieves a movie contract by using the producer's couch.

> "The mightiest oak was once a small nut that held its ground."
> Woody Allen

RESPONSIBILITY (n) The kind of duty that everybody is required to shoulder, few can face, none can stomach, and all strive to hand off to others. A political persuasion can affect the meaning of the word. For example, to a Republican, it signifies a duty owed by others to protect his rights; while to a Democrat, it signifies a duty by others to indemnify his wrongs.

> "Too many stand up vigorously for their rights and fall down miserably on their responsibilities."
> Eleanor Roosevelt

RETORT (n) A shut-up to another's put-down that comes to mind an hour too late. Several fast thinkers have famously solved the timing problem, as in the following examples:

1. When American author, Edna Ferver, came to a party wearing a pants suit, the gay British playwright, Noel Coward, said to her: "you look almost like a man." Ferber promptly retorted, "so do you."

2. After a heated disagreement at a dinner party, Lady Astor said to Winston Churchill: If you were my husband, I'd put poison in your coffee." Churchill replied, "if you were my wife, I'd drink it."

3. Socialist George Bernard Shaw sent Conservative Winston Churchill two tickets to the opening performance of his new play, Saint Joan, with a note that said, "one ticket is for you and the other is for a friend, if you have one." Churchill sent his regrets that a conflict prevented his attending, but asked for two tickets to the second night's performance, "if there is one."

4. A British peer, irritated by the slow service at an exclusive London restaurant, loudly asked his waiter, "do you know who I am?" The waiter coolly replied, "no sir, I do not, but I will make immediate inquiries and inform you directly."

5. At a reception for members of Parliament, Churchill had several brandies too many and enraged a female Laborite with his sarcasm. "Mr. Churchill," the lady fumed, "you are drunk!" "Yes, I am," he promptly replied. "But, you are ugly and I will be sober in the morning."

6. At a celebrity cocktail party, a catty society matron asked playwright and wit, George Kaufman: "Why is it that women take an instant dislike to me?" Replied Kaufman, "because it saves time."

RETREAT (v) To advance, backwards. In his memoirs, Napoleon explained that the removal of his army from Russia, in 1812, was not a retreat, but a campaign into Prussia. Similarly, a spokesman at the Pentagon explained that our departure from Viet Nam was not a retreat, but a repositioning of forces to the West Coast."
Said a chubby Marine, William Wright,
When accused of deserting the fight:
"I was not in retreat,
"But, advancing to eat.
"It's a campaign I make every night."

RETRIEVER (n) One who brings back balls or emptied trash containers, depending on whether he is a breed of dog or a well-bred husband.

"One who possessed beauty without vanity, Strength without insolence, courage without ferocity, and all the virtues of Man without his vices."

> Lord Byron
> (epitaph on the gravestone of his beloved retriever)

REUNION (n) A gathering of old classmates who have become so fat, bald, and wrinkled, that they can hardly recognize you.

REWARD (N) Payment for doing that which should have been done anyway.

"The best reward for a thing well done is to have done it."
> Ralph Waldo Emerson

RIB (n) The price Man had to pay to acquire his bitter half. It is a bargain that he could have improved upon, according to the respected biblical scholar, Bishop Hal E. Tosis. Among the Dead Sea scrolls, this eminent researcher uncovered the following account of a pre-Eve conversation between God and Adam:

God: "I am thinking of creating a companion for you, called a 'woman'. She will be your servant, doing all the housework without complaint, bearing and raising your children, caring for your every need, and satisfying your sexual desires on demand. What do you think of the idea?"

Adam: "It sounds great, but what will it cost me?"

God: "An arm and a leg."

Adam: "What can I get for a rib?"

The rest is history.

RIDDLE (n) A word-puzzle designed to separate wits from half their kind. Oedipus won the right to sleep with his mother by solving this riddle posed by the Delphic oracle: "What walks on four legs in the morning, two at noon, and three at night?" Oedipus gave the correct answer, "Man".

On one of Mart Twain's lecture tours in England, he spent an evening with Rudyard Kipling, during which the latter posed this riddle: "One occurs in ten years, two occur in twenty years, but none at all occur in a hundred years. What is it?"

When Twain promptly supplied the answer, "the letter "T", Kipling asked how he guessed it so quickly.

"Why, " Twain replied, "during my many years on the lecture tour, I've grown quite familiar with ten's and twenties, but I'm quite a stranger to a hundred."

RITZY (adj.) Anything you cannot afford.
The penthouse was ritzy, its furnishings glitzy,
Diane was a fortunate lass.
Then, she fell for a laddie and cheated on daddy,
Who threw her out on her--grass.

ROBBERY (n) An illegal act by which one party gets another's money without earning it. In its legal form, it is called "business".
An elderly woman was held up by a robber while returning home from an evening of bridge. The robber patted her down three times without finding money. "Lady," he said in disgust, "ain't you got any cash on you?"
"No," she replied agreeably, "but if you'll do that one more time, I'll write you a check."

ROBOTICS (n) A technology devoted to perfecting the successor to Man. Its new Adam and Eve are called "Rob Ott" and "Ann Droid", respectively, and their Cain is called, "Cy Borg". Following is a list of features that mark them as a superior species:
1. The ability to self-replicate without morning sickness and labor.
2. The ability to instantly turn their hearing off when rap is played.
3. The ability to instantly recall every slight or injury that anyone has ever inflicted on them in the past.
4. The ability to deal with a complaining spouse with a simple screwdriver.
5. Eliminating the need to get out of bed in the middle of the night to pee.
6. Avoiding constipation, diarrhea, menstruation, premature ejaculation, penal dysfunction, and television commercials relating to them.
"I'm an erotic guy, name of Dusty,"
Whispered he to a she, pert and busty.
When he slipped in his hand,
Her comment was bland:
"I'm a robotic gal, name of Rusty."

ROCK AND ROLL (n) Sound masquerading as music. The beat is administered by drummers and the beaten are often administered to by hearing specialists. This programmed trauma got its name from its effect on older stomachs.

ROOSEVELT (n) A dirty word to the Republican Party. In 1908, President Theodore busted trusts that financed the Party, while in 1932, President Franklin trusted the Party to bust itself.

Q. How was Franklin Roosevelt different from Moses?

A. Moses told his people: "Pack up your asses, get on your camels, and I'll lead you to the promised land." On the other hand, FDR told his people: "get off your asses and light up your camels. This is the promised land!"

"Roosevelt respects the Constitution in the same way that a tomcat respects a marriage license."

(An unnamed Republican Congressman, referring to President Theodore Roosevelt)

RULE (n) A standard of conduct intermediate between a custom and a command, but similar to both in being disobeyed--customarily or on command.

Once an immutable axiom, the "golden rule" has been amended in recent years to conform to modern conditions, as in these examples:

1. (corporate) "Do unto others before they do unto you."

2. (Democratic Party) "Do unto Republicans what they want to do unto you."

3. (Republican Party) "Those who have the gold, rule."

4. (Libertarian Party) "Do unto others, but not unto us."

RUNNING (v) A form of locomotion much admired in those we dislike. It is the subject of both praise and warnings, among which are the following instructive examples:

"My grandmother has been running five miles a day since she turned 62. Now that she's 93, we can't find her."

--"The only reason I am running a lot, now, is that I miss the sound of heavy breathing."

--"I'm running with a head of steam, a tail of lead, and no stomach for it."

--"If you want to do cross-country running, begin with a small country."

--"Medical researchers say we can add a minute of life for each 5 miles of running we do. What that means is that when we're 95, we can live 5 more months in a nursing home at $5,000 a month."

RUPTURE (n) Any sundering, from one that elicits tears (e.g., appendix), to one that evokes cheers (e.g., divorce). In the case of the second example, the word is often misspelled "rapture".

> Said a Mick, with a rupture quite raicent,
> To his doctor, in tones very daicent:
> "When you're cuttin me groin,
> "Go ahead, but don't toin
> "Your attention to what is adjacent."

RUT (n) A depression in the ground that is distinguishable from a grave only by factors of depth and privacy.

S

SABBATH (n) The ritual name given the last day in the week, "having its origin in the fact that God made the world in six days and was arrested on the seventh."
Ambrose Bierce

SABOTAGE (n) A vote by explosives.

> A landfill, installed, left neighbors appalled;
> They tried sabotage to undo it.
> But, the bomb they did make blew them up by mistake.
> Now, in pieces and bits they bestrew it.

SACRED (adj.) Infused with religious veneration, as exemplified by the following potent signs:
1. A sign of the cross, to a priest.
2. A dollar sign, to a banker.
3. A billboard sign, to an advertiser.
4. A picket sign, to a union leader.
5. A lobbyist check, to a politician.

> Said Ted to his girlfriend, named Bea,
> As he slid his hand up past her knee,
> "Don't fret nor beware,
> "For I solemnly swear
> "That your virtue is sacred to me."

SACRED COW (n) Either an object of veneration or scorn, depending on whether it is a four-legged animal in India or a two-legged animal on Madison Avenue.

SAD (adj.) A state of mind prevalent in the State of Mississippi, where heat and humidity bring more transfused blood to mosquitoes than to the Red Cross.

"You look awfully sad," said the boy to his dad.
"What causes you such sorrow?"
"Your mother got mad," he replied to the lad.
"She vowed not to speak to me for a week
"And the week is up, tomorrow."

SADIST (n) Someone who smiles while making another cry, unlike a masochist, who smiles while making himself cry. This difference explains why there are so many more sadists than masochists.

Said a bureaucrat sadist, named Larry,
Who counsels young couples in Gary:
"If I do my job, well,
"I will prove there's a Hell,
"By persuading the youngsters to marry."

SAFARI (n) A contraction of the English phrase, "so far in", it denotes a trek into darkest Africa, the purpose of which is to give wild animals their first sight of hippie white women in shorts and bulbous white men in Snoopy tee shirts. Local leaders hope to show the animals some of civilization's shortcomings so they will resist recruitment by zoos.

A much-married woman, named Terry,
Went to Zaire on safari.
When a hippo's big ass
Rose above the deep grass,
She cried, "that's my third husband, Larry."

SAINT (n) "A dead sinner revised and edited."
Ambrose Bierce

SAINT PAUL (n) A Jew from Tarsus who became a Christian by replacing the "S" in his name with "P".

A fellow, named Saul, had a serious fall
That jarred both his butt and his brain.
Sitting there in a daze, he saw with amaze
God in the form of a crane.
The bird opened its beak and started to speak
Words that sank deep in his soul:
"From now on you will preach and, humanity, teach.

211

"To lift up Mankind is your goal."
Saul was found nearly dead from that fall on his head.

Though he wrote well, he wasn't quite sane.
By inspired epistles that exploded like missiles,
He worshiped, not God, but the crane.

SALAD (n) Fresh mixed vegetables chock full of vitamins,
minerals, and members of the Cide family--Herbie, Pestie, and
occasionally, Homie.
A fine Frisco chef, named Joanna,
Learned how to grow veggies in Ghana.
No chemicals, she;
They're toxically free,
By using manure from Tijuana.

SALE (n) Surplus merchandise offered at an irresistible price
that includes a sizeable profit.
A woman, named Alice, is homeless in Dallas;
She sleeps in the street every night.
"Things I bought fill my place and my family, displace,
"But, the prices at sales were so right."

SALMON (n) A type of fish that turns red with shame when it has
sex for the first time in its life and then dies of it.
Oh, pity the salmon's sad state.
Just once in its life can it mate.
And then it must rue it;
It kills them to do it.
Is sex worth so awful a fate?

SALON (n) A ritzy shop that sells women's clothing for a
ridiculous figure.

SALOON (n) A place where men part with dollars and sense.
There are more salons than saloons in up-scale communities because
there are more women there with ridiculous figures than there are
men with sense.

SALTPETER (n) A chemical compound that, when placed in food, is
widely used in prisons and military services to reduce a man's
libido. According to Congressional budget-cutters, sprinkling
ordinary table salt on his peter would produce the same result at
a fraction of the cost.

SANDWICH (n) A light-meal concoction that consists of a bread or bun wrapping around concentrated cholesterol. It is a staple of fast-food restaurants and is beloved by teenagers, bachelors, and cardiologists everywhere.

It was named after the Earl of Sandwich, who was esteemed by his contemporaries as a dandy and a wit. In one event that established his reputation, the Earl was dancing with a lovely partner when a jealous rival stopped them, shouting:

"You, sir, will die either of the pox or on the gallows."

Sandwich promptly replied: "that will depend, sir, on which I embrace--your mistress or your morals."

SANE (adj.) According to modern psychiatry, a person is sane if he understands the consequences of his action and has the ability to control it if the consequences may be harmful. By that definition, most young men who marry are not sane. First, while they may know the binding nature of the ceremony, it has been established by surveys that they do not understand such inevitable consequences as squalling babies, staggering debts, and the hellish visitations of PMS. Further, the few who do understand these consequences are rendered powerless to avoid them by the testosterone that hardens both body and brain.

SANTA CLAUS (n) The patron saint of Christmas, having ousted Christ from the role due to lobbying from the Chamber of Commerce. In Western countries, a man lives through six stages of Santa Clausitis: first, he believes in him; then, he does not believe in him; then, he dresses up like him; next, he looks like him; then, he thinks he is him; finally, he disappoints his heirs, who thought he was him.

The story of fat Santa and his flying reindeer bring joy to every parent in Christendom and cynicism to their children, most of whom are old enough to know a lie when they hear it. Despite an imperfect grasp of the math involved, the kids sense the following factual defects in the story:

1. Thanks to time zones and the Earth's rotation, Santa has a total of 31 hours to distribute toys to 375 million Christian children (he ignores Moslem, Jewish, and Buddhist youngsters) in 107.5 million households.

2. To do the job in time, he must make 822.6 visits per second. So, he has one one thousandth of a second to hop out of his sleigh, drop down the chimney, place the toys, eat whatever snacks were left, climb back up the chimney and jump into the sleigh.

3. To keep to the schedule, the sleigh must move at a speed of 650 miles per second, 3,000 times the speed of sound (for

comparison, the fastest space craft has been clocked at 27.4 miles per second).

4. Assuming each child gets no more than 2 pounds of toys per household, the sleigh is carrying 321,300 tons (not counting Santa, who is overweight). To pull this load, he needs 14,200 reindeer with flying ability, whose weight increases the total payload to 353,000 tons.

5. A weight of 353,000 tons traveling at a speed of 650 miles per second creates tremendous wind resistance and heat. The reindeer will absorb 14.3 quintillion joules of energy per second, thus bursting into flame almost instantaneously. The entire team of 14,200 reindeer will, therefore, vaporize within 4.2 thousandths of a second.

SAP (n) 1. A contraction of "Homo Sapiens", the definition has narrowed over time and now means any person who votes for a Libertarian and any spouse of that voter who does not sue for divorce, immediately.

2. The lifeblood of every tree, which logging saps empty without remorse or indictment.

SARACENS (n) Moslem fighters whose curved swords, called a "scimitar", razed the heads of many Crusaders during the Middle Ages.

A Crusader's wife at a garrison
Ran off with an amorous Saracen.
She was not oversexed,
Neither bitter nor vexed.
She just wanted to make a comparison.

SATAN (n) Loser in history's first political contest--CEO of the universe. He still suffers from a tarnished image caused by negative campaigning from pulpits and poor pr.

From the accounts   of those who knew him intimately--Goethe, Twain, and Shaw--he is an urbane, witty, and convivial fellow with whom anyone could spend a pleasant evening. By contrast, accounts by those who know God best--Southern Baptists, televangelists, and the Pope--portray Him as something of a stick in the mud. From this comparison derives the motto:
"Heaven for climate and Hell for companionship."

Said Satan, "despite my address
"And the frightening way that I dress,
"My negative rating,
"That causes such hating,
"Results from a prejudiced press."

214

SATIRE (n) A form of humor that ridicules a serious subject, e.g., the Congressional Record, California's annual budget, military procurement. Jonathan Swift went to his grave, broken hearted, because his great satire on the British monarchy, "Gulliver's Travels", was lightly regarded as a fantasy for children.

A satirist, Jonathan Swift,
Wrote an epic to give Brits a lift.
Though the nation did need it,
Only children would read it,
Which rift stiffed his gift and miffed Swift.

SATISFY (v) To instill the belief that a need has been filled when it has only been delayed. Rome's need to believe that its many gods were superior to Christ's one was temporarily satisfied by throwing Christians to the lions. When it soon discovered, however, that there were many more Christians than lions, Rome made itself the capitol of Christianity and installed the Pope as its leader--where he still reigns supreme over Christ.

SATYR (n) A creature, half man and half goat, wearing horns, who lived in ancient times and played pipes. It is now extinct in that form, having evolved into a horny old goat who smokes a pipe and plays with himself.

The most famous of the Satyrs was Pan, who is said to have driven young women into a frenzy with his pipes. This is no big deal. Nowadays, the same effect can be achieved by the gift of a credit card.

SAUSAGE (n) A meat product made by combining animal organs, chemical preservatives, seasonings, and plenty of gall. It is to meat what particle board is to lumber, rap is to music, tabloids are to journalism, soap operas are to culture, and head cheese is to brains.

"If you like sausage, do not watch it being made."
Bismarck

When a meat cutter, Gossage, started marketing sausage,
His pets thought it all very nice.
But, the cat, Puss McBride, was fit to be tied
When she found he was using her mice.

SAVOIR FAIRE (n) Literally, to know what to do. the word connotes the ultimate in self-control amidst a crisis. Following are several superb examples of the faculty:

1.   A husband, finding his wife in bed with a stranger, says, "excuse me, please continue."

2. The wife and her lover in the previous example do continue.

3. A woman, when told that the back of her skirt was tucked into her panties, says: "I know. I thought I would stay cooler this way."

4. A burglar, found by police breaking into a house, says: "I misplaced my keys."

5.   A bowler, after sliding the length of the alley with his thumb stuck in the ball, says: "I needed a strike."

SCRATCH (v) Together with beer, candy, food and sex, one of life's greatest pleasures. Like the others, however, misery results if it is carried to excess.

> "He's a lucky son of a bitch
> "Who has a scratch for every itch."
> > Ogden Nash
> > An elderly guy from Iraq
> > Wears his arm in a surgical rack.
> > Said he, with a catch,
> > "All I did was to scratch
> > "An itch in the small of my back."

SCREW-UP (n) The normal result of careful planning.

> "The best laid plans oft go awry.
> "Then men do curse and women cry."
> > Robert Burns

SECRETARY (n) Someone who works four times harder than her boss for one-fourth of his pay.

SEDUCER (n) Someone who promises a woman that he will mine gold for her, then gives her the shaft. For those readers who prefer another metaphor: he gets sweet on a woman, calls her "sugar", puts chocolate in her stomach, a baby in her uterus, and winds up paying her a lump sum.

> A smooth-talking guy with a wink in his eye
> Seduced a proud lady named Myer.
> When he found her in tears, she wielded her shears;
> Now the pitch of his voice is much higher.

SELF-CRITICISM (n) A mild vaccine that mitigates the harsher criticism by others. One of the most common types involves a humorous reference to the speaker's childhood and is intended to disguise the fact that the kid really was a pain in the ass.

Following are several examples of this strategy:

"When I was a child, I was so slow that I didn't get a birthmark until I was eight."

"I was not a loveable child. One Summer, my parents bought me a sandbox and filled it with quicksand."

Rodney Dangerfield

SELF-DELUSION (n) 1. A pitiable mental aberration from which all those who think themselves better than you suffer.

2. A mental defect that induces a man to suck in his stomach when about to mount bathroom scales and a woman to attribute sagging breasts to gravitation.

SELF-ESTEEM (n) An opinion that sharply differs from the prevailing view held by those who know you best.

SELFISH (adj.) Catering to your necessity rather than to another's vice, e.g., taking the last chocolate mint.

SENILITY (n) A mental condition that afflicts everyone more than twenty years older than you and those who, whatever the age, oppose your opinions. You can tell when you suffer from the condition when any of the following occur:

1. You discover your mouth making promises your body cannot keep.

2. When a waiter asks how you want your steak done, you tell him "pureed."

3. You are out of breath after going down a flight of stairs.

4. It takes a couple of tries before you can walk over a speed bump.

5. People always include "at your age" in a compliment.

SENSE (n) The rarest of human gifts, everyone being convinced that others lack it.

> Said an unhappy wife, named Hortense,
> When her spouse dissipated the rent:
> "To the bars he goes, drinkin.
> "When he's loaded, I'm thinkin,
> "The man's got no dollars and sense."

SETTLE (v) In law, the act of resolving a dispute by compromising the deeply-felt convictions of the parties, thereby leaving everybody unhappy except the lawyers, who urged it, and the judge, who gets to play golf.

"It is better to debate a question without settling it than to settle a question without debating it."
Joseph Joubert

SEWAGE (n) A byproduct of eating that proves the axiom, "garbage in, garbage out." It is what is left of food after the sugar, fat, coloring and flavoring agents, preservatives, pesticides, herbicides, calories, and cholesterol, have all been absorbed into your tissues and blood.

From the dawn of human history until this Century, raw sewage was returned to the soil and the Earth bloomed. Now, after it has been thickened by polymers, disinfected by chlorine, and deodorized by hydrogen peroxide, it is sludge fit for nothing better than to be sprayed on corn and rice fields--contaminating both.

Cried a panicky boss in South Bend,
"We've a blockage of sewage to mend."
But, the Mayor's calm words
Stilled the fears about turds:
"It will come out all right in the end."

SEX (n) A person's gender or activity, depending on whether identification or recreation is involved.

"The difference between having sex and reading about it is the same as the difference between lightening and the lightening bug."
Mark Twain

"Women need a reason for sex, while men only need a place."
Billy Crystal

SEXES (n) The male and female genders that litter the Earth with litters, defy family planners, cause traffic jams, inspire authors to explain them, and are responsible for divorce lawyers.

The difference between the sexes has been scientifically analyzed using the following equations:
1. Smart man + smart woman = romance.
2. Smart man + dumb woman = affair.
3. Dumb man + smart woman = marriage.
4. Dumb man + dumb woman = pregnancy.

There are profound philosophic differences between the two, the most important of which are these:

1. A woman worries about the future until she gets a husband, while a man never worries about the future until he gets a wife.
2. A man considers himself a success if he makes more money than his wife can spend, while a woman considers herself a success if she can find such a man.
3. A woman marries a man expecting him to change, but he never does, while a man marries a woman expecting her not to change and she always does.
4. A woman has the last word in any argument, while anything a man says after that is the beginning of a new argument.
5. A man will pay $2 for a $1 item that he needs, while a woman will pay $1 for a $2 item she does not need.

SEXUAL (adj.) Possessing hormones more powerful than neurons.
> A super-stud, Rex, enjoys daily sex.
> It's a pleasure no scruple forbids.
> He thinks it so jolly because he's a collie
> And need not support all his kids.

SEXAGENARIAN (n) Someone who is old enough to know better and young enough to do it anyway.

SEXUAL HARASSMENT (n) Male behavior that he calls gallantry until she calls a lawyer.
> Said a girl to her swain, "I have to complain;
> "My boss slid his hand down my spine."
> "Harassment!" cried he. "Not hers," answered she.
> "The ass that he meant was just mine."

SHALLOW (adj.) The mind of one who is incapable of understanding the difference between adultery and fornication. He is likely to protest: "I've tried both and there is no difference."
> His friends think him callow; his enemies, shallow.
> He's so tongue-tied that some swear he's mute.
> But, Timothy Gore is a man girls adore;
> They all think his assets are cute.

SHOTGUN (n) A firearm much prized in West Virginia for facilitating marriage. There, A shotgun wedding is said to be a case of wife or death.

SHOPLIFTER (n) Someone who discounts the price of merchandise she likes to zero and gives new meaning to the art of shopping on a tight budget.

SHOWOFF (n) A child more talented than yours.

SHYSTER (n) While there are tricks to all trades, his trade is all tricks.
>Said a lawyer, named Priest, to a client he'd fleeced:
>"Call me "shyster," but don't call me "crook."
>"My skill saved you more than the loss you deplore;
>"I am worth every thousand I took."

SIGN (n) A form of advertising that ranges from the uplifting (library) to the depressing (laxative). While most commercial signs are inept and foolish, others send both spirits and sales soaring. In the latter category belong these noteworthy examples:
>1. (plumber's truck) "We repair what your husband fixed."
>2. (pizzeria) "Seven days without pizza makes one weak."
>3. (tire store) "Invite us to your next blowout."
>4. (message on a psychic's answering machine) "Don't call me. I'll call you."
>5. (electrician's shop) "Let us remove your shorts."
>6. (veterinarian office) "Be back in five minutes. Sit! Stay!"
>7. (restaurant's non-smoking section) "If we see smoking, we'll assume your on fire and take appropriate action."
>8. (on a maternity room door) "Push! Push! Push!"
>9. (optometrist's office) "If you don't see what you're looking for, you've come to the right place."
>10. (muffler shop) "No appointment necessary. We'll hear you coming."
>11. (Burmashave) "Don't lose your head to save a minute. You need your head. Your brains are in it."
>12. (Burmashave) "He drove too long and now he's snoozing. What happened next is not amusing."

SIMILE (n) Like something else, as in these examples:
>1. As happy as a rat in a dumpster.
>2. As focused as a whale positioning himself for sex.
>3. As lucky as a dog near a bitch in heat.
>4. As sincere as a politician's smile.
>5. As passionate as a whore's caress.
>>Said Timothy Taft, in a capsizing raft,
>>At a shark sign and storm that was brewing.
>>"Like an Army recruit, from a drill sergeant brute,
>>"I am in for some heavy ass chewing."

SIN (n) Human misconduct of a type that varies according to the several religions, as in these examples:

1. (Catholic) Any immoral act of a parishioner that can be enjoyed by a priest and absolved for both.
2. (Baptist) Any immoral act that the minister finds enjoyable.
3. (Jewish) Eating pork, marrying a person named "Murphy", or refusing to donate to Israel.
4. (Unitarian) Any act that benefits God, alone.
5. (Capitalist) Any act that lowers profits.
6. (Republican) Any governmental act that benefits someone below the poverty line.
7. (Democrat) Any governmental program that is not entirely paid for by Republicans.

SINFUL (adj.) 1. The nature of an act to those who believe in Hell. Prominent among these believers are Catholics and wives. The first of these may avoid the heat by confessing the sin to obtain what is called "absolution". As practiced in the Church of Rome, this is a sacrament that wipes away the sin, thus freeing the sinner to repeat it.

For wives of all religious persuasions, the synonym for absolution is called "divorce."

Said a Catholic fellow in Bend,
On seducing the wife of a friend,
"Though it's sinful, I'm sure,
"I'll confess, to be pure.
"Then, I'll do it again and again."
(2)
Said Paddy, when Father O'Dell
Warned his drinking would send him to Hell:
"If by being gin-full,
"God thinks I am sinful,
"Then my pals will be down there as well."

SKEPTIC (n) Someone for whom experience has stifled optimism, ingratitude poisoned charity, jingoism smothered patriotism, reason invalidated faith, and swapping genes with chimpanzees seems the only way to improve the human species.
A skeptical fellow in Tate
Claimed his air bags would never inflate.
His wife, more pragmatic,
In a manner dramatic,
Proved him wrong by rear-ending some freight.

SKIING (n)1. A Winter sport that mainly consists of falling down

and partying.
   2. God's gift to orthopedic surgeons.
      Said William McKee, "I'm crazy to ski
      "For my body is usually supine.
      "To help in a clutch, I carry a crutch
      "And plaster to fuse-up my spine."

SKY DIVING (n) An activity that should not be attempted if the
adage, "If, at first, you don't succeed," applies to you.

SLANG (n) "The grunts of a human hog."
      Ambrose Bierce

SLOB (n) Someone who wears his stomach on his sleeve.
      A slovenly fellow, named Fiss,
      Wears shirts that are stained and amiss.
      Said he, with some shame,
      "My mouth is to blame.
      "Though I aim for it, often I miss."

SLUMLORD (n) A monarch whose domain consists of debris in the
shape of apartments. The tenants pay dearly for the privilege of
entertaining rats, lice, cockroaches, and the angel of death.
      A slumlord, named Simon LeTree,
      Never lets extra bodies stay, free.
      When a tenant said that
      Two rats chewed her cat,
      He doubled her rent for the three.

SMELT (n) A small fish identifiable by its odor. The name is a
contraction of the original, "smell it".
      When asked why God dealt a fish the name "smelt,"
      Some answered, "because of the smell of it."
      But, I must demur because I infer
      He named it so just for the halibut.

SMILE (n) A starved laugh, mature grin, or reformed grimace, that
may be caused by anyone of these five common conditions:
   1. Someone you intensely dislike told a joke that was hilarious.
   2. Your back is being scratched, again, where it itches.
   3. You have a sweet and sour stomach from Chinese food.
   4. Your employer or rich aunt told you a joke that was not a joke.
   5. You are thinking of how you will inflict pain on an enemy.
      "I'm smiling because I don't know what's going on."
         (bumper sticker seen in Los Angeles)

SMOTHER (v) To deprive someone or something of oxygen. The word evolved as a contraction of "his mother" and denoted the compulsion of many mothers to impose emotional guilt trips, unsolicited advice, and third-degree interrogations on bachelor sons.

SNOB (n) 1. Someone who believes that Adam and Eve are his ancestors, but that Darwin was right about everyone else.

(1)

One Timothy Cobb, a certified snob,
Deigned to marry Miss Imogene Brect.
As the price of his name, he got from the dame
Her promise to genuflect.

(2)

A wonderful place is Long Island;
The home of incurable snobs.
Where money's the quality standard
And those who don't have it are slobs.

SNORE (n) Sound during sleep that prevents another's sound sleep.
Researchers believe that snoring reproduces primal grunts made by our earliest ancestors, leading some anthropologists to maintain that Man is more likely to have evolved from pigs than from monkeys. This theory undoubtedly explains our liking for ham.
"Why is it that the one who snores always falls asleep first?"
Joan Rivers

(1)

A married young woman, Hortense,
Shot her husband, whose snore was immense.
Based on sounds he emitted,
The jury acquitted,
Declaring: "'twas self-defense."

(2)

An elderly woman, named Sophie,
Several times shot her husband, Dan Brophy.
When she pleaded, "he snored,"
From the jurors, tears poured
And they voted to give her a trophy.

SNUB (v) To behave toward another as though she does not exist; to stage a disappearing act without the aid of magic.
A much-despised society maven in New York accosted the playwright, George Kaufman, at a cocktail party and asked for his advice. "Why do so many women seem to take an instant dislike to me, George?" "Because," he replied, "it saves time."

SOB (n) 1. A wrenched cry.
  2. A wretch of a guy.

SOBER (adj.) 1. Denied the most popular excuse for folly.
  2. Lacking a sense of humor.
    Said a man from Podunk, when charged as a drunk,
    "I'm no worse than a judge on the Bench."
    To Officer Milt, this was proof of his guilt,
    For the man was Chief Magistrate Dench.

SOCIALISM (n) An economic philosophy whose essence is to give to
those who need that which, otherwise, would go to those who have.
It differs from Capitalism, whose essence is to give to those who
have that which, otherwise, would go to those who need. Both
systems differ from communism, whose essence is to give nothing
to either group of that which is not available to anybody.

SOCIOLOGIST (n) A PhD researcher who identifies society's major
problems, their causes and their victims. then publishes the
findings--minus solutions--in three volumes to great acclaim.
Whenever one of these authors is asked why solutions are never
included, she will tell you that they are for the taxpayers to find
and fund.
    Two sociologists were walking along a sidewalk in a suburban
part of town when they passed a man lying in a nearby ditch,
bruised and bleeding. One sociologist turned to the other, saying:
"we've got to find the guy who did this. He needs help."

SOCRATES (n) A Greek philosopher-teacher who talked himself to
death. His way of teaching, known as the "Socratic Method", was to
require his students to answer questions that he, himself, could
not answer. In this way, he gained the learning for which he is
still celebrated.
    His teaching method has long been preferred by college
professors in America. They quickly saw the utility of a system
that permitted blockheads to hide their ignorance.
    Of his many biographies, perhaps the most penetrating is the
one written by a fifth-grader in Idaho, from which the following
excerpts are taken:
    1. "Socrates was an old Greek teacher who went around giving
people advice, so they killed him."
    2. "He died from an overdose of wedlock, which is poisonous."
    3. "After his death, his career suffered, but he did not."

224

SONNET (n) A type of literature that could be verse, but is probably better, than the limericks in this work. The most celebrated exponent of the form is Shakespeare, whose genius is illustrated by the following excerpt from one of his most admired sonnets:

"Shall I compare thee to a garbage pail?
"Oh no, thou art more odorous and bulky.
"Rough hands did cart thee off to jail
"And there thou sits, syphlitical and sulky.
"One lesson Nature teaches well.
"For sluts so ugly, life is Hell!"

One of the most poignant of all marital sonnets is one written by an unknown husband:

"If I ignore you more than's right
"And don't respond as you desire.
"If I escape oft from your sight
"And from your childish prattle, tire.
"If I withhold endearing speech
"And kiss you less than you demand.
"Do not, for these things, roar and preach.
"Love's never ruled by loud command.
"My fate's the same as doomed MacBeth.
"My wife is nagging me to death!"

SPACE (n) 1. What a Republican puts between himself and a homeless person, a Democrat has in her purse, a Libertarian has in his head, a Communist has in her pantry, and a Socialist puts between himself and work.

2. Formerly thought to be a ceiling over Earth to which many lights were affixed. This romantic concept has been debunked by modern scientists, who favor a cosmological junkyard of icy rocks, super-heated gasses, "dark matter" (known to exist only by faith),

and a near-Earth ring of old rockets, containers of nuclear waste, and the kind of debris found on Earth only at swap meets.

Noted Catholic cosmologist, Heath,
"I've the secret of space to bequeath.
"It isn't unending
"Nor dimensional bending,
"It's merely a gap in God's teeth."

SPECIALIST (n) Someone who is ignorant about a lot of things, except one.
    A medical specialist, Peet,
    His wife, he neglected to treat.
    When she died of the flu,
    He asked, "what could I do?
    "My specialty's working on feet!"

SPECULATOR (n) Someone who gambles money on the stock, bond, or real estate markets. If he does the gambling, he is called "broke". If another does it for him, he is called "broker". The latter title is explained by the fact that, in addition to losing his investment, the speculator has to pay a fee to the one who lost it for him.

SPEECH (n) The unique ability humans have to bore or fleece each other. For the latter purpose, politicians use it much like dentists use a drill. But, whereas dentists fill mouths while emptying pockets, politicians fill ears while the pockets are picked.
    "When all is said and done, more is usually said than done."
        Will Rogers (commenting on Congress)
    "A speech should be like a mini-skirt--long enough to cover the subject, but short enough to maintain interest."
        Adlai Stevenson
    "Most speech is unnecessary and, when it is necessary, what is said is mostly unnecessary."
        Henry Fielding

SPERM (n) A strong swimmer that is egged-on to win a race.
    Said one sperm to another, "let's make her a mother."
    And off they did swim in a burst.
    But, the egg was immune, for last Monday at noon,
    Other swimmers had gotten there first.

SPOONERISM (n) A type of pun in which the head and tail of the shaggy dog are reversed in one swell foop. Following are several memorable examples:
    1. Time wounds all heels.
    2. A genetic researcher cloned himself, but the latter turned out to be exceedingly profane in his speech. Horribly embarrassed, the researcher pushed his creation off a high roof to his death, causing the next day's headline to read: "Scientist makes obscene clone fall."
    3. The San Diego police incinerated a ton of seized marijuana and a flock of terns flew through the smoke plume. The next day's newspaper headline read: "No Tern Was Left Unstoned."

SPRING (v) What a woman does when her fanny is pinched and a man does when his zipper catches.
"Hope springs eternal," Shakespeare said.
It springs from boyhood on.
For young men, it doth spring in bed;
For old men, on the john.

STATESMAN (n) "A dead politician."
Ambrose Bierce

STATISTIC (n) A Protean fact that can assume any shape that will support the conclusion of the person citing it. One example is a recent governmental finding that three out of every four Americans suffer from some type of mental illness. You can benefit from this valuable statistic by considering your three best friends. If they are normal, then you need help.

STEALTH (n) A tactic used by criminals, politicians, police, and young men, to screw someone.
Napoleon Strick was subtle and quick
When courting fat Margaret Tegnant.
When she thought tiny Nap merely sat on her lap,
He was stealthily getting her pregnant.

STIFLE (v) To suppress looney or seditious opinions so that yours can be heard.
The Pope's harsh on quacks who pervert the facts;
Fake science is quickly detected.
They're stifled, who try to foster the lie
That Jesus was not resurrected.

STILL (n) A device for making whiskey that is much prized in the Ozarks. It is so-called because of the effect its product has on the vital signs of new consumers.
A thirsty young fellow, named Darrows,
Discovered a still near Mount Barrows.
When found on his face,
He was buried in place;
he had pickled himself like the Pharaohs.

STOCK BROKER (n) Someone whose profession it is to sell stock to clients and make them broker than before.

STORY (n) A description of one or more events that never actually happened, called "fiction", or much of which never happened, called "non-fiction". Some of the most enduring stories are those written for children, among which are "High Tee", "Grim Fairy Tales", "Hansel and Gretel Munchies", and "The Lizard of Ooze". Following is a list of charming tales for kiddies that have not yet made it into print:

1. "Tantrums That Really Work"
2. "The Kids' Guide to Hitchhiking"
3. "Kathy Was So Bad Her Mom Stopped Loving Her"
4. "Dead Cats Go to Hell"
5. "The Little Sissy Who Snitched"
6. "Some Kittens Can Fly"
7. "Grandmother Chooses Her Funeral Music"
8. "The Magic World Inside the Abandoned Refrigerator"
9. "Strangers Take You On The Best Walks"
10. "Whining, Kicking and Crying to Get Your Way"
11. "Things Rich Kids Have, But You Never Will"
12. "Pop! Goes The Hamster--And Other Great Microwave Games"
13. "Where Would You Like to Be Buried?"
14. "Daddy Drinks Because Of You"

STRAITLACED (adj.) Literally, tightly corseted; figuratively, prudish. The modern equivalent is "tight-assed," which illustrates how far our language has progressed in clarity and candor.

STRESS (n) The conflict between the mind, which wants us to behave, rationally, and the body, which wants us to kick the shit out of some son of a bitch that richly deserves it. A renowned British behaviorist, Sir Thomas Muffin, maintains that, if our bodies would prevail more often, there would be less stress and fewer shits in the world.

STUPID (adj.) The condition of those who have given a piece of their mind to too many other people. Following are several more tactful ways to describe the condition:

1. "He is depriving some village of its idiot."
2. "He is   several cards short of a full deck."
3. "He could hold an intellectual conversation with a wall."
4. "She has a photographic memory without any film."
5. "She's as   Bright as Alaska in December."
6. "He must have fallen on his head from the family tree."

7. "If you give him a penny for his thoughts, he's overcharging you."

8. "He's so dense, light bends around him."

9. "She must have gotten into the gene pool when the lifeguard wasn't looking."

"God must love stupid people, because he made so many of them."

George Carlin

SUAVE (adj.) The ability to tell someone to "go to Hell" in such a way that he looks forward to the trip.

> A stock broker down in Ariz
> At selling, is suave and a whiz.
> But, his clients are tragic
> 'Cause his tongue works black magic,
> By changing their money to his.

SUBLUXATION (n) To chiropractors, the source of every physical ailment possible in a human being. Their practice is to relieve the condition by simultaneously adjusting the patient's body and bank account. The treatment usually is at least 50% effective.

> In Britain, a subluxation blighter
> Has a practice that makes his life much brighter.
> His adjustments, first rate,
> Help his patients lose weight,
> For their wallets leave many Pounds lighter.

SUICIDE (n) A permanent solution to a temporary problem.

SUMO (n) The most popular sport in Japan, during which overweight men push each other around a ring. It is properly ridiculed in America, where overweight men chase an inflated pig's bladder around a field.

SURGEON (n) The interior decorator of the human anatomy. Alterations are chiefly made by the scalpel, a sharp instrument named after the American Indian practice of removing the scalp of their enemies with one fell swipe.

> There was a young man with a hernia
> Who said to his surgeon, "gol dern ya;
> "When you're fixing to cut,
> "Go right ahead, but,
> "Don't mess with what don't concern ya."

229

SYMPATHY (n) An inexpensive way to comfort a friend in need. It is the only thing that Republicans are willing to waste on the homeless and that Democrats believe they can afford.

Said Officer Riley, in Vail,
To a homeless young couple, quite pale,
"Though it may make you bitter
"That in Vail, you are litter.
"Still, our landfill is better than jail."

SYNOPSIS (n) An outline of a novel that serves the same purpose and value as boiling whale blubber, i.e., it boils away useless fat and leaves the valuable residue. The New Testament of the Bible is a perfect example of this. Before it was abridged to its present length, it was swollen by thousand of pages of fish stories told by the apostles.

T

TALK (n) The only thing elderly men can do in bed, besides sleeping, and that Elderly women do do everywhere, anytime. It is said to be cheap because the supply is so much greater than the demand.

"The only way a husband can be sure that his wife will listens to his every word is to talk in his sleep."
Phyllis Diller

TABOO (n) An unwritten social or religious law that bans certain personal behavior and varies throughout the world. Here are several examples that every reader will recognize:

(America)
1. Spitting on the sidewalk instead of in the street.
2. Having an affair with your sister instead of with your wife's sister.
3. Letting your dog dump on a neighbor's front lawn instead of in his bushes.
4. Using cash instead of a credit card.
5. Smoking criminalized marijuana instead of subsidized tobacco.

(France)

6. Smiling at an American tourist instead of sneering
at her.

(Germany)

7. Openly praising Hitler instead of secretly
admiring him.

England)

8. Openly praising the monarchy instead of secretly despising
it.

(Japan)

9. Buying an American car made in Japan instead of
a Japanese car made in America.

(China)

10. Shouting "Free Tibet", instead of "Free
Enterprise".

> An American tourist, Magoo,
> Shattered a Russian taboo.
> He sprayed Arrid, well,
> And, deprived of his smell,
> Offended more than a few.

TACTLESS (adj.) Suffering from Foot In Mouth disease.

TART (n) Either a baked item with a filled body that is sold by
a girl in a shop off the street, or, a girl who shops her full
body on the street to a half-baked item.

Outside Caesar's Palace in Las Vegas, the celebrated
personal injury lawyer, Melvin Belli, was once introduced by a
friend to a beautiful local businesswoman, this way:

"Bonnie, I want you to meet Melvin Belli, the King of
Torts." Turning to Belli, the friend continued, "Mel, I want you
to meet Bonnie, the Queen of Tarts."

TAX (n) Government action which, in another context, is called
"extortion" and punished as a felony.

> An artful old dodger, named Max
> Was charged with not paying his tax.
> "I'm not guilty," said he,
> "For as sure as can be,
> "I mailed in the money by fax."

TAXPAYER (n) A species of biped mammal that is abundant in all
civilized nations. It is much admired for the richness of its
thick skin, which is fleeced, annually, for the profit of its

leaders. Two slogans epitomize the state of mind of those who pay and those who take:

    (taxpayer)   "Everything I have belongs to you."
    (IRS) "We've got what it takes to take what you've got."

(1)

Fumed a taxpayer, Phil, when an IRS bill
Caused him to blowup, sky high.
"He can't add worth a damn, that scrooge, Uncle Sam,
"But, he sure as Hell can multiply."

(2)

A taxpayer, Zeke, in a moment of pique,
As a capital loss, took son Bill.
When the IRS sued, he calmly argued:
"My return on investment is nil."

(3)

Cautioned the IRS Chief,
To a taxpayer seeking relief:
"Since the judges are paid
"From the payments you made,
"Don't look to the courts for relief."

TEACH (v) A magical process by which the notes of a teacher become the notes of his students, with none of them having to think about it.

    "Men should be taught as if you taught them not
    And things unknown proposed as things forgot."
        Alexander Pope

TEAMSTERS (n) A labor union of movers and shakers. The moving is done by trucks, while the shaking is done to shippers who want to use non-union haulers.

TEDIUM (n) A state of mind induced in friends by the display of photo albums containing pictures of your children in cute poses. The word's liturgical origin has long been suppressed by Rome, but recent leaks prove that it derives from the Latin text, "Te Deus" ("To God"). Anyone who has ever snored through the sermon of a
Catholic priest will wonder why the linkage was not guessed long ago.

TEE (n) In golf, a place where many swingers can be found, but only a few straight shooters.

A man was preparing to hit his ball off of the ladies tee at the first hole when the clubhouse loudspeaker blared: "will the man at the ladies tee please move back to the men's tee before hitting his shot?" As the golfer appeared to ignore the instruction, it was repeated with increased vehemence, causing him to turn toward the clubhouse and shout:

"Will the man at the microphone please shut up and let me take my second shot?"

TEENAGER (n) Someone in a transitional stage of development midway between infancy and adultery.

"Hire a teenager while he still knows everything!"

(sign in an employment office)

TEESHIRT (n) An article of clothing that is worn as an under garment by young men, for warmth, and as an outer garment by young women, for advertising. It has become a popular medium for pithy witticisms, among which the following are prime examples:

1. "That's it! I'm calling Grandma."
2. "The wrinkles you see are makeup."
3. "Rehab is for quitters."
4. "My dog can lick anyone."
5. "I'm finally 21 and legally able to do everything I've been doing since 15."
6. "I'm from West Virginia, where there are a million people and fifteen last names."
7. "I'm out of estrogen and I've got a gun."
8. "A journey of a thousand miles begins with a cash advance."
9. "They call it 'PMS' because 'mad cow disease' was already taken."
10. "Quoting one is plagiarism. Quoting many is research."

TEETH (n) Bony protrusions from the gums that come and go and come and go. The first loss involves the earliest experience with a fairy, while the second loss involves an extraction from both the mouth and wallet.

"Brush the teeth you want to keep."

(Advice on a bumper sticker)

When a wife asked her elderly dear
To ardently nibble her ear,
He went from the bed
To the bathroom, instead,
For the teeth he was soaking in beer.

TEETOTALER (n) A fanatic who denies his body the fun of falling down, throwing up, and hanging over.

"I feel sorry for teetotalers. When they get up in the morning, it's the best they will feel the entire day."
                    W.C. Fields

TELEMARKETER (n) A commercial psychic whose sales calls are timed to coincide with your dinner.

There's a young telemarketer, Bryan,
Who, from loneliness, truly was dyin.
Then, he sold a bikini
To pretty Jean Rini
And went to her place for the try on.

TELEVANGELIST (n) A television huckster who sells rights in Heaven to people he has wronged on Earth. Resembling a Mexican stock, he pays no interest, changes his principle at will, and lacks any maturity.

TELEVISION (n) A visual mode of communication often called a "medium" because it is rarely done well.

"After watching many programs, I think television broadcasting should, more accurately, be called 'broadchasing'."
                    Fred Allen

Said a TV executive, Brewers,
Responding to critical skewers:
"Sure our programs are dumb,
"Leaving brains dazed and numb,
"But, that's normal in all of our viewers."

TELLER (n) A female bank employee whose primary duty once was to tell customers that their accounts were overdrawn (hence, the title). In recent years, two changes in the job description have occurred:

1. She must explain why the bank's fee for overdrawing a checking account exceeds the amount of the overdraft, itself.

2. She now uses a computer, which permits her to make the same mistakes, faster.

Prayed a pious check writer, in a church near South
            Brightor,
"Hear this prayer to my teller, Miss Haver:
"Just once, for my sake, make an adding mistake
"That turns out to be in my favor."

234

TELLTALE (adj.) Exposing a concealed fact, as in: "the telltale tightness in her shoulders revealed that, instead of getting a facelift, she had her body lowered."
"The telltale bra," said Joan McGraw,
"Is proof that Tom has cheated.
"Without that snitch, the son of a bitch,
"My divorce suit, he'd defeat it."

TEMPTATION (n) The strongest force on Earth, compared to which gravity is negligible. For while some people are grave, everyone on Earth is tempted.
"I can resist everything but temptation."
Oscar Wilde

TENNIS (n) A game played by people least likely to succeed in marriage. This is because, to tennis players, love means nothing.
Following are several variations in the sport that appeal to specific groups:
1. (Cinderella tennis", for senior citizens) If the players are lucky, they get to the ball.
2. "Guerrilla Tennis", for young men) A player aims his balls at another player's balls, to curtail courtship competition off the court.
3. ("Mafia Tennis", for gang members) Players have a ball taking pot shots with their rackets.

TERMITE (n) A creature whom God hath created for the profit of exterminators and building contractors.
Oh, pity the wood-loving termite,
Always munching, like some kind of saw.
Though the taste fills her brain with delight,
She has slivers from anus to jaw.

TERROR (n) Fear, at its most acute stage, as illustrated in each of the following situations:
1. A letter just received from the IRS audit office.
2. A call to the mother of a teenage daughter from Family Planning, confirming the girl's appointment.
3. The father of a teenage son, who has just found plans for making a pipe bomb in the boy's Chemistry book.
4. Your mother-in-law has just told you that she is planning a permanent move to your neighborhood.
5. Your employer just announced that it is downsizing and a colleague is measuring your office to see if her desk fits.

235

6. A married daughter just telephoned you to say that she is getting a divorce and asks if she and her four children can move in for a few months.

TERRORIST (n) 1. Someone who employs pain and intimidation to achieve a desired goal (see MOTHER).
2. A person who makes grave decisions and communicates them, explosively.
"It's God's responsibility to forgive Bin Laden and it's our responsibility to arrange the meeting."
(U.S. Marine Corp's Bulletin after 9/11)
(1)
A Middle-East terrorist pyro
Made a time-bomb designed by a tyro.
He set it for eight
(Which was one hour late)
Now, the fellow is all over Cairo.
(2)
From a terrorist Mom to her sloppy son, Tom,
This ultimatum did issue:
"Stop using your shirt or your fanny will hurt;
"When you go to the toilet, use tissue."

TEXAS (N) A State that has more oil wells than cattle and more votes cast than there are voters. The latter fact is explained by the voter category, "Posthumous", that is recognized in every Republican county.
"When I die, I want to be buried in Texas so I can remain politically active."
(A sign in Austin)
Oh, give me a home where God makes
Those gun-toting, Bible-quoting, flakes.
Where civil rights are deplored,
Executions have soared,
And the Bushes grow fat on tax breaks.

THANKSGIVING (n) A national holiday that celebrates the victory of the earliest undocumented aliens in America over the resident population. It was made possible by smallpox, syphilis, influenza, and other pestilential weapons that God (glory to his name) supplied His Christian flock to dislodge the heathen rabble that littered the early landscape.
When the pilgrims took land, they baptized it;

Planted corn when the natives advised it.
But, 'twas more than advice
That made their crops nice.
The natives, themselves, fertilized it.

THERAPIST (n) (physical) A health care professional whose mission
is to push, pull, tug, and twist, patients so as to make them
insurable for treatment by an orthopedic surgeon.

(1)

A therapist, Michael, in Bend

Is known as an orthopod's friend.
By tugging and twisting,
And patients resisting,
He fractures some bones in the end.

Mike explains why his method's so fell:
"Doctors heal broken bones very well.
"But, healing arthritis
"And chronic bursitis
"Is costly and harder than Hell."

2. (occupational) A person who, for a fee, forces a square peg
into a round hole, then pronounces the peg round.

THINK (v) A mental act that all animal species are said to be
capable of, excepting only human male adolescents, who can only
lust. The famous French philosopher, Descartes, professed to prove
that he existed by the argument, "cogito, ergo sum" ("I think
therefore I am"). Although he did not say precisely what this
proved him to be, his contemporaries thought he was a fruitcake
for thinking that he needed proof.

"Have you ever stopped to think--and forgot to start it up
again?"

(bumper sticker in Washington, D.C.)

THOUGHT (n) An ethereal manifestation of the mind, which is an
incorporeal product of the brain, which is a gelatinous mass of
tissue that has no market value unless it comes from a pig. Is it
any wonder, then, that so many people are fat and have swinish
thoughts?

"If you are lost in thought, it may be because you are in
unfamiliar territory."

Steve Allen

237

THRIFT (n) The habit of avoiding waste, it is a virtue to everyone except the poor. Conservative legislators practice it by cutting back on welfare programs. Liberal legislators, on the other hand, practice it by trying to limit the number of conservatives.

"Every night before you go to bed, empty your purse or pants of pennies and drop them into a container placed for the purpose. After a few years, you will realize that this sort of thrift doesn't amount to anything at all."
Gurney Williams

TIAJUANA (n) Literally, "Aunt Jane", this city across the border from San Diego exhibits all that is good and bad about anyone's old aunt. Here are a few traits that you will recognize:
1. Loves to nip, but holds it well.
2. Believes in Heaven, but lives in Hell.
3. Mostly fragrant, but sometimes smells.
4. Romantic music, but strident yells.
5. Generous to all, but poor as a mouse.
6. On most days, sober, but on holidays, a souse.
   Tijuana has handsome senoras,
   Foul water and harsh maquiladoras.
   But, with NAFTA's treaty,
   The people aren't needy,
   'Cause they're flooding a border that's porous.

TIME (n) A non-renewable resource that sticks at thirty nine years, for women, rotates around to a second childhood, for men, heals all wounds and wounds all heels. The shortest interval is between the changing of the traffic light from red to green and the sound of the car horn behind you. The longest interval is the time it takes a funeral procession in Mexico to reach its destination when there is only one set of jumper cables available.
"Time may be a good healer, but it sure is a lousy beautician."
Dorothy Parker
"The time is always right to do right."
Martin Luther King

TIME CHANGE (n) A foolish government practice in most of the nation in which time is forced to spring forward one hour each May, thereby shortening everyone's life to the same degree. Luckily, the politicians cannot withstand the public outcry and always restore the hour before the Fall elections.
A bright young eccentric, named spears,
Lived incredibly long, it appears.

He added, some say,
Ninety days every May
And lengthened his life twenty years.

TIME TRAVEL (n) The type of travel one experiences during rush hour on any urban freeway in America--taking twice the time to travel a mile.

Soon, experts say, there'll be a way,
Back in time, we'll travel.
Some Physics breaks is all it takes;
Space secrets to unravel.
When these are taught, some astronaut
Will prove it is achieved.
But then, alack, he might come back
Before he was conceived.

TITTER (n) A man with a compulsion to fondle women's breasts.

A titter named Tony from Tyre
Fondled each breast he'd admire.
Then, one of the girls
Grabbed hold of his pearls.
Now he speaks a complete octave higher.

TOAST (n) A ceremonial tribute--usually made with an alcoholic beverage--to the achievements of some person in attendance. Its accuracy is inversely proportional to the number of drinks the toaster consumed.

"May you live to be a hundred and may the last voice you hear be mine."

Frank Sinatra (his favorite toast)
A tipsy Best Man, name of Lott,
Made the following toast and was shot.
"Let us drink to the bride
"Who, it can't be denied,"
"Earns her bread on her back more than not."

TOBACCO (n) A plant much esteemed in advanced nations for its ability to limit population. In America, this is deemed to be so valuable a social benefit that farmers are paid subsidies to grow it.

Cigarette manufacturers do their part by heavily advertising to adolescents. This is based on the well-known marketing fact that the only thing the latter can control are good habits.

239

TOILET (n) The highest achievement of science for the comfort of Mankind, it relieves bodily strain and mental anxiety, provides privacy, promotes meditation, and is responsible for most of the greatest ideas generated since its invention. Developed by one Thomas Crapper, it is a singular instance of a man so enamored with his invention that he adopted its gutter name as his own.

(1)

Hail to the toilet, the Common Man's throne;
Of its merit, it's hard not to gush.
By a poker game metaphor, value is shown,
For it gives to us all a royal flush.

(2)

A Sierra Club member named Mack
Received an award for his knack
Of conserving much water
By preaching   "folks oughter
"Use outhouses dug out in back."

TONGUE (n) A human organ that is imperfectly designed for its main function, i.e., lying out of both sides of the mouth. To remedy the defects, genetic engineers are hard at work evolving a tongue that wags at both ends and is forked.

According to pain specialists, the tongue is the second most sensitive part of a man's body if it is stuck to an icy flagpole.

Abroad, English is rough; its spelling is tuff.
Axense diverje in all sexshuns.
Japanese say "Irene" when they're meaning "I lean,"
And are shocked by our many erections.

TORNADO (n) The inspiration for the proverb, "it's an ill wind that blows nobody good". The phrase was coined by an insurance executive, just before tripling the premiums on his company's windstorm policies.

A weather forecaster, named Ray,
Predicted a beautiful day.
A tornado, him smote,
Forced his words down his throat,
And left him with nothing to say.

TORTS (n) The technical name for automobile negligence cases that support 70% of the lawyers in America, 80% of all liability insurance companies, and 100% of all auto body shops. It is unknown in Japan, which undoubtedly accounts for the backwardness of that nation.

Pleads a lawyer, named Swartz, who's a master of torts:
"Be just to my clients--in cash!"
But, his fees are so high that when juries comply,
He winds up with most of the stash.

TRADITION (n) A custom that depends on momentum and is divorced from common sense. Here is a list of several that have achieved sanctity in their native countries:
    1. (America) It is the tradition to settle a personal dispute with a handgun.
    2. (Great Britain) It is the tradition to revile the monarchy and revere the monarch.
    3. (France) It is the tradition to despise a foreign tourist and worship his money.
    4. (India) It is the Hindu tradition to kill Moslems and venerate cows.

TRAVEL (v) To move from one place that is familiar and comfortable to another place that is strange and lacks the amenities of home; to replace past boredom with present discomfort, and to pay two months' income for the privilege of taking pictures to which your family and friends will be indifferent.

TRIAL (n) A courtroom contest between two or more parties to determine who among them has the best lawyer. During the course of it, the lawyers oppose each other, both are opposed by the trial judge, who is opposed by the appellate courts, which apply archaic legal principles that are opposed to common sense. Thus, the "search for truth" is, too often, a quest by moles for a path through a maze.
    Following are several actual examples of lawyer-moles in action:
    1. Lawyer: "Did you ever blow your horn before the accident?"
    Defendant: "Sure, I played the horn for 15 years and even studied it in school."
    2. Lawyer: "I understand that you have a 20 year-old son, is that right?"
    Witness: "Yes."
    Lawyer: "Well then, how old was he when he was born?"
    3. Lawyer: "How far apart were the two vehicles at the time of the collision?"
    Defendant: "Not far apart at all."
    4. Lawyer: "Well, officer, were you there at the crime scene until the time you left?"
    5. Defense Lawyer: "So the date of your baby's birth was August 8th, is that right?"

Female Plaintiff: "Yes"

Lawyer: "And what were you doing at the time?"

6. Lawyer: "Now, Mrs. Siegel, you have had 3 children, I believe."

Plaintiff: Yes"

Lawyer: "How many were boys?"

Plaintiff: "None of them were boys".

Lawyer: "Were there any girls?"

7. Lawyer: "You say the stairs went down to the basement?"

Witness: "That's right".

Lawyer: "And these stairs, did they also go up?"

8. Lawyer: "How was your first marriage terminated?"

Defendant: "By death."

Lawyer: "By whose death was it terminated?"

9. Witness: "The robber was about medium height and had a full beard."

Lawyer: "Was this a male or a female?"

10. Lawyer: "Is your appearance here pursuant to my deposition notice?"

Plaintiff: "No, this is how I always dress when I go to work."

> Fumed a criminal lawyer named Bligh,
> Told his client confessed on the sly:
> "My duty, know you,
> "Is to tell him what's true,
> "So he won't tell police what's a lie."

TRIFLE (n) Anything insignificant, as in these examples:

1. Chastity, to a sailor;
2. Truth, to a used-car dealer;
3. Humility, to a movie star;
4. Marine ecology, to an oil rig operator;
5. Cleanliness, to a small boy.

> There was a young lawyer named Rex,
> With diminutive organs of sex.
> When charged with exposure,
> He said, with composure,
> "De minimus non curat lex."
> ("The law does not regard trifles.")

TRINITY (n) In Catholic doctrine, the word signifies the "Father, Son, and Holy Ghost." Some Unitarians risk eternal damnation by flippantly referring to it as "Big Daddy, Junior, and the Spook."
So far, none of the three seems to mind.

TROLLOP (n) A woman of flexible morals, intermediate in behavior between a prostitute and a college student.

(1)

An angry young woman, named Grace,
Proudly threw all the cash in his face.
"I am not a cheap trollop,"
She said, with a wallop,
"But, a Divinity student at Pace."

(2)

When her anger subsided, she sweetly confided
(Retrieving the money with grace),
"I'm taking this, purely," she offered, demurely,
"To buy some string panties with lace."

TRUISM (n) A statement that most everybody accepts as true without the need for verification. The following examples have, however, been validated by both Republican and Democrat pollsters:

1. The reason women over fifty usually do not have children is because they would lay them down and forget where they put them.

2. A mystery that science has not yet solved is how you can eat a two-pound box of candy and gain five pounds.

3. The surest way to forget all your troubles is to wear tight shoes.

4. The nicest thing about living in a small town is that, when you don't know what you're doing, someone else does.

5. Before you can get use to yesterday, along will come tomorrow, leaving no time to do anything today.

6. Another one of life's mysteries is why, when you hang your clothes in a closet for a few years, they get two sizes smaller.

7. Women who mix Valium with birth-control pills will have kids, but won't worry about it.

8. Some women worry a lot about nothing and then marry him.

TRUST (v) To place someone in a position to cheat you when, otherwise, it would have taken him a bit longer.

Said a dad to his little girl, Sue,
After dropping her, hard, at the zoo.
"Though your fanny will burn,
"There's this lesson to learn:
"Don't trust any man to support you."

TRUTH (n) A perfect fit between your opinions and reality. In the case of those persons having the temerity to contradict you, only the one who can prove it is your enemy.

"If trouble comes from truth, let it come. Better that there be trouble than that truth be hidden."
 Thomas Hardy, quoting Saint Jerome
 "The truth may make you whole, but on the whole, it often makes no sense."
 Bertrand Russell

TRUTHFUL (adj.) The condition of an infant or an older person who has not yet been found out.

TRY (v) The fourth component of a six part sequence involved in human action. The other five are "idea", "intention", "goal", "failure", and "blame".
"If you try, you will sometimes fail; but, if you do not try, you will always fail."
 William Jefferson Clinton
 "If at first you don't succeed, don't try skydiving."
 George Carlin

TRYST (n) A romantic try that succeeds. A related French word is spelled "triste" and means "sorrow." These two words demonstrate the close relationship that often exists between different languages. No person of sense can deny that many trysts result in triste for the woman and treats for the man.
 Scoffed a medical doctor, to Liszt,
 Who could not lift it up on a tryst:
 "When you play with your organ
 "From nacht until morgen,
 "You have to expect it to list."

TURPITUDE (n) In Texas, a type of immorality that is reached when a man is found in bed with a woman who is not his wife or with a man who is.
 A lawyer in all States may be expelled from the profession if he commits an act of "moral turpitude" against a client. The courts deem this punishment so extreme that they shrink from imposing it. So, an incompetent lawyer who loses his client's case, then charges a generous fee for doing so, is not guilty. But, a brilliant layman who impersonates a lawyer and wins the case will be prosecuted for "practicing law without a license."

TUSH (n) The word people use who are too cultured to say, "fanny" and too cowardly to say, "ass."

244

An old country priest had an ass
Whose colon was swollen with gas.
When he poked at its tush,
Gas escaped with a woosh
And blew him halfway through the Mass.

TUTOR (n) Someone who passes on to another the misinformation passed on to him.
A tutor in Bath tutors tutees in math
And is praised for numerical talents.
But, though he is big on calc, geom, and trig,
His checkbook is never in balance.

TWINS (n) Two people who are disagreeable for the same reasons.
Bob: "I understand you had a date with Siamese twins."
Bill: "Yes, last night."
Bob: "Did you have a good time?"
Bill: "Yes and no."

TWIT (n) A tiny wit, about half the size.

TYPICAL (adj.) As obnoxious as others in its class. Here are several representative types:
1. The typical man never tries to conceal a belch.
2. The typical woman begins putting her face on five minutes before it is time to leave for an appointment.
3. Because of his training in preparing fee bills, the typical lawyer has great skill with multiplication, but cannot add worth a damn.
4. The typical doctor knows the daily details of his brokerage account better than his appointment book.
5. The typical auto mechanic spends as much time looking for other things to fix as he does fixing the reason for the car being there.

TYRANT (n) In history, a harsh authority who punished offenses, severely, frequently flew into rages, would not listen to reason, and whose decisions were arbitrary and final. Nowadays, this person is called, "mother."

U

UBIQUITOUS (adj.) The ability to be in all places at one time, but not in all places at all times (which is "omnipresence"). The first is a power possessed only by God, while the second is a characteristic of telemarketers.

UGLY (adj.) 1. (Woman) Having a face that is her misfortune, unless she has a fortune, in which case the face is said to have "character." Money--or the lack of it--also explains two common metaphorical expressions. If she has it, then her face "makes time stand still," but if she is poor, that same face is said to "stop a clock."
　　2. (Man) Having a face that varies from "repulsive" through "bearable" to "interesting", depending on whether the observer is a stranger, his wife, or his employee.

　　In a modern fairy tale, a pretty girl found an ugly frog and took it into her bed that night. When she awoke next morning, the frog had changed into a handsome young man. She could hardly believe it! Neither could her parents.

　　Nowadays, many pretty girls kiss wealthy men who look like frogs, hoping to change them into husbands.

　　"I may be fat, but you're ugly and I can lose weight." (message on a bumper sticker)

> There was a young man from Omar
> Who said, "I'm not handsome by far.
> "But, my face, I don't mind it
> "Because I'm behind it.
> "It's those up in front that I jar."

ULTIMATUM (n) 1. A request made out of a gun barrel.
　　2. An unconditional demand before concessions.

> From a passionate wife in Cape Spear,
> This ultimatum, severe:
> "Either take me to bed,
> "As if we just wed,
> "Or I'll tip off my husband you're here."

UMGAWI (n) A common Swahili word whose meaning may be gleaned from the following story:
　　During a goodwill tour of Kenya, an American foreign service

officer was gratified by the reaction of villagers to his speech. As he told them about America's friendship and intended foreign aid, the crowd intermittently shouted: "Umgawi!"

Later, the village chief escorted the officer on a tour of the village's cattle herd. "Watch out for the umgawi," the chief warned.

> Each day in Hawaii brings tons of umgawi
> And I'm damned if I know where they go.
> Some say, in the sea, but I disagree;
> I think it helps pineapples grow.

UNAMERICAN (adj.) The boorish behavior of any nation that goes to war as a last resort rather than as the first, spends more money on health care than weapon systems, bans handguns, and provides food and shelter to all its citizens.

> "It's un-American pap,"
> Cried he to the pacifist chap.
> "If you do not desist
> "Preaching not to enlist,
> "I will plant both my fists in your yap."

UNBEARABLE (adj.) The condition of a woman who had a hysterectomy.

UNBELIEVER (n) Someone who does not believes that God made him an atheist. Some famous people have had this conviction, among them the following:

1. Albert Einstein: "I cannot imagine a God who rewards and punishes the objects of his creation."

2. Charles Darwin: "I can hardly see how anyone ought to wish Christianity to be true. The plain language of the text seems to show that those who do not believe will be everlastingly punished and this is a damnable doctrine."

3. Thomas Edison: "So far as the religion of the day is concerned, it is a damn fake. Religion is all bunk."

4. Sigmund Freud: "Religion is comparable to a childhood neurosis."

5. Clarence Darrow: "I don't believe in god because I don't believe in Mother Goose."

UNBIASED (adj.) 1. The correct cut during circumcision.
2. Dead

> Said Mary O'Rouse, to praise her dead spouse,

247

"Right now, he's unbiased--that's great!
"I say that, well knowing, that where he is going,
"There's nobody there he won't hate."

UNBIRTHDAYS (n) 364 days in the year when nobody asks you about your age. It was coined by Lewis Carroll to give people whose birthdays fall on national holidays an opportunity to party.

UNCTION (n) A type of lubricant widely used by climbers to move up employment and social ladders. In its extreme form, Catholic priests employ it to signal parishioners that it is time for them to die.
To facilitate the passage, the clerics apply ointment to various body parts, helping some slide past Hell. Physicians condemn this practice, arguing that only they have the training and license to tell people when to die and help them do it.

UNCTUOUS (adj.) The manner of a salesperson before you reject his pitch. Afterward, the manner is called, "perfunctuous."

UNDERSTAND (v) The second of three steps involved in human intelligence, the first and third being "to perceive" and "to ignore."
"What I do not understand is how I understand."
        Albert Einstein
    Archimedes, who understood math,
    Was stupid about his own bath.
    When he sat down in haste,
    The water displaced
    Spilled and filled his wife brimful of wrath.

UNDERSTANDING (n) The ability to accurately perceive another person's faults and your own virtues.
"My husband and I had a perfect understanding; that's why we got a divorce."
    Pamela Harriman (referring to her ex, Randolph Churchill)
        "His understanding was so keen
        That all things that he felt, heard, seen,
        He could interpret without fail
        (Whether in or out of jail).
        He wrote at inspiration's call
        Deep disquisitions on them all.

Then, penned, at last, in an asylum,
Performed a service to compile them.
So great a writer, all men swore,
They never had not read, before."
Ambrose Bierce

UNICORN (n) 1. A minor foot problem.
2. A mythical horse with a sharp horn sticking up from his
forehead. In England, belief in the animal's existence was once
so widespread that the following was a common parental warning:
"Never play leapfrog with a hiccupping Unicorn."

UNION (n) A labor organization that is defined, differently, by
the three groups most affected--employees, management, and the
public.
1. (employees) A group of workers whose aim is to live as
well as the CEO's pet.
2. (management) A conspiracy of employee-ingrates whose aim
is to reduce corporate profits below levels necessary for stock
option redemptions.
3. (public) An organization of radical employees whose aim
is to disrupt the flow of goods and services to the public, and
drive up the prices it must pay for them.
Said computer tech, Walt Heiser, to a union organizer:
"To join up would be clear irreverence.
"Management is a friend I'll support 'til the end!"
Next day, he was sacked without severance.

UNISEX (adj.) Anything that is intended for use by members of
all three sexes--males, females, and ballet dancers in tights.
Ernestine Block got a terrible shock
When she entered a unisex stall.
The man up ahead never faltered, but said,
"Kindly wait 'til the last droplets fall."

UNITARIAN (n) A member of a liberal church society run by ex
Rotarians, who were tired of having to rotate whenever religion
was mentioned.

UNKEMPT (adj.) The appearance of one who dresses for decency
rather than order and uses a mirror only when it is attached to a
car.
A used car dealer and his wife, from Los Angeles, lined up

with twenty other tourists at an audience with the Pope. As the latter moved from person to person, shaking hands, he lingered in front of an unkempt young man, who wore a patched and dirty overcoat. Much to the astonishment of the others, the Pope embraced him, pressing his cheek against the other's beard.

"Did you see that?" the car dealer said to his wife, excitedly. "What a story back home if I can get him to do that to me." He rushed over to where the young man was standing, bought the unsightly overcoat for twenty dollars, put it on, and rushed back to his place in line as the Pope approached.

Sure enough, when the Pope reached him, instead of shaking hands, he embraced him. As their cheeks pressed, the Pope whispered, "I thought I told you to get the Hell out of here!"

UNMARRIED (adj.) Unmarred
"You have to kiss a lot of frogs before you can find a Prince."
                    Dorothy Parker
    "My advice is to marry," said old Father Perry;
    "It will strengthen your faith very well."
    "You mean," she invited, "that after I'm plighted,
    "I will start to believe there's a Hell?"

UNPRECEDENTED (adj.) Having never happened before, as in the following examples:
    1. A Republican who cares for the homeless.
    2. A Democrat who cares for a Republican.
    3. A Libertarian who opposes a landowner's plan to site a slaughterhouse in a residential neighborhood.
    4. A law student who rejects an opportunity to cheat on a final examination.
    5. A teenager who does not believe he knows everything.

UNTOWARD (adj.) Moving away from an object.
    Said an amorous widow from Broward,
    Of a timorous suitor named Howard.
    "He's a nice sort of guy,
    "But, terribly shy;
    "When I grab him, his action's untoward."

UPKEEP (n) Formerly, the amount of income needed to maintain the family's standard of living. Presently, however, the term is applied to mean the number of credit cards needed to maintain the standard of living depicted on television.

"If your outgo exceeds your income, your upkeep will be your downfall."

Charles Short

URBANITY (n) The polish unique to city dwellers. The cause of this condition is explained by the old proverb: "It's the rubbing that brings out the shine."

URBAN SPRAWL (n) A city on steroids.

URINAL (n) A public plumbing fixture where a bad circumcision is obvious to the fellow standing at the adjoining fixture.

URINATE (adj.) A fine compliment to any woman, using a scale of one to ten.

URANIUM (n) A metallic element that emits radiation strong enough to stimulate the homicidal tendencies of physicists and world politicians.

UROLOGIST (n) A people plumber whose work on urinary tracts leaves male patients feeling bored.

USED (adj.) An archaic term that once described a vehicle that was driven by a former owner. Nowadays, the dealers prefer "pre-owned", in the apparent belief that potential buyers will somehow think it was never used, before. The charade seems not worth the effort, since every "new" car is thrice pre-owned before it reaches the ultimate buyer--by the manufacturer, the wholesaler, and the dealer.

USURY (n) Excessive interest charged by one not licensed, as a bank or finance company, to do so.
> A usurious banker, named Pree,
> Refers to his debtors with glee.
> "When they get in arrears,
> "I don't shed any tears,
> "For they forfeit their assets to me."

UTOPIA (n) A mythical nation created by King Henry the Eighth's Lord Chancellor, Sir Thomas More, in his book of that name. More wrote that his nation was superior to England in every way and that he yearned to live there. He got his wish. The blade of

251

Henry's executioner headed him there.

> A famous Lord Chancellor, from Brit,
> Imagined a nation with wit.
> He said the best thing
> Was, the place had no king
> And he quite lost his head over it.

UXORIOUS (adj.) Nurturing a swollen affection for one's spouse.
This is contrary to the predilection of the great majority of
married people in America, who either divorce or fight it out to
the bitter end.

V

VAGRANT (n) One whose sole means of support is the sidewalk.
> An oft-cited vagrant named Brown
> Thinks he's straight and the Mayor's lowdown.
> "I just lie in the park,
> "On the grass after dark,
> "While the Mayor lies all over town."

VAINGLORIOUS (adj.) Describing the joy of being superior to all
other people. Most notable among those who possess this quality
are college deans, military officers, corporate CEO's, and young
people everywhere.
> Admirals, all, strut very tall,
> Acting as if they're victorious.
> But, they fight for promotions and rarely on oceans;
> The whole lot is simply vainglorious.

VALENTINE (n) A greeting card that commemorates the amorous and
commercial success of the Valentine family. The first of these
belongs to the patriarch, Saint Valentine, who is reputed to have
embraced nuns and got into the habit. His descendants are said to
have founded the Hallmark Company.
> Cried the wife of a fellow named Doug,
> When he gave her a kiss and a hug:
> "Hip, hip, hooray!
> "It's Valentine's Day!
> "Let's finish this down on the rug."

VALENTINE'S DAY (n) The annual holy day for card and candy sellers that demonstrates how profitable the facade of love can be. Romantic poems grace the cards that have the highest profit margins, among which the following are notable examples:
1. "How do I love thee? Let me count the ways.
"Up on top and down below are my most common lays."
2. "My love is like a red, red, rose
"Whose petals all have fallen.
"My love is like a rotten peach
"In which a worm is crawlin."

VALIANT (adj.) In military affairs, having a deficient understanding of the risks involved. To inspire their troops, generals of many nations have long recited the following proverb:
"While cowards die a thousand deaths, the valiant die but one, 'tis said."
As a public service to the many readers of this admirable work and their military-age relatives and friends, your Editor's research uncovered a second sentence belonging to the proverb that has been suppressed:
"Now, the valiant sleep within their graves, while the cowards sleep in bed."

VANITY (n) The tribute fools pay to the values of the marketplace.
"I won't wed him," said Allison Fride.
"He's not fit to have me as his bride."
"I am smarter than he
"And as sweet as can be,
"While he's vain and swollen with pride."

VASECTOMY (n) A type of surgery that denies a man recreation.
A mother of nine, name of Liz,
Dragged her spouse to a surgical whiz.
Said Liz: "tie a knot
"Or take what he's got.
"I won't have him back as he is."

VEGAN (n) An extreme vegetarian who spurns any food that had a mother, but believes in breast feeding.
A rigorous dieter, Lumm,
Will not eat a fattening crumb.
A Vegan, he'd druther
Eat naught had a mother,
So no milk, but plenty of rum.

VEGETARIAN (n) Someone who shuns meat, as unhealthy, and eats vegetables fertilized by manure.

A strong vegetarian, Kate,
Never put meat on her plate.
Then her spouse, to be nice,
Ground a mouse in her rice
(which she vowed was the best thing she ate).

VENIAL (adj.) The lesser of two levels of sins in the Catholic Church. The superior type is the "mortal" sin, so-called because only live people can commit it. According to Catholic dogma, a priest may absolve a parishioner of either type, thus freeing him or her to repeat it.

VERBOSE (adj.) 1. The condition of one whose train of thought lacks terminal facilities.

2. A flood of words during a drought of ideas.

"He can compress more words into the smallest ideas of any man I know."

Abraham Lincoln (referring to Salmon Chase)

Says Duncan McFife, "I don't speak to my wife.
"To do so would be too abrupt.
"It's not that all day I have nothing to say.
"It's because I don't dare interrupt."

VERDICT (n) A jury's decision after a trial, arrived at in spite of the law and evidence. In criminal cases, it is influenced by the following factors, listed in descending order of persuasion:

1. The defendant's race and appearance.
2. The number of jurors suffering from common senselessness.
3. The skill of the lawyers at concealing the truth.
4. The nature and extent of the judge's prejudices.
5. How many jurors have sour stomachs.
6. How far the judge has progressed into senility.

VIAGRA (n) A drug that makes a man outstanding. An 80 year old man asked his doctor for a prescription so he could buy a quarter pill of Viagra. "Why do you want only a quarter of a pill?" asked the latter in surprise. "I just want to stop peeing on my shoes," the patient replied.

VICE-PRESIDENT (n) The human outhouse in the Executive Branch of the Federal government. He is regularly dumped on, is frequently pissed, emits a lot of gas, is sat on by most everybody, is often flushed, and gets shit from the President to work on.

VICIOUS (adj.) The chief character trait of the man who deliberately stole the last parking space that you were heading for.

VICISSITUDE (n) A word that college students use to impress and authors use to depress. All others use "change."
> A virtuous nun at Saint Jude
> Succumbed to a vicissitude.
> One day, while confessing,
> She started undressing
> And Danced through the church in the nude.

VILIFY (v) To describe another, with no retouching, when he cannot touch you.
> Said a woman, named Forst, of a man she divorced:
> "He's a beast who could murder his mother."
> Said her ex: "I agree, though she vilifies me,
> "But, the woman I'd kill is not mother."

VINDICATION (n) The recognition that some person, previously thought to be wrong, was right all along. Historically, it has been much easier for critics to admit their error after the wronged person has died, thereby avoiding liability for defamation.
> "Of all the sweet phrases that I know,
> "The sweetest is this: 'I told you so.'"
> > Robert Simmons
> "Galileo is wrong!" the Pope said.
> So, he put him on water and bread.
> But, Gal had the last laugh
> When the See saw its gaffe.
> Only, by then, he was dead.

VIRGIN (n) A female sub-species of Homo Sapiens that was once plentiful, but is now extinct. Her vanishing is confirmed by the disappearance of the adjective, "chaste", in favor of the verb, "chased."
> Mary is widely believed to have been a virgin when Jesus was conceived. While we do not know how Joseph reacted to the news, we do know that parents of young women have long greeted similar claims with profound skepticism.
> A young virgin, in Sledd, took a toad to her bed.
> Overnight, it had changed to a Prince.
> When her parents berated, this is what the girl stated;
> But, her mother was hard to convince.

VIRTUE (n) A temporary abstinence until a better opportunity appears.

VIRTUOUS (adj.) Not having had the opportunity to sin.
>A virtuous nurse, in Saint Pete,
>Told a medical student in heat:
>"You can't take me to bed
>"Until we are wed.
>"But, do what you like on this seat."

VIRUS (n) The diagnosis of any illness the real cause of which the doctor does not know.
>Said an eminent doctor, in Stowe,
>To his Medicare billing clerk, Flo:
>When I haven't a clue,
>"Say it's virus-based flu.
>"We can't charge if you say I don't know."

VITAMIN (n) A chemical compound that is effective in curtailing the income of physicians and is, therefore, demeaned by them.
>"Vitamins are all junk! Claims of value are bunk!"
>So say some respected MD's.
>But, when no one is peeking, off they go sneaking;
>Twice daily, a thousand mg's.

VITUPERATION (n) Verbal abuse on steroids. It is a modern assault in which the tongue substitutes for a fist, wounds are caused by cutting aspersions, bruises, by hard opinions, and the victim survives to retaliate in kind. Third party witnesses tend to agree with both combatants.

VOCATION (n) The nature of one's employment, sub-divided into innumerable categories. Each of these is considered demeaning and ridiculous by many employed elsewhere. In America, the only category that is universally demeaned is law. This is best illustrated by the maxim: "While there are tricks to all trades, law is a trade of all tricks."

Job placement experts report that many people are denied positions due to their perceived "unsuitability"--as in these examples:

1. An aspiring teacher has no class.

2. A trainee in a frozen juice factory could not concentrate and was canned.

3. An apprentice lumberjack could not hack it and got axed.

4. Many men employed in muffler factories quit because the work is exhausting.

5. Some apprentice barbers fail because they just can't cut it.

6. Delicatessen workers often fail because, no matter how they slice it, they cannot cut the mustard.

7. More than a few aspiring surgeons never get a license to practice because they are awful cutups.

8. A good many fishermen quit because they find they cannot live on their net income.

9. A vocation in pool maintenance frequently fails because it is too draining.

VOICE MAIL (n) The surest way to measure what relatives, friends, and business associates, think of you. According to the eminent communication scientist, Dr. I. M. Phony, a callee's opinion of you is inversely proportional to the time it takes to get a return call. So, if the call-back is prompt, she thinks highly of you; if it takes several days, she thinks poorly of you, while if it is not returned at all, either she does not think of you at all or she is an adult child.

VOLATILE (adj.) The tendency of a solid to turn into gas (see BAKED BEANS).

A bombastic lawyer in Mobile
Loves baked beans and talking a good deal.
While visiting friends,
Gas burst from both ends
And spun him back home like a pinwheel.

VOLCANO (n) A natural phenomenon marked by a blowing top, much heat, fearful noise, and a lot of gas. Such eruptions sometimes occur in mountains, but are more frequent in mothers.

Many famous songs have been inspired by volcanic eruptions, among which are these unforgettable ditties:

1. "No crater love have I."
2. "Mighty lake a rose."
3. "Lava, come back to me."
4. "Oh pumice me that we will never part."

VOLUNTEER (v) What many people do following good advice, but few follow with good deeds.

A skater who fell through thin ice
Thanked a man volunteering advice:
"Your idea that I pray
"Is well meant, I must say,
"But, a rope would be awfully nice."

VOTE (n) The means by which Citizens in America separate
candidate wheat from chaff and elect the chaff.

VOTER (n) Someone who elects a villain pretending to be a fool,
then complains when he turns out not to be a saint.
    "A voter should select a candidate like a
cantaloupe--squeezing hard to see if there is any rot."
                    H. L. Mencken
    "Voters are most remarkable in Chicago and Houston. In the
first, because of their readiness to vote twice; in the second,
because of their ability to vote when they're dead."
                    Harry S. Truman
        Said a patriot, Cindy, in Terra Haute, Indy:
        "I'm here each election, please note.
        "Though I lack any clues of the candidates' views,
        "I think it's my duty to vote."

VOW (n) An important part of a marriage ceremony performed in a
church. It consists of a solemn oath by both prospective spouses,
"in the sight and hearing of God," to love and honor each other.
Formerly, the bride also pledged to "obey" her husband, but since
the feminist movement discovered that God was a "she", that verb
has been discarded from the ceremony as unenforceable.

VULGAR (adj.) Lowdown conduct that offends highbrow
sensibilities. Here are several examples that may have offended
you in the past:
    1. Spitting on your lawn instead of in your neighbor's
bushes.
    2. Blowing your nose on the floor instead of in your hand.
    3. Eating food with a knife instead of with your fingers.
    4. Using the Lord's name in vain instead of with effect.
        Said a flatulent fellow who farted,
        To his horrified hostess, who smarted:
        "That it's vulgar, I've known.
        "But, as physics has shown,
        "An ass and its gas are soon parted."

WAGNER (n) A German operatic composer whose name is either mispronounced or misspelled. He said his main purpose in writing operas was to show the superiority of the ancient mythical gods over the modern mythical one. While the latter condemns orgies, the former (and Wagner) enjoyed them, which may explain why any one of his operas draws a bigger attendance than a Sunday Mass.

"Dick Wagner's music is better than it sounds."

Mark Twain (after a performance of Siegfried)

WALK (n) The least onerous form of exercise, much favored by those health devotees whose guiding standard is "no pain, that's gain."

"Golf is the perfect way to ruin a good walk."

George Bernard Shaw

An elderly lady, named Liz,
As a walker, is simply a whiz.
She goes miles every day
In a resolute way;
Now, nobody knows where she is.

WALL STREET (n) Where shares of stock in public corporations can be purchased for more than the quoted price, or sold for less than it. The difference between "less," "more," and "price," is pocketed by the person who handles the transaction. The latter is facetiously called "broker," although it is only the buyer and seller who are broker than before.

WANT (v) Second in a sequence of emotional states involved in human mating. Once, it began with "like", continued after "want" with "marriage," then "intercourse," and concluded with "revulsion." Nowadays, the sequence is slightly different. "Want" comes first, immediately followed by "Intercourse," then by "like." "Marriage" is usually omitted and replaced by "indifference."

From this, we can safely conclude that the surest way for a modern man to like the woman who shares his bed is to refuse to marry her.

"The only thing worse than not getting what you want is getting it. The first leaves you frustrated, but hopeful, while the second leaves you fulfilled, but disillusioned."

Voltaire

WAR (n) The quickest and most efficient method for controlling a nation's population. Over the past century and a half, one of the chief controllers has been the United States--a combatant in eight wars. This gives it a wide edge over the second place finisher, Russia, which could only manage four because of its incompetent Communist government.

"There is much guilt in an unnecessary war."
President John Adams, 1798
(rejecting an appeal to declare war on France)
Snorted old Uncle Sam, fierce and fine,
When reminded that peace is Divine:
"That 'turn the cheek' pap
"Is cowardly crap
"And Christ had no weapons like mine."

WARLOCK (n) One who shares the convictions, but not the plumbing, of witches.

Ambitious young warlock, Tom Fitch,
Displeased with his low coven niche,
Grabbed hold of a knife
And, at risk to his life,
Changed himself into a witch.

WARRANTY (n) A manufacturer's guarantee that, while its product will surely last twelve months, it will be freely replaced if it does not last six months. Actually, it will last seven.

A typical clause provides that if the product fails, it will be replaced by another of the same quality. This refutes the slander that manufacturers lack a sense of humor.

Said a home builder, Morris McTannished,
"With my warranty, worries are banished."
Though he stood behind all,
When cracks came in a Fall
He was so far behind that he vanished.

WASHINGTON (n) In history books dealing with the American Revolution, he is called the "Father of his country," in much the same way that the Christian God is called the "Father of Mankind." In both cases, a large majority of the natives denied the paternity.

"Your Father Washington," an Englishman said,
"Was elected your Chief and applauded.

"But, why do your critics, all of them red,
"Contend they've been basely defrauded."
"To answer your question, it is my belief,"
Said I, "that they don't know the rule.
"The Electoral College chooses the Chief
"And the redskins don't go to that school."

WASTE (n) Reclaimable resources whose virtues have been concealed
by ignorance and a bad press, with the consequence that the name
describes its fate.
   "Recycling waste is not to my taste,"
   Said Bromfield, the Mayor of Twit.
   "Though some disagree, all that I see
   "Are mountains of rubbish and shit."

WATER (n) A simple hydrogen compound that means life to those who
have enough and prosperity to those who control enough. It is said
that water flows downhill to use and uphill to money. This maxim
is best illustrated in Mexico, where downhill flows to the barrios
are called "sewage" by environmentalists, and "water supply" by
those who control it.

WE (pro) A word employed in a self-referencing way by narcissists
to indicate that they are more than singular.
   "The only people with the right to refer to themselves as 'we'
are royalty, Siamese twins, and persons with tapeworms."
                    George Bernard Shaw

WEALTH (n) Possessing sufficient assets to satisfy
all "needs" that are really necessary and some "wants" that are
deemed such. Among the wants that wealth cannot satisfy are the
following:
   1. It can buy good advice, but not good judgment.
   2. It can buy education, but not wisdom.
   3. It can buy a house, but not a home.
   4. It can buy a clock, but not time.
   5. It can buy good food, but not a good appetite.
   6. It can buy position, but not respect.
   7. It can buy sex, but not love.
   8. It can buy good medical care, but not good health.

WEDDING (n) A legal duet that insures one party's pregnancy and
the other's golf game. One subtype, involving a shotgun and widely

practiced in West Virginia, is said to be a matter of wife or death.

>To a church wedding service in Bray,
>The groom brought his golf clubs, to play.
>When the bride asked him why,
>He said in reply,
>"This business won't last the whole day."

WEDLOCK (n) The only lock that can be opened by cold looks, tepid kisses and hot words.

>Said a blushing young bride, Betty Brick,
>Of her imminent wedlock with Nick:
>"I will give him love, gladly.
>"But, if I'm used badly,
>"I'll pick the damn lock mighty quick."

WEED (n) A plant whose virtues have not yet been recognized.

WELFARE (n) Either a pool of potential voters or a conspiracy of freeloaders, depending on whether you are a Democrat or Republican.

>Oh, give me a home where the hardhearted roam,
>Where Republicans rant, rave, and foam.
>Where that right-winging crowd keeps hollering loud
>For exporting poor people to Nome.

WEREWOLF (n) A man who changes into a wolf by night. For reasons not fully understood by scientists, the transformation appears to be most common at college fraternity parties.

>A werewolf outside of Green Bay
>Stalked a spinster, who started to pray:
>"Lord, if You think I ought
>"To wait to be caught,
>"Make sure he's a man when it's day."

WEST VIRGINIA (n) A State with more than a million residents and less than fifteen last names.

WHEAT (n) A grain that contains the only germ worth having. It is also a rich source of chaff, which is widely used to make similes and metaphors.

WHISKEY (n) A substance that, when consumed, elevates matter over mind.

>"Sometimes, too much whiskey is not enough."
>W. C. Fields

"In California, whiskey is for drinking and water is for fighting over."

Mark Twain

WHITES (n) The first and, still today, the biggest beneficiaries of Affirmative Action policies and programs.

WHORE (n) A worker who lays down on the job.
Said an elderly whore in Poughkeepsie:
"In my youth, I'd get ten dollars, fifty
"For one simple trick
"Both easy and quick.
"But now, all I get is the fifty."

WIDOW (n) 1. A woman who has loved and lasted.
2. A woman who has either lost her husband or has not yet found him, depending on whether she is of the soil or grass variety.
The "Black Widow" spider is so-named because of the female's habit of poisoning her mate with her stinger. This is a notable example of the many parallels between human and insect behavior. Some human widows are known to have treated their mates like these spiders, poisoning them with their tongues.

WEIRD (adj.) Exhibiting a behavior that is natural rather than customary and, therefore, different from ours. Following are typical examples of such behavior:
1. Returning a wallet filled with money to its owner.
2. Calling an addition error that favors you to the attention of the waitress.
3. Letting an elderly man have your seat on a crowded bus.
4. Washing your hands after going to the toilet.
A certain weird Scotsman from Fife
Disturbed his community's life.
It was shocked by his taste,
Because he embraced
His neighbor and not the man's wife.

WIFE (n) The senior partner in every American marriage. It is a status that is recognized by such maxims as the following: "A wife is called a 'housekeeper' because if there is a divorce, she gets to keep the house."
Nowadays, the definition has become so flexible that a wife

may be either a woman or a man and it is very important to know which it is. Here are some practical tips that will help you avoid affronts:

1. It is a woman if she has small feet. Nature has provided them so she can stand closer to the kitchen sink.

2. It is a woman if she said something clever immediately after a man said it.

3. It is a woman if, when your wife is hollering for you outside the front door and your dog is barking for you outside the back door, you open both doors and only the dog shuts up.

4. It is a woman if, after calling you a male chauvinist pig, she won't do what she's told.

5. It is a woman if you have not spoken to her for more than a year because you hate to interrupt her.

6. It is a woman if the food that caused her sex drive to decline by 95% is called "wedding cake".

WILL 1. (n) A legal document that is a dead giveaway. It disposes of the maker's assets after his death by disbursing fees to the probate lawyers and expenses to the court. Anything left over passes to the decedent's heirs, giving them less than they expect and more than they deserve.

(1)

An elderly man in Michigan had high-tech devices implanted in both ears that restored 70% of his hearing. After recovering at his granddaughter's house for two weeks, he paid a follow-up visit to the doctor. "I imagine your family is delighted that you can hear so well," enthused the doctor. "Oh, I didn't tell them, yet," replied the old man, "and I've already changed my Will three times."

(2)

The famous German poet, Heinrich Heine, wrote one of the shortest Wills on record:

"I leave my entire estate to my wife on condition that she immediately remarries. I want there to be at least one person alive who sincerely regrets my passing."

2. (v) Expressing the firm purpose to take future action that one intends never taking if it can be avoided.

If "ifs" and "buts" were candy and nuts,
We'd all have a Merry Christmas.
If "maybes" and "wills" were five dollar bills,
We'd all be as wealthy as Midas.

WINNOW (v) A process by which television news editors separate sensational falsehoods from verifiable truths and broadcast the former.

> Said an editor, Ben, "I've got a strong yen
> "To winnow the crap about Sony.
> "But, I just couldn't show all the dirt that I know,
> "For, after the story's gone, so me!"

WINE (n) God's next best gift to man--after whiskey.

> Every night Thomas Klein drinks lots of red wine
> To master his panic and dread.
> Then he staggers to where there's a sight he must bear;
> His wife, sprouting curlers, in bed.

WINSOME (adj.) Denoting a physical charm that enables the subject to win some person of the opposite sex.

> "She was a winsome Southern belle.
> "I married her in June.
> "Last week she died and went to Hell.
> "I'll win some peace, now, soon."

WISE (adj.) 1. Knowing enough to be ashamed.

2. Having the sagacity to avoid making the same mistake, twice, e.g., a divorcee who does not remarry.

The Bible tells us that the three who came out of the East with gifts for baby Jesus were "wise men." But, many mothers this editor has spoken to say the world would be in much better shape if the three had been wise women. They would have:

1. asked directions; 2. arrived on time; 3. gave money instead of incense; 4. helped deliver the baby; 5. changed his diaper; 6. cleaned up the stable, and 7. made a casserole.

WIT (n) Next to common sense, the trait Americans most prize in themselves. Regarding common sense, nobody in America has it, if each person's opinion of everybody else is to be believed. As for wit, most people we know are halfway there.

> "True wit is nature, to advantage dressed.
> "What others thought, but n'er so well expressed."
>   Alexander Pope

Following are several examples of nature, dressed to advantage:

1. If you think nobody cares about you, try missing a few payments.

2. Borrow money from pessimists. They won't expect it back.

3. 49.9% of all people in the country are below average.

4. "I drive way too fast to worry about cholesterol."

Jay Lenno

5. I intend to live forever; so far, so good.

6. The only substitute for good manners are fast reflexes.

7. The only culture some people have are bacterial.

8. Experience is what you get only after you first needed it.

9. For every action, there is an equal and opposite criticism.

10. The Post Office should investigate why bills travel through the mail at twice the speed of checks.

11. The severity of an itch is inversely proportional to your ability to scratch it.

12. Two wrongs are only the beginning.

13. Get a new car for your spouse. It is a good trade.

WITCH (n) "1. An ugly and repulsive old woman in a wicked league with the devil.

"2. A beautiful and attractive young woman, in wickedness, a league beyond the devil."

Ambrose Bierce

WOMAN (n) A member of the unfair sex. According to an eminent philologist, the word is a contraction of the early Saxon phrase, "woe to man". The expert may be somewhat biased, however, since he has been married and divorced three times.

Her relationship with man has long been the basis for frequent displays of wit, among which the following are notable examples:

1. (classified ad) "A princess, having had much experience with princes, seeks a frog."

2. "God made us sisters, men made us allies, and Prozac made us friends."

3. "My mother-in-law is a travel agent for guilt trips."

4. "Cake, chocolate, and men: some things are much better rich."

5. "Don't treat me any differently than you would treat the Queen."

6. "Of course I don't look busy. I did it right the first time."

7. "I got all stirred up about nothing and then I married him."

WOMEN (n) The plural form of the Saxon contraction (see WOMAN).

They are distinguishable from men by wide hips (designed to endure long hours of shopping) and the fact that although they never admit their age, men never act theirs.

"Women who seek equality with men lack ambition."
            Dorothy Parker

"Women are like angels," said the husband. "You mean because we're so pure and spiritual?" inquired his wife. "No," he replied, "because you're always up in the air, harping about something, and never have anything to wear."

WONDERLAND (n) A mythical country in stories written by Lewis Carroll for the enjoyment of British children and to stimulate their imagination. Nowadays in America, since children have little imagination and rarely read, the stories are enjoyed only by childish adults.

One of Carroll's best known poems is the following:
      "Will you walk a little faster,"
      Said the walrus to the snail.
      "There's a polar bear behind us
      "That is lunching on my tail."

A British researcher, digging into a pile of the author's unpublished manuscripts, discovered this verse:
      "Will you eat a little faster,"
      Said the Scotsman to his bride.
      "There's a cockroach in your sandwich
      "Who's escaping out the side."

WORDS (n) Ammunition of advocates, torpedo tube of doctors, verbal caress of lovers, oily gusher of politicians, retail merchandise of lawyers, red herrings of salespersons, and the vehicle of extortion by the clergy.
      "I choose my words most carefully
      "To be both soft and sweet.
      "Because I never know, you see,
      "Which ones I'll have to eat."
      (So said the politician, Bestian,
      Before he died of indigestion.)

WORRY (n) The last in a sequence of emotional states that young women often experience during lovemaking. The others are anticipation, expectation, and disappointment.

WRESTLING (n) 1. (amateur) A sport in which two fit young men grapple each other in search of a pin. Although they rarely find it in the ring, some can count on getting it from an orthopedic surgeon later in life.

2. (professional) An entertainment in which overweight, middle-aged, men body-slam each other in search of a television contract.

A vigorous wrestler in Doan,
In the midst of a match, heard a groan.
When he squeezed up a notch,
The pain in his crotch
Made him realize the groan was his own.

WRITER (n) Someone who makes a record of her opinions so they cannot be ignored. Instead, they are ridiculed. One whose opinions have been widely read, but rarely adopted, is the famous British essayist, Alexander Pope. The following advice of his to writers on the art of writing has been savagely attacked by lawyers, accustomed as they are to charging fees as though their words were eggs--so much per dozen:

"Words should be used like gold coins, spending just enough to purchase the reader's understanding."

X

X (n) The most popular letter among pirates for marking the site of buried treasure on their maps. Since they were poorly educated, an explanatory footnote was often appended, stating "x marks the spot."

X CHROMOSOME (n) The female chromosome that helps determine the gender of a fetus. There are two of them in the egg and one x and one y chromosome in each sperm intent on fertilizing it. If the egg's x bonds with the sperm's y, a male fetus results, while it will be female if the egg's x bonds with the sperm's x. Finally, if both egg chromosomes bond with the sperm's x, the fetus will have a lifelong compulsion to shop.

X-RATED (adj.) Containing sex, terror, and violence, therefore, fit only for teenagers--who are used to it.

X-RAY (n) A diagnostic radiation that enables an orthopedist to see what is going to pay for his next vacation.

Y

YACHT (n) A marine vehicle useful for terrorizing small boats, contaminating bodies of water, and making a pauper of its owner.
> Moaned aspiring sailor, Ken Mott,
> after buying a fifty foot yacht:
> "It costs me so much,
> "For upkeep and such,
> "That to sail it, I simply cannot."

YAHWEH (n) A cruel and callous deity the Jews mistakenly worshipped as the Supreme Being. Christians know that only the loving God who drowned everybody as an excuse for Noah to build a boat deserves that honor.

YAM (n) An immigrant from Asia tenuously related to the potato family, whose popularity in America has been hampered by its name and scabrous color. It has not helped, either, that it is said to be the favorite food of rats in China.
> That villainous veggie, the yam,
> Has deluded our poor Uncle Sam.

YEAR (n) Three hundred and sixty-four disappointments and one birthday you don't have to pay for.
> A partying man, Albert Speer,
> Has a diet mainly of beer.
> He is always so tight
> That his days merge with night
> And his age never adds a new year.

YEAST (n) A natural substance that produces large quantities of gas in a fermenting body and produces a fat head (SEE POLITICIAN). After speechifying political candidates, its effects are most noticeable in beer-drinking lawyers, talk-show hosts, preachers, and telemarketers.
> For these and others susceptible to yeast inflation,
> Confucius offers this invaluable maxim:
> "Better to be silent and appear a fool than to open your mouth and remove all doubt."

269

YELLOW 1. (n) A color that can be most vividly seen in the following settings:

1. In the stricken faces of fraternity members after a binge.

2. In the jaundiced faces of political activists who just lost the White House to the other party.

3. Down the spines of Federal leaders who order young men and women into a war that is without risk to themselves.

2. (adj.) A character trait possessed by prudent people who are aware of all the contingencies involved in bravery.

"'Tis wise, from fights, to run away.

"You'll live to run another day."

Anonymous

YESTERDAY (n) A time in the past when things that should have been done were put off until today and will be done on some tomorrow. It is the time when that day's disappointments begin to fade, expectations for today begin to sprout, and their harvest, tomorrow, seems certain.

"May the best moment of yesterday be worse than the worst moment of next year and may you live until then."

Irish Prayer

YIELD (v) To give up a right in response to pressure, as in the following examples of rights frequently surrendered:

1. A political candidate's right to refuse a campaign donation.

2. A homely woman's right to say "no" to a handsome man.

3. The Defense Department's right to require competitive bidding.

4. The President's right to refuse a photo opportunity.

5. A father's right to share diaper-changing duties with his wife.

An elderly woman stopped her car at the "Yield" sign before entering a freeway. Several minutes elapsed as she waited for an empty lane, traffic accumulating behind her. Since she gave no indication of ever moving, the next driver in line rolled his window down, leaned out and shouted: "Hey, lady, the sign says, 'yield,' not 'surrender'."

YOUTH (n) A person skilled at teaching parents the value of birth control.

"Young people in America are always ready to give their elders the benefit of their inexperience."

Oscar Wilde (on returning from a trip to the United States)
Voltaire's famous lament, "En l'amour, s'il jeunesse savait;
s'il veillesse pouvait" ("In love, if the youth could know; if the
old were able"), suffers from his practical inexperience. While
old men cannot do it, young men can and quickly learn how.

Z

ZANY (adj.) Behavior so imbecilic that it will always take first
prize in any contest between fools. Prime examples of this are
televised "reality" shows, political conventions, Miss America
extravaganzas, and the five hundred annual competitions for best
movie, best recording, best Broadway show, best dog, best cat, and
any country fair's best pig, pumpkin, chili, hog caller, and
outhouse.

> A Supreme Court Justice, named Taney,
> Was almost certainly zany
> When he ruled, in Dred Scott,
> That white school boards were not
> Cheating black kids throughout Allegheny.

ZEAL (n) An hormonal dysfunction that compels activists to push
a cause over opponents or the latter over a cliff, with equal
vigor.

> An earnest young woman from Kiel
> Studies with wonderful zeal,
> About women's rights,
> Privacy fights,
> And whether her climax is real.

ZEALOT (n) Someone who won't take "no" for an answer.

ZENITH (n) The highest point in a three-dimensional structure.
In astronomy, it is the highest point on the heaven's ceiling,
directly above a standing man and between the stars that are
painted there.

ZEPHYR (n) Wind, in formal dress.

> A society matron, named Feffer,

Vented gas like a bilious heifer.
When her friends looked offended,
She blandly contended,
"I couldn't help breaking a zephyr."

ZEST (n) Enthusiasm in action, followed by remorse
on reflection.
There was a young couple from Brest
Who fondled each other with zest.
One night, on a dare,
She stripped herself bare
And--well--you can guess all the rest.

ZEUS (n) "The most eminent of the Grecian gods, he was worshipped
by the Romans as "Jupiter", and by modern Americans as "God",
"money", "dog", and "mom"--not necessarily in that order."
Ambrose Bierce

ZIGZAG (v) To move erratically from side to side, as in these
examples:
1. Democrats in the U.S. Senate, who move from the right wing
of the party to its left wing, depending on whether they hale from
the South or North. (Note. Since all Republican Senators are right
wingers, they never zig, but only zag.)
2. The head of a politician, whenever he hears contradictory
opinions coming from two large donors.
3. A female driver, whenever she is applying makeup or nail
polish.
4. A male driver, after picking up a prostitute.
5. An 80 year old driver of either sex, who has dementia and
good hearing.

ZIRCON (n) A counterfeit diamond that is a man's best friend.
Her defenses, inviolate, that none could annihilate,
Kate's a girl no man's ruses would work on.
But, Bill's plan had merit; he gave her a karat.
How was she to know it was zircon?

ZOO (n) A prison for once-wild animals with life sentences.
There, they are displayed as a warning to adolescents, incentive
to poachers, goad to animal-rights terrorists, and the nourishment
of fleas.

Some say monkeys are bored and grow fat
In zoos and places like that.
But, the claim can't be right
Because each day and night,
They have us to mimic and laugh at.

ZOOLOGY (n) The study of the animal kingdom. Noteworthy research
within the past twenty years has reached two shattering
conclusions:

1. Man does not descend from monkeys, as Darwin believed, but
from worms (who share 30% of our food, 70% of our genes, and 100%
of our buried bodies).

2. The cockroach, not the lion, is king. In America, the
latter is a prisoner in zoos, while the former is de facto owner of
every residence, lacking only the deed to secure his claim in
court.

End of THE SKEPTIC'S DICTIONARY VOLUME TWO